THE MISCELLANEOUS WORKS OF JOHN BUNYAN

General Editor: Roger Sharrock

VOLUME V

THE BARREN FIG-TREE
THE STRAIT GATE
THE HEAVENLY FOOT-MAN

JOHN BUNYAN

The Barren Fig-Tree
The Strait Gate
The Heavenly Foot-man

EDITED BY
GRAHAM MIDGLEY

CLARENDON PRESS · OXFORD
1986

Oxford University Press, Walton Street, Oxford OX2 6DP
Oxford New York Toronto
Delhi Bombay Calcutta Madras Karachi
Petaling Jaya Singapore Hong Kong Tokyo
Nairobi Dar es Salaam Cape Town
Melbourne Auckland
and associated companies in
Beirut Berlin Ibadan Nicosia

Oxford is a trade mark of Oxford University Press

Published in the United States
by Oxford University Press, New York

British Library Cataloguing in Publication Data
Bunyan, John
The barren fig-tree; the strait gate; The
heavenly foot-man.—(Oxford English texts)—
(The Miscellaneous works of John Bunyan; v. 5)
1. Puritans—Doctrines
I. Title II. Midgley, Graham III. Bunyan, John.
The strait gate IV. Bunyan, John. The heavenly
foot-man V. Series
230'.59 BX9318
ISBN 0-19-812733-2

Library of Congress Cataloging in Publication Data
Bunyan, John, 1628-1688.
The barren fig-tree.
(The Miscellaneous works of John Bunyan; v. 5)
(Oxford English texts)
Includes bibliographies and indexes.
1. Theology—Collected works—17th century.
I. Midgley, Graham. II. Title. III. Title: Barren
fig-tree. IV. Title: Strait gate. V. Title:
Heavenly foot-man. VI. Series: Bunyan, John, 1628-
1688. Selections. 1976; v. 5.
BR75.B73 1976 vol. 5 230'.583 s 86-2631
ISBN 0-19-812733-2 [252'.0583]

Set by Hope Services, Abingdon, Oxon
Printed in Great Britain at
The University Printing House, Oxford
by David Stanford
Printer to the University

FOR
WILLIAM AND ERIC
Mark 7: 28.

GENERAL EDITOR'S PREFACE

SINCE the middle of the nineteenth century, there has been no complete edition of Bunyan's works. The author who is known to the world for *The Pilgrim's Progress* was a prolific preacher and writer. As his first editor and friend, Charles Doe, the comb-maker of Southwark, said: 'Here are Sixty Pieces of his Labours and he was Sixty Years of Age.' Apart from his spiritual autobiography, *Grace Abounding to the Chief of Sinners*, and the three allegorical fictions, *The Pilgrim's Progress*, *The Life and Death of Mr Badman*, and *The Holy War*, these include sermons, theological treatises, biblical commentaries, and controversial works directed against the Quakers, the Latitudinarians (in the person of Edward Fowler), and the strict-communion Baptists; all these works are cast in the form of the popular sermon, with analysis of the text, abundant quotation from Scripture, a frequent employment of numbered heads and a meeting of objections by a series of questions and answers, and 'uses' or applications of the doctrine extracted from the text (these last usually conclude the work).

The purpose of this edition is to present all that Bunyan wrote in a text based on the earliest available editions, but incorporating those additions and revisions in later editions published during the author's lifetime which may reasonably be judged to have been made by him or to have received his approval. In fact, the method is that observed in the Oxford editions of *Grace Abounding, The Pilgrim's Progress*, and *The Holy War*. As in those editions, colloquial forms and irregular grammar (such as plural subjects with singular verbs) have been retained. The punctuation, capitalization, and italicization are those of the originals, though here the editors have corrected obvious printers' errors and inconsistencies, and anything in the accidentals which might be merely confusing to the reader. A short textual introduction with title-page transcriptions precedes each work; it includes information on the printers, a list of seventeenth-century editions, and a mention of later reprints that are of any importance.

The reader of Bunyan's *Miscellaneous Works* is as likely to be a social or ecclesiastical historian, a theologian or a psychologist, as a literary student. The introductions to the various works thus aim to give an adequate account of the background of Nonconformist life in the period, as well as of Bunyan's own life and career as minister of the Bedford separatist church and visitor to its associated churches in the eastern counties and in London. Explanatory notes have been kept to a minimum. However, a good measure of individual freedom has been left to editors in respect of the introductions and notes; it seemed, for instance, that *The Doctrine of the Law and Grace Unfolded*, Bunyan's chief theological treatise, required a fairly full consideration of his particular version of the theology of the two covenants, a dialectical system which may be said to provide the basic structure informing every work in these volumes, and indeed underlying the drama of salvation and damnation in *The Pilgrim's Progress* and other allegories.

The first attempt at a complete edition was that of Charles Doe in the Folio of 1692. This was announced in an advertisement in *Mercurius Reformatus* for 11 June 1690:

Mr. *John Bunyan*, author of *The Pilgrim's Progress*, and many other excellent Books, that have found great acceptance, hath left behind him Ten Manuscripts prepared by himself for the Press before his Death: His Widow is desired to print them (with some other of his Works, which have been already printed but are at present not to be had), which will make together a book for 10s. in sheets, in Fol. All persons who desire so great and good a work should be performed with speed, are desired to send in 5s. for their first payment to Dorman Newman, at the King's Arms in the *Poultrey*, London: Who is empower'd to give receipts for the same.

A year later, Doe issued a pamphlet, *The Struggler* (1691), telling of his efforts to bring out a collected edition of his friend's works. But when the Folio finally appeared, it contained only ten works apart from the previously unpublished ones obtained from Bunyan's widow and her son John. These were, in the order in which they appeared: *Saved by Grace, Christian Behaviour, I Will Pray with the Spirit, The Strait Gate, Gospel-Truths Opened, A Vindication of Some Gospel-Truths Opened, Light for Them that Sit in Darkness, Instruction for the Ignorant, The Holy City: Or, The New Jerusalem, The Resurrection of the Dead*. It seems likely that Doe ran into trouble over copyrights, and was therefore not able to bring out the second volume that he had planned. It is noteworthy that none of Bunyan's best-selling books is represented in the Folio; it is difficult to imagine Nathaniel Ponder, another publisher in the Poultry, surrendering his control over that valuable property *The Pilgrim's Progress*; and it is significant that the Folio was finally published by William Marshall, and not by Dorman Newman, who had issued both editions of *The Holy War*. The Folio was published by subscription, and the many copies extant suggest that the subscription-list was a long one.

A second edition of the Folio was issued in 1736–7, and this included the second volume with those writings which Doe had been unable to assemble. The edition was edited by Ebenezer Chandler and Samuel Wilson (the son of Bunyan's friend John Wilson) and published by E. Gardner and John Marshall (the son of William Marshall). Three books were still not included, but these are found in the third edition of the collected works which appeared in two volumes in 1767, and was thus the first truly complete edition. There is a preface by George Whitefield. Another collected edition in six volumes by Alexander Hogg appeared in 1780.

In 1853 the complete works were re-edited by the devoted Bunyan scholar, George Offor. In the twentieth century this has continued to be the only collected edition available to the scholar. It contains an amount of painstaking if amateurish bibliographical information, and a verbose and often melodramatic evangelical commentary; as John Brown (Bunyan's biographer and minister of Bunyan Meeting, Bedford, 1854–1903) said: 'His notes ... are occasionally a little superfluous, sometimes indeed raising a smile by their very simplicity.' Offor's edition was revised and reissued in three volumes (Edinburgh and London, 1860–2). There was also an edition in four volumes by Henry Stebbing (1859).

The great disaster of Bunyan studies was the fire which destroyed a great part of the Offor collection when it was to be auctioned at Sotheby's in 1865 (Tuesday, 29 June). Many of the surviving volumes came into the possession of Sir Leicester Harmsworth, and at the sale of the Harmsworth Collection at Sotheby's in February 1947 passed into various public libraries. Some remained in the family or were bought back by it, and at the death of Richard Offor, George Offor's grandson and former Librarian of the University of Leeds, were presented to Elstow Moot Hall in Bunyan's birthplace. Several of the copies consulted by the present editors are bady charred books from the Offor collection.

Coleridge once drew a distinction between the Bunyan of genius and the Bunyan of the conventicle. If we accept this, the bulk of the works in this new edition represent the Bunyan of the conventicle; but Coleridge's romantic premisses, which we have in part inherited, draw a far sharper line between genius and the man rooted in his historical accidents than accuracy will admit. There is much strong, plain, effective exhortation in the awakening sermons; many of the poems in *A Book for Boys and Girls* are real poems; more important, the *Miscellaneous Works* bring us up against the raw material, the subsoil, on which the ethos of English Puritanism, which we meet in *The Pilgrim's Progress* and experience in its historical succession, is founded.

ROGER SHARROCK

CONTENTS

REFERENCES AND ABBREVIATIONS

[The place of publication, unless otherwise stated, is London]

BUNYAN'S WORKS

The Works of That Eminent Servant of Christ, Mr. John Bunyan, ed. Charles Doe	*1692 Folio*
The Works of John Bunyan, ed. George Offor (3 vols., Glasgow, Edinburgh, and London, 1860–2)	Offor
The Miscellaneous Works of John Bunyan, general editor Roger Sharrock (Oxford, 1976–)	Oxford Bunyan
Grace Abounding to the Chief of Sinners, ed. Roger Sharrock (Oxford, 1962)	*G.A.*
The Pilgrim's Progress from This World to That Which Is to Come, ed. J. B. Wharey, rev. Roger Sharrock (Oxford, 1960)	*P.P.*
The Doctrine of the Law and Grace Unfolded, ed. Richard L. Greaves (Oxford, 1976)	*Law and Grace*

OTHER WORKS

The Term Catalogues, edited by Edward Arber (1903–6)	Arber
John Brown, *John Bunyan: His Life, Times, and Work*, rev. edn. Frank Mott Harrison (1928)	Brown
Oxford English Dictionary	*O.E.D.*
M. P. Tilley, *A Dictionary of Sixteenth and Seventeenth Century Proverbs and Proverbial Phrases* (Michigan, 1951)	Tilley

INTRODUCTION

(i)

BUNYAN'S power as a preacher was the beginning and basis of his rise to eminence in his own congregation, and an equal reason along with *The Pilgrim's Progress* for his reputation in the seventeenth century. It is one which subsequent criticism has accepted and reaffirmed, yet the direct evidence for that power consists almost completely of hearsay, hearsay which is nevertheless continuous and consistent from the time when the meeting at Bedford desired him 'to speak a word of Exhortation unto them' and he did 'with much weakness and infirmity, discover my Gift amongst them; at which they not onely seemed to be, but did solemnly protest, as in the sight of the great God, they were both affected and conforted, and gave thanks to the Father of Mercies for the grace bestowed on me.'[1] When he began to preach more publicly in the countryside his listeners 'received [his word] with rejoicing at the mercy of God to me-ward, professing their Souls were edified thereby'.[2] In prison, surrounded by a considerable congregation of other sufferers for the faith, the power of his preaching was recorded by a fellow-prisoner: 'In the midst of the hurry which so many new comers occasioned, I have heard Mr Bunyan both preach and pray with that mighty Spirit of Faith and Plerophory of Divine Assistance, that has made me stand and wonder.'[3] Agnes Beaumont, whose connection with Bunyan was to bring pain and scandal, tells how her father, moved by Bunyan's affecting preaching, 'heard him with a broken heart, as he had done Several others . . . he was mightly convinced'.[4] This ability to move his hearers' emotions and stir their hearts is the theme of Charles Doe's account of his first hearing Bunyan preach: 'But Mr. *Bunyan* went on, and Preached so *New Testament*-like that he made me admire and weep for Joy, and give him my Affections. And he was the first Man that ever I heard Preach to my new enlightened Understanding and Experience, for me thoughts all his Sermons were adapted to my Condition and had apt

---

[1] *G.A.*, p. 83.   [2] Ibid.   [3] Brown, p. 170.
[4] *Narrative of the Persecution of Agnes Beaumont*, B.L. MSS. Eg. 2128. folio 27.

Similitudes, being full of the Love of God, and the manner of its secret working upon the Soul, and of the Soul under the sense of it, that I could weep for Joy most part of his Sermons.'[1] The years saw Bunyan's reputation strengthening and widening as he preached not only in Bedfordshire but in London, not only to simple country folk but to congregations of eminence and learning. Charles Doe is again our witness for his reputation and its effect: 'When Mr. *Bunyan* preached in *London*, if there were but one days notice given, there would be more people come together to hear him preach, than the Meeting-house would hold. I have seen to hear him preach (by my computation) about twelve hundred at a Morning Lecture by seven a clock on a working day, in the dark Winter-time. I also computed about three thousand that came to hear him one Lord's day at *London*, at a Townsend Meeting-house, so that half were fain to go back again for want of room, and then himself was fain at a back-door to be pull'd almost over people to get up stairs to his Pulpit.'[2] This chorus of praise continues into the nineteenth century, loud and certain in all the commentary of his pious editor Offor and his biographer John Brown, who never tires of asserting the 'heart-stirring power' of his hero 'whose preaching came like a fresh breeze from the mountains'.[3]

Yet when we come to test the truth of this cloud of witnesses, we find ourselves without touchstones. As with all preachers silenced by death, we cannot hear the tone and cadence of voice which must, we suppose, have been a major factor in the moving and convincing effect of his sermons. In Bunyan's case I cannot find even a description of his voice. We know, for example, of Whitfield's mighty boom and Newman's silvery delicacy, but of the sound of Bunyan's voice there is no record. Over and above this, there has survived only one sermon out of the hundreds he must have preached, a fate attending a large proportion of dissenting preaching, much of it extempore; and, as Tindall has somewhat tartly remarked, 'Because few of the Baptist mechanicks were as lavishly addicted to print as the Quakers, most of their social preaching was lost with the winds to which they had intrusted it.'[4] The surviving piece of evidence is *Mr. Bunyan's Last*

---

[1] *A Collection of Experience of the Work of Grace* (1700), p. 52.
[2] *The Struggler, etc., 1692 Folio,* p. 874. [3] Brown, p. 383.
[4] W. Y. Tindall, *John Bunyan, Mechanick Preacher* (Columbia, 1934), p. 104.

Sermon: Preached August 19th. 1688[1] and published in 1689, which is a dull and lifeless performance, hardly likely to persuade us of the preacher's ability to arouse tears and joy and convincing awakening. It is brief—taking about twenty-five minutes to preach—much less than the time most commonly accepted as normal sermon-duration. Bunyan himself allows an hour—'Time is precious, an hour's time to hear a sermon is precious'[2]—and the usual references are to an hour, the running of an hour-glass, though sermons running up to three hours are recorded.[3] This last sermon has, even in its brevity, the basic construction and method of the fuller published sermon-treatises which are our concern in this volume and, though not very striking in itself, is of interest as the sole specimen of what, so far as we can surmise, was the kind of seed from which not only Bunyan's treatises but his full-scale allegories ultimately grew.

(ii)

The purpose and context of the three treatises in this volume is not such a matter of surmise. They form a coherent trio for many reasons, one being the special nature of this aim and audience, which separates them rather from the main themes and intentions stressed by Bunyan in his own account of his development as a preacher.

The key word to most of his homiletic work is 'awakening', to awaken men to a sense of their own sin, their helplessness to help themselves, and their need of Christ to save them. His earliest sermons, influenced very much by his own experience, aimed, as he said, 'to condemn all flesh, and to open and alledge that the curse of God, by the Law, doth belong to and lay hold on all men as they come into the World because of Sin'.[4] Soon he saw a change in his preaching as he made a more positive offering of hope. 'I did much labour', he writes, 'to hold forth Jesus Christ in all his Offices, Relations, and Benefits unto the World, and did strive also to discover, to condemn,

---

[1] Offor, ii. 755.   [2] *The Life and Death of Mr. Badman*, Offor, iii. 687.
[3] George Fox preached for 3 hours at Leominster (*Journal*, 1694, p. 145) as did Edward Rainbow in a funeral sermon on Lady Anne Clifford. (*A True Memorial of the Life of Lady Anne Clifford* (1848), p. 282.
[4] *G.A.*, p. 85.

and remove those false supports and props on which the World doth lean, and by them fall and perish'.[1] From then on he realized that his special power and calling was not in the doctrinal disputes which had employed his first energies, but that they 'did run in another channel even to carry an awakening Word; to that therefore did I stick and adhere'.[2] This was a belief he frequently reasserted: 'I found my spirit leaned most after awakening and converting Work, and the Word that I carried did lean itself most that way.'[3] The harvest he sought to gather through this preaching was one of 'awakened men' whom he described as 'such as through the Revelation of their Sin and Misery, groan under the want of Jesus to save them, and that continue sensible that they needs must perish if his benefits be not bestowed upon them'.[4]

These three treatises, however, have something more particular than this general evangelical purpose, being addressed not so much to the unawakened sinners, but to those who have awakened to their sin, their need for Christ, and have been received as professors of that faith into the body of the faithful. Their aim is to awaken the awakened to their falling away, their hypocrisy and formalism, and to destroy the false belief that there is saving worth in a mere profession of faith and an observance of outward acts of piety. They are the work of a man on whose shoulders has now fallen the care of the churches, and the pastor here seeks to guide his own sheep, rather than bring more in from the fields of sin.

It was a guidance which Bunyan knew was needed only too well in the years which saw the appearance of these works. The Bedford Church Book records a variety of ways in which the faithful fell away, and the continual need to admonish and discipline is illustrated in such entries as:

1672. 25 May. At a full assembly of the Congregation was with joynt consent of the whole body, cast out of the Church, John Rush, of Bedford, for being drunk after a very beastly and filthy maner ...

1673. 18 Nov. ... was cast out of the Church the wife of our brother Witt, for railing and other wicked practises ... disorders among

---

[1] Ibid., p. 86.   [2] Ibid., p. 87.   [3] Ibid., p. 89.
[4] *Light for them that sit in Darkness*, Oxford Bunyan, viii. 127.

som in the congregation, specialy for that som have run into debt more than they can satisfie, to the great dishoner of God and scandall of religion.

1674. 10 May.   . . . our Sister Elizabeth Maxey had bin admonished for disobedience to her parents, to witt, for calling her father lier, and for wicked carriages to her mother.

29 June.   . . . was our sister Eliz. Burntwood openly rebuked for her immodest company keeping with carnal and light young fellows at Elstow faire.

1676. 23 March.   . . . our sister Sarah Caine was admonished of . . . fond carages towards young men and neglect of hir business.

1678. 6 March.   . . . the miscarages and abominable sines of William Man did find that he was guilty of commiting fornication . . .

1678. 24 July.   . . . our sister Mary ffosket (after private admonition given her before) was publikly admonished for receiving and privatly whispering of an horrid scandal (without culler of truth) against our Brother Honylove . . .

1679. March.   . . . our brother John Stanton was admonished by the Church of his evil in abuseing his wife and beateing hir often for very light matters.

The recurrent and various backslidings caused grave general concern, as well as particular reaction. On 15 September 1679 there was a general Church meeting and 'it was taken notice of that the church was much decayed in hir faith and loue . . . it was proposed to the Church that care might be taken to consider of wayes and meanes how we might Joyntly reforme and performe our dutyes one unto another According to what our relation in the fellowship of the gospel calls for'.[1] These three sermons are very much part of the 'wayes and meanes how we might Joyntly reforme and performe our dutyes'. No one realized more clearly than their preacher the danger to the church of its erring and false members. He knew, as well as the Devil, 'that a loose professor in the church does more mischief to religion than ten can do to it that are in the world';[2] and throughout his work, not only in these special diatribes, he returned to their denunciation. As he asserted, 'Whoso have a form of godliness, and deny the power thereof, from such we must turn away'.[3] These are they 'whose religion

[1] *The Church Book of Bunyan Meeting 1650–1821*, ed. G. B. Harrison (London & Toronto 1928).
[2] *The Jerusalem Sinner Saved*, Offor, i. 99.
[3] Ibid.

lies in a few of the shells of religion'.[1] Better never profess, he cries, 'than to make profession a stalking horse to sin, deceit, to the devil and hell',[2] for 'all those that retain the name, and shew of religion, but are neglecters, as to the power, and godly practise of it . . . will live like *Dogs* and *Swine* in the house, they pray not, they watch not their hearts, they pull not their hands out of their bosoms to work, they do not strive against their lusts, nor will they ever resist unto blood striving against sin.'[3]

Primarily a reaction from his experience within the limited sphere of the Bedford church, this rottenness within is sometimes seen by Bunyan as part of a wider degeneracy, made more distressing by a nostalgic belief in a better past, that 'Were but our times duly compared with those that went before, we should see that which now we are ignorant of. Did we look back to the *Puritans*, but specially to those that but a little before them, suffered for the word of God, in the *Marian* days, we should see another life than is now among men, another manner of conversation, than now is among professors.'[4] But that 'life now among men' is spoken of here not only among his Bedford flock but on a national scale:

Wolves in sheep's clothing swarm in England this day; wolves both as to doctrine, and as to practice too. Some men make a profession, I doubt, on purpose that they may twist themselves into a trade; and thence into an estate; yea, and if need be, into an estate knavishly, by the ruins of their neighbour. Let such take heed, for those that do such things have the greater damnation. Christian, make thy profession shine by a conversion according to the gospel; or else thou wilt damnify religion, bring scandal to thy bretheren, and give offence to the enemies . . . Christian, a profession according to the Gospel is, in these days, a rare thing . . .[5]

In this setting, local and national, these treatises were written, directed to the backsliding believer to arouse him to reform, to make his 'profession shine by a conversion according to the gospel'.

This special purpose brought with it a different theological emphasis from that which prevails in the evangelical sermons of

---

[1] *The Desire of the Righteous Granted*, Offor, i. 765.
[2] *The Life and Death of Mr. Badman*, Offor, iii. 632.
[3] *A Treatise of the Fear of God*, Oxford Bunyan, ix. 27.
[4] *A Holy Life the Beauty of Christianity*, Oxford Bunyan, ix. 345.
[5] *The Life and Death of Mr. Badman*, Offor, iii. 594.

conviction and conversion. There the doctrine of grace and imputed righteousness had to be stressed above all. The hearers must be convinced of their sin, convinced that they had no power of themselves to help themselves nor to do any good work which could wipe away their sin; that only through the grace of God freely given and the imputed righteousness of Christ, could man come to salvation. In this preaching, the place of good works is not neglected but is given a subordinate place. Such treatises as *Justification by an Imputed Righteousness* and *Saved by Grace* illustrate this emphasis, where the writer's need to exclude the works of sinful man as a means of salvation tips the balance. Bunyan was not unaware of this as he clearly shows in the *Epistle to the Reader* of *Christian Behaviour*: 'Having formerly writ some small matter touching the doctrine of faith, as justification by grace through the faith of Christ's blood, &c., I do here, as the second to that doctrine, present thee with a few lines touching good works . . .'.[1] The essential difference which must be established is between good works done to achieve salvation—the way of the Law, justification by works—and good works done by those who have been justified by faith. 'Now the principle is this', Bunyan writes in *The Doctrine of the Law and Grace Unfolded*, 'not to do things because we would be saved, but to do them from this, namely, because we do really believe that we *are* and *shall* be saved.'[2] Good works should be the natural and inevitable results of the working of the Spirit in the believer, who 'comes with the gospel down from heaven to such an one, and fills his soul with good; by which he is capacitated to bring forth fruit, true fruit, which are the fruits of righteousness imputed, and of righteousness infused, to the glory and praise of God'.[3] Grace, he again asserts, 'manifesteth matter of joy and rejoicing; so it causeth much fruitfulness in all holiness and godliness . . . Yea, it so naturally tendeth this way, that it can no sooner appear to the soul, but it causeth this blessed fruit in the heart and life.'[4] It was a necessary doctrine to preach alongside the doctrine of justification by imputed righteousness, to counter possible charges of libertinism, the rejection of any need for a

---

[1] *Christian Behaviour*, Offor, ii. 549.
[2] *Law and Grace*, Oxford Bunyan, ii. 73.
[3] *The Desire of the Righteous Granted*, Offor, i. 766.
[4] *Saved by Grace*, Oxford Bunyan, viii. 220.

moral rule which some extreme sects indeed justified and practised. Bunyan sees good works as an inescapable result of the impelling power of God in the pardoned sinner, so that a rejection of morality and a failure to perform good works would for him be a sign that Grace was not at work. Facing the danger in *Justification by an Imputed Righteousness*, he states that 'To prevent this doctrine from being impeached with a tendency to weaken man in the discharge of his moral duties, the same Divine power which thus pardoned sin has decreed that a sense of pardoning love should impel the redeemed to walk in newness of life—and that it is only while thus walking in holy obedience that they have an evidence of being members of Christ's mystical body'.[1] Good works, at the Day of Judgement, are made an acceptable offering to God through a similar inextricable relationship with the acceptability of the sinner himself, both effected through Christ, for 'as Christ presents thy person before God, acceptable without thy works, freely and alone by his righteousness, so his office is to take away the iniquity of thy holy things, that they also by him may be accepted of God'.[2] It is, as it were, a double imputation of righteousness, to the sinner so that he is seen by God only in Christ, and to the sinner's attempts at good, presented as purified and made perfect in Christ. The doctrine is presented at length and clearly in *Israel's Hope Encouraged*:

Not that a believer casts off to do good, for he knows that what good thing is done in faith and love, is acceptable to God, and profitable to his neighbour . . . We must therefore conclude that there is an acceptation, and acceptation: acceptation of the person, and acceptation of his performance. Acceptation of the person may be considered with respect to justification from the curse, and so acceptation there can be none, but through the one offering of the body of Jesus Christ once for all. Also the acceptation of a duty done by such a person is, by virtue of the self-same offering, the person being considered as standing just through Christ before God.[3]

Again, in *Justification by an Imputed Righteousness*, Bunyan expounds it with a consistency and similarity of phrase which spring from a carefully codified and obviously orthodox statement of belief:

Our works, even the works of faith, are no otherwise accepted but as they come

---

[1] Offor, i. 300. [2] *Paul's Departure and Crown*, Offor, i. 738.
[3] *Israel's Hope Encouraged*, Offor, i. 617.

through Jesus Christ, even through his intercession and blood. So then, Christ doth justify both our person and our works, not by way of approbation, as we stand in ourselves or our works before God, but by presenting of us to his Father by himself, washing what we are and have from guilt in his blood, and clothing us with his own performances. This is the cause of our acceptance with God, and that our works are not cast forth of his presence.[1]

This is the doctrine, then, behind these three treatises, with their stress on good works and the holy life among those who profess the faith of Christ crucified, as they live and work in the world, as they pursue the pathway to heaven, and as they come to the gate of heaven and judgement. God, says Bunyan in a fine phrase, 'expecteth that there should in our whole life be a blessed tang of the Gospel'[2] in humility and condescension to others, in pity, love, and compassion, in truth and faithfulness and forgiveness. So when, in these sermon-treatises, he turns with particular attention to the professors of faith within the church, it is with the uncompromising text 'God's people are fruitful in good works according to the proportion of their faith; if they be slender in good works, it is because they are weak in faith.[3] This image of fruitfulness and its opposite, the barren tree, is one which has shaped his thought in many passages outside the treatise which bears that title: 'whoever pretends to sanctification', he quotes as another text, 'if he shows not the fruits thereof by a holy life, he deceiveth his own heart, and professeth but in vain';[4] for 'the tree must be good before it bear good fruit, and so also must a man . . . Hence the fruits of the Spirit are called the fruit of that tree.'[5] To come closer to the subject and metaphor of the first of these treatises, and to fit them neatly into the theology of good works which we have seen Bunyan expounding, we have these words from *A Holy Life the Beauty of Christianity*:

A Professor is a Professor though he hath no good Works; but that, as such, he is truly godly; he is foolish that so concludeth. Not that Works make a Man good; for the Fruit maketh not a good Tree, it is the Principle, to wit, Faith, that makes a Man good, and his works that shew him to be so. What then? why, all Professors that have not *good Works* flowing from their *Faith*, are naught; are Bramble bushes; are nigh unto Cursing, whose end is to be burned. For

---

[1] Offor, i. 326.   [2] *Saved by Grace*, Oxford Bunyan, viii. 225.
[3] *Christian Behaviour*, Offor, ii. 552.
[4] *The Desire of the Righteous Granted*, Offor, i. 751.   [5] Ibid., p. 749.

Professors by their fruitlessness declare that they are not of the planting of God; nor the Wheat: but Tares and Children of the Wicked one.[1]

Such is the doctrine and such is the peculiar pastoral purpose of these three treatises, but for many readers, removed from and unmoved by the general problems of Faith and works or the local problems of the church at Bedford, these pieces have a greater interest and importance as part of Bunyan's development as a creative artist, being a step in his discovery of different ways of putting things, by statement, by rhetoric, by similitude, by typologies, by allegory.

(iii)

In order to establish some understanding of the peculiar genre of these works with which we are dealing, and the criteria by which, in construction and style, they are to be judged, it is necessary, as a first step, to trace the process of development from the preached word to the printed text, or at least the relationship between preached sermons and printed sermon-treatises.

This process is an uncertain and a conjectural one, even from its very beginning, in the nature of the sermon text itself. Voices of advice and record in the century differ, but the widely held belief that dissenting sermons were free and extempore effusions, as contrasted with the prepared and written sermon, cannot be entirely upheld. W. F. Mitchell's opinion was that 'Throughout the whole century the Puritans favoured the carefully written sermon, delivered *memoriter*, although some of their number considered notes sufficient, and probably only wrote up their sermons for printing after they had been preached.'[2] Certainly there is evidence for the fully written-out sermon text. William Strong, for instance, left all his sermons in a full text in his difficult handwriting, needing the services of a lady who knew his hand to transcribe them for the press.[3] There is, indeed, distrust of extempore preaching and a realization of its dangers. James Arderne, in his *Directions Concerning the Matter and Stile of Sermons*, warned that '. . . 'tis true, you may after long exercise in preaching, adventure upon

---

[1] *A Holy Life the Beauty of Christianity*, Oxford Bunyan, ix. 251.
[2] W. F. Mitchell, *English Pulpit Oratory from Andrewes to Tillotson* (1930), p. 26.
[3] William Strong, *XXXI Select Sermons* (1656) in Henry Wilkinson's 'To the Reader'.

extempore enlargements; but this must be the fruit of long studies and the reward of continu'd labour, whereby your stile is secur'd against the dangers of that easie and plausible way.'[1] On the other hand, influential voices alerted the would-be preacher to the deflating and inhibiting power of the fully-written text. John Wilkins is quite unequivocal in his opinion that 'it will not be convenient for one that is a constant Preacher, to pen all his discourses, or to tie himselfe unto Phrases . . . A man cannot ordinarily be so much affected himselfe (and consequently he cannot so easily affect others) with things that he speakes by wrote . . . such a fitting confidence, as should be in that oratour, who is to have a power over the affections of others, which such a one is scarce capable of, who shall so servilely tie himself to particular words and expressions, from which he dares not vary for feare of being out.'[2] In another widely-read preaching manual, William Perkins seems to suggest that a fully worked-out scheme embodied in full and methodical note form is the farthest the written form of a sermon should be taken. He advises a general memorizing of the sermon, in its method, proofs, application of doctrines, and its illustrations of applications, but 'in the meantime nothing careful for the words'. He urges against full verbal memorizing as laboursome and liable to lead to stumbling and the hindering of a true delivery.[3] It is impossible to say where, in this variety of method, Bunyan's own practice was. The state of *Mr. Bunyan's Last Sermon* is suspect. It is too short to be a full sermon, yet it is fully written out in connected prose rather than in abbreviated note-form language. In the lack of any proof that notes of the sermon were found in Bunyan's handwriting, one is tempted to accept Offor's hypothesis that 'it bears strong marks of having been published from notes taken by one of the hearers'.[4] Bunyan himself says little to help us, but there is a remark in *A Relation of my Imprisonment* which establishes one fact. 'I would willingly', he says, 'take the pains to give any one the notes of all my sermons.'[5] Add to this the near-contemporary assertion of John Wilson that, among

---

[1] Published 1671, p. 94.
[2] John Wilkins, *Ecclesiastes, Or, A Discourse concerning the Gifts of Preaching as it falls under the rules of Art* (1646), p. 74.
[3] William Perkins, *The Art of Prophecying* (1592), Englished by Thomas Tuke in 1617. Chapter IX, p. 670, in the *The Workes* (1617), vol. ii.
[4] Offor, ii. 755.   [5] *G.A.*, p. 124.

Bunyan's many virtues, was a 'Memory tenacious, it being customary with him to commit his Sermons to Writing after he had Preached them'.[1] The stages of growth seem to be from a skeleton schematized set of notes, such as Perkins had advised, preached on and expanded, fleshed out and enlivened with anecdote and the phrase of the emotional moment, and then this full-bodied sermon committed to paper from memory, in grammatical and syntactical correctness, but the affecting rhetoric of the actual delivery surviving. This was, then, the basis for the next stage in enlargement and development, embodying the here-and-now quality of the sermon and the urgency of the speaking voice, to be preserved or submerged according to the varying degree of polishing and expansion it was subjected to in its progress towards the sermon-treatise.

This expanding of sermon into treatise was not, of course, confined to Bunyan, but was a widely practised form of composition in the century. Richard Baxter tells us that his *Treatise of Conversion* was made up of 'some plain sermons on that Subject', his treatise *The Crucifying of the World by the Cross of Christ* was enlarged from an Assize Sermon, and that *The Divine Life* was constructed from 'popular Sermons preached in the midst of diverting Businesses'.[2] John Gauden, speaking of his published discourse, *Funerals made Cordials*, outlines the process from sermon notes and memory of the actual hour's preaching to the expanded form: 'The ensuing discourse is now much enlarged beyond the Horary limits of a sermon, exceeding in length most of the ancient Orations. For in recollecting and ruminating my meditations they easily multiplied, and in transcribing my notes, as I had prepared them, I added with Baruch (Jer. 36, 32) many like words to what I had preached and penned, but omitted, being necessarily and so excusably contracted in the Pulpit, but now more dilated in the Presse . . .'[3] Frequently a minister preached several sermons on one biblical text or theme, and these would then be conflated and published as a treatise.[4]

The continued production of sermon proper and sermon treatise,

---

[1] John Wilson, in the *Epistle to the Reader* in the 1692 folio.
[2] Richard Baxter, *Reliquiae Baxterianae* (1696), pp. 114, 116, 120.
[3] John Gauden, *Funerals made Cordials* (1658).
[4] See W. P. Ingoldsby, *Some Considerations of Nonconformist Sermon Style, 1645–1660*, upublished Oxford B. Litt. thesis, p. 17.

rather than a simple printing of the preached sermon, is based on a recognition of the related but different form and purpose of the two. In the 'Address to the Reader' at the beginning of William Strong's *XXXI Select Sermons*, this is clearly and succinctly expounded. Preachers of sermons should 'confine themselves to the *express scope* of that particular place which they have in hand, that the point and branch of Doctrine proper thereunto may be more earnestly and industriously inforced . . . truths many times come in *fresher* and *sweeter* upon the soul, as being drawn more immediately from the fountain, and without the intervention of *our logick* and *discourse*.'[1] From this necessarily confined, moderately argued and organized form, the discourse could move to a wider treatment, expanding from its centre to related themes, making use of a more complex argument and logical structure. As these writers of the *Address* put it: 'There is a double way of edification now in use in the Church of God, either by *Long Tracts*, or by *short* and *pithy discourses*: . . . *Treatises* have their use, & so have *single Sermons*: . . . sometimes tis good to see truths, not by *piece-meal*, but in their *dependance* and *frame*, that the whole Doctrine may be brought together, and digested into a method: On the other side, to say all that may be said in an argument, is a *burden* and a *prejudice* to the common sort of hearers . . .'.[2]

A large proportion of Bunyan's published work, apart from the major allegories, falls into this kind. The three treatises in this volume, which will be discussed more fully below, are obvious examples, to which we could add others, vouched for as of this genre by Bunyan himself. Speaking of *The Jerusalem Sinner Saved*, he says, 'I have found, through God's grace, good success in preaching upon this subject, and, perhaps, so I may by my writing upon it too.'[3] The foundation of *The Holy City* was an early sermon, preached in prison, which 'so increased in my hand, that of the fragments that we left, after we had well dined, I gathered up this basketful. Methought the more I cast mine eye upon the whole discourse, the more I saw lie in it. Wherefore setting myself to a more narrow search, through frequent prayer to God, what first with doing, and after that with doing again, I thus did finish it.'[4] *The Greatness of the Soul* grew from a London sermon, as the

[1] William Strong, *XXXI Select Sermons*, A2[r–v].
[2] Ibid., A2[r].   [3]. Offor, i. 68.   [4] Offor, iii. 398.

title-page informs us—'First Preached at *Pinner's Hall*, and now Enlarged, and Published for Good.'[1] Many others show in their method and style their unmistakable origin in sermons, and one must agree with Offor when he comments that *Israel's Hope Encouraged*, as it is printed, was 'pretty close to the sermon original, and follows the sermon method closely',[2] that with *The Resurrection of the Dead*, 'The form in which it is prepared, with minute divisions to assist the memory, and its colloquial language, indicate that it was first intended for the pulpit and then enlarged to form a more complete treatise; while the frequent recurrence of the words 'I say', shew the unpolished style in which he was in the habit of committing thoughts to paper, when he became an author,'[5] and that *Paul's Departure and Crown*, found in manuscript, prepared for the press, after Bunyan's death, 'bears the marks of having been composed, and perhaps preached, towards the end of his pilgrimage. Had his valuable life been spared a few months longer, this work would, very probably, have been enlarged, and the sub-divisions somewhat improved.'[4]

The sermon origin of this large part of Bunyan's work needs to be stressed, not merely as a bibliographical fact, but because it provides the stylistic and constructional patterns on which the elaborated literary structure was built, and because the colloquial nature of the original, mixing in varying degrees with the more self-conscious literary mode of the finished product, appears to account for the varying degrees of vitality in the work of treatise writers in general and Bunyan in particular.

The patterns—almost rules by the middle of the century—for the organization of sermons had been discussed in an extensive literature of which, I believe, Bunyan was not ignorant even in his early days, and in which, from the evidence of the work, he must have become increasingly conversant. I cannot accept the entirely unfounded hypothesis of C. F. Richardson that some polishing and elevating amanuensis stands between Bunyan's preaching and his printed word. 'What probably happened', Richardson suggested, 'was that after taking down the sermons by shorthand, a devoted follower transcribed his notes with an eye to dignifying the work of a man who was scorned by the educated clergy. The preferred method of sermon-construction

---

[1] Oxford Bunyan, ix. 135. [2] Offor, i. 577. [3] Offor, ii. 83.
[4] Offor, i. 721.

was considered an evidence of scholarly training . . . Reasonably, then, an admirer of Bunyan would wish him to appear in print not in the habit as he lived, but to some degree according to the manner of the preachers whose work and persons won respectful attention.'[1] Early in life, as a listener to sermons rather than a deliverer of them, Bunyan was aware of some of the technicalities and the technical jargon of sermon style. He recounts his attending a sermon on the text 'Behold thou art fair, my love; behold, thou art fair', and how the preacher 'made these two words, *My love*, his chief and subject matter; from which after he had opened the text, he observed these several conclusions: . . . only when he came to the application of the fourth particular, this was the word he said . . .'.[2] Indeed, it is probably as a listener that he first gave his attention to the parts and divisions of a sermon as an aid to remembering the discourse, to meditate upon it or report it. As a good Puritan he would not be counted among that congregation where, as he wrote, 'The heads, also, and the hearts of most hearers are to the Word as the sieve is to water; they can hold no sermons, remember no texts, bring home no proofs, produce none of the sermon to the edification and profit of others.'[3] When called forth from his fellows to preach that Word, what more likely than that he would receive instruction from his fellow-preachers, and that he would study more closely the art of his new calling in the extensive body of preaching manuals with which the century abounded, and which, in varying degrees of complexity, lay down the generally accepted framework on which properly constructed sermons, and all these sermon-treatises were built.

William Perkins, whose *The Art of Prophecying* of 1592 has already been referred to, was the most recommended and quoted authority among the dissenting sects. At the end of his lengthy work, he sums up:

> The Order and Summe of the sacred
> and onely methode of Preaching.
> 1) To reade the Text distinctly out of the Canonicall Scriptures.

---

[1] C. F. Richardson, *English Preachers and Preaching* (London and New York, 1928), p. 74.

[2] *G.A.*, p. 29.

[3] *Christ a complete Saviour*, Offor, i. 214.

2) To give the sense and understanding of it being read, by the Scripture itselfe.

3) To collect a fewe and profitable points of doctrine out of the naturall sense.

4) To apply (if he have the gift) the doctrines rightly collected, to the life and manners of men in a simple and plaine speech.

Here the three main divisions, which we meet with in all subsequent discussions, are expounded—Explication of the text, the 'collection' and proof of doctrines from it, and the Application, 'whereby the doctrine rightly collected is diversly fitted according as place, time, and person do require'.[1] Some thirty years later we find this same basic scheme, but now sophisticated and elaborated. John Wilkins, as we have seen, published in 1646 his *Ecclesiastes, or, A Discourse concerning the Gifts of Preaching as it falls under the rules of Art*. He offers, in directions and diagrams, the fullest exposition of the maximum sectioning and subsectioning of a sermon. He lays down three main divisions, Explication, Confirmation, and Application. 'Explication' is of the text itself, its difficulties of sense, words, historical reference, translation problems, and so on, and it also deals with doctrines derived from the text. Wilkins, excessively analytical as he seems, nevertheless warns against 'That common practice of dissecting the words into minute parts and enlarging upon them severally . . . a great occasion of impertinency and roving from the chief sense.' 'Confirmation' moves on to bring positive proofs of the truth of the text and its doctrines from Scripture, in notions and practical examples, and from Reason, in argument and practical observation. It also offers solutions to any doubts and questions on the doctrines expounded which may arise in the hearers' minds. The third main section, 'Application', is partly doctrinal, pointing out the possible personal application of the doctrine in self-examination or in deeper faith and understanding, and partly practical, in reproof, dissuasion from sin, and directions for reform; in consolation by promises and by removing unnecessary scruples; and in exhortation where, by showing the dangers and profits involved in disobedience and obedience, the affections of the hearers are excited to act, and practical ways of action are offered. In this last part he insists that 'the severall heads or uses we are to insist upon,

[1] p. 664.

must not here be handled, in a generall notionall way, as in the doctrinall parts, but in such a home and applicatory manner, as may have some perculiar reference to the hearers.'[1] This method persisted, honoured and observed in most dissenting pulpits throughout the century. Little change of idea can be discovered in such a late example of preaching manuals as James Arderne's *Directions Concerning the Matter and Stile of Sermons*, published in 1671, which still offers as the best basic construction 'that of Proposition, Confirmation, and Inference' or 'Doctrine, Reason, and Use' even though there are 'many Preachers at present, who are very shie in naming these words, because they were so frequent amongst the dissenting Ministrie'.[2]

Such shyness amongst the established clergy of speaking in a language with such unpleasant associations can well be understood, for this dividing of the text and the dividing of the sermon had become the butt of satire before the century was out. Sir John Berkenhead in 1662, with deflating imagery, mocks the preacher who '*Butchers* a Text, cut's it (just as the *Levite* did his *Concubine*) into many dead Parts, breaking the Sense and Words all to pieces, and then they are not Divided, but shatter'd, like the Splinters of *Don Quixot's* Lance'.[3] John Eachard, in 1670, writes of this part of the sermon with excited apprehension: 'In the next place, he comes to divide the Text . . . Now come off the Gloves . . .' and wearily records that 'I have known, now and then, some Knotty Texts, that have been divided seven or eight times over, before they could make them split handsomely, according to their mind', substantiating his attack with many ludicrous examples.[4] Joseph Glanvil was of a similar opinion, and in his discourse on preaching in 1678, while accepting the need of a shapely structure, asserted that 'Of all the Vanities in Preaching there is none less accountable than this, of dividing Texts into indivisibles; and mincing them into single words; which makes them signifie nothing . . . your divisions should be into solid and main parts, obvious in the Text, and apt to yield occasion for serious, and substantial Discourse.'[5] He might well have had in mind those complex diagrams in Wilkin's *Ecclesiastes* when he attacked the

---

[1] pp. 12–15. [2] pp. 27–8. [3] *The Assembly Man* (1662), p. 16.
[4] *The Grounds and Occasions of the Contempt of the Clergy and Religion Enquired into* (1670), pp. 66–7.
[5] *An Essay Concerning Preaching* (1678), pp. 46–7.

'tedious Prolixity' of the Applications section of sermons preached by men who 'run their Applications into numerous, coincident *Uses*, as of *Information, Confutation, Instruction, Reproof, Exhortation, Dehortation, Comfort, Direction* and the like . . .'.[1] But such satire in its own time and throughout the following century does not seem to have shamed the dissenting preacher from his method. It persisted well into the nineteenth-century chapels as Emily Brontë must have known when she created Mr. Lockwood's delirious nightmare about 'seventy Times Seven, and the First of the Seventy First. A Pious Discourse delivered by the Reverend Jabes Branderham, in the Chapel of Gimmerden Sough'. With horror he records 'and he preached— good God! what a sermon; divided into *four hundred and ninety* parts . . .'.[2]

While Bunyan never reaches this nightmare extremity, the treatises in this volume, 'composed', as Tindall says, 'with the purpose of his sermons, logical extensions of the art of familiar preaching',[3] are constructed with varying degrees of intricacy on this honoured and accepted pattern of division and subdivision.

Of equal concern to the preachers of the word and the expositors of their art was the language and rhetoric of the discourses they sought so strictly to divide and organize. The dissenters saw themselves in reaction against the preaching style of the earlier establishment, condemning it as over-elaborate in its rhetoric and figured prose, over-learned in its Greek and Latin tags and patristic quotations, even profane in its use of non-scriptural authors and modern knowledge, 'the learning of this world and the wisdom of the flesh'. Their critics had no doubts about why the old style could not be maintained by the new preachers. John Eachard, looking back on the sermons of the century, saw the change as inevitable. 'Nor is it any Miracle,' he wrote, 'that Preaching was abused in those days, when a learned Orthodox Clergy was silenced for their malignant *Loyalty*, and their Pulpits filled with Shoe-makers, Taylors, Weavers, Threshers, Coblers, Tinkers, Brewers, Bakers, Fishmongers, Wool-Combers, and all manner of Russet-Rabbies, and Mechanick Divines: No wonder if there was rare work made with *Texts* and *Preachments*.'[4] This

---

[1] Ibid., p. 52.   [2] *Wuthering Heights*, Everyman edn., p. 18–19.
[3] W. Y. Tindall, *John Bunyan, Mechanick Preacher*, p. 179.
[4] *The Grounds and Occasions*, p. 74.

line of attack, founded on educational and class prejudice, was constant and unvaried, and the great Tinker was only one of many who patiently suffered and ignored it, strengthened by a deep belief in the need for a new language in a new situation and with a new task to perform, 'simple and perspicuous, fit both for the peoples understanding, and to expresse the Maiestie of the spirit'.[1] Moreover they believed they had a divine pattern and justification of their simple style in the teaching of Jesus. 'The Lord', wrote John Downame, 'in the profunditie of wisdome could have written in such a loftie stile as would have filled even the most learned with admiration, yet he useth a simple easie stile fit for the capacity of all, because it was for the use of all, and necessarie to salvation to bee understood of all sorts and conditions.'[2] This necessity 'to bee understood of all sorts and conditions' and to move the hearers to repentance and faith rather than admiration, is the motive which the apologists and instruction manuals return to again and again. The influential John Wilkins is typical when he asserts that '... it will not become the Majesty of a Divine Enbassage, to be garnished out with flaunting affected eloquence. How unsuitable is it to the expectation of a hungry soul, who comes unto this ordinance with a desire of spiritual comfort and instruction, and there to hear onely a starched speech full of puerile worded Rhetorick.'[3] Bunyan himself, in *The Holy City*, addressing The Learned Reader, adds edge to the claim: 'Besides, Sir, words easy to be understood do often hit the mark, when high and learned ones do only pierce the air. He also that speaks to the weakest, may make the learned understand him; when he that striveth to be high, is not only for the most part understood but of a sort, but also many times is neither understood by them nor by himself.'[4]

The prescriptive criticism springing from this general idea is, for the most part negative, a listing of devices the preacher should avoid, habits he should repress, a recipe for cleansing and purifying. William Perkins decrees that 'neither the words of art nor Greeke and Latine phrases and quirkes must be intermingled in the sermon', that 'the telling of tales and all profane and ridiculous speeches must be

---

[1] William Perkins, *The Art of Prophecying*, ii. 670.
[2] John Downame, *The Christian Warfare* (1612), p. 341.
[3] John Wilkins, *Ecclesiastes*, p. 72.   [4] *The Holy City*, Offor, iii. 398.

omitted', and he forbids his preacher to 'feed his auditorie with Philosophie, or fables, or lying legends ... poeticall fictions, Thalmidical dreams, Schoolmens quiddities, Popish decrees, or humane constitutions, or to tickle the itching eares of his auditorie with the fine ringing sentences of the Fathers'.[1] This quoting of the Fathers and other writers seems to have been particularly obnoxious, suspected no doubt as a sign that when a preacher had to speak through the mouths of others he spoke not from his own heart. John Wilkins, in what on the whole is a moderate discourse, is quite firm in his views. 'To stuffe a Sermon with citations of Authors, and the witty sayings of others', he writes, 'is to make a feast of vinegar and pepper, which may be very delightful being used moderately as sauces, but must needs be very improper and offensive to be fed upon such as diet.'[2]

It would be wrong, however, to think that the diet offered by the dissenting preachers and treatise writers was entirely plain meat. It had its own spices and sauces not seen as such by those who used them, because they were accepted and their own; but they were distinctive enough to be isolated, defined, and often as severely criticized by the establishment as the high style had been by the Puritans. In other words, the dissenting pulpit created its own peculiar rhetoric which its practitioners did not clearly recognize as such, and to the excesses of which they could be oblivious.

The rejection of secondary authorities, the Fathers and other divine or profane authors, led inevitably to a constant appeal to scriptural authority, word, and example. In many preachers this obviously became an excessive 'Concordance' method which soon found its critics deprecating 'the ridiculous, senseless and unintended use, which many of them make of Concordances', when preachers 'must bring into the Sermon, to no purpose at all, a vast heap of Scripture'.[3] Joseph Glanvil echoes this when he advises the preacher that 'you should not prove by your Concordance but by your understanding and Judgment; not by the sound of words, but by the Sense of things. And you are to look upon it as an abuse of Scripture, to heap Texts to no purpose.'[7]

[1] William Perkins, *The Art of Prophecying*, ii. 670.
[2] John Wilkins, *Ecclesiastes*, p. 13.
[3] John Eachard, *The Grounds and Occasions*, pp. 78–9.
[4] Joseph Glanvil, *An Essay concerning Preaching*, 2nd edn., (1703), p. 51.

The age-old rhetorical trick of repetition both of word and phrase, to increase emotional pressure and build up climax, was by no means despised by these plain preachers. Bunyan was himself a skilful practitioner of the method, in its many variations, who managed to avoid most of the abuses its cruder users committed. Zachary Grey, collecting examples of such abuses in his *English Presbyterian Eloquence*, offers one fine example from Rutherford's Fast Sermon to the House of Commons in 1643, an attempt to apply rhetorical pressure without adding anything to the meaning:

We are all for Time; We are for a Time Court, a Time Glory, a Time Prince, a Time Friend, a Time Husband, a Time Brother, a Time Heaven and Happiness, a Time Deliverance in Trouble, Time Riches, Time Joy, and Time Pleasure, Time Triumphing, and Time Life &c. But we may find in the King of Ages, the same good things, of another Nature, as we find in God. Eternal Court, Eternal Glory, an Eternal King, an Eternal Friend, an Eternal Happiness, Eternal Riches, Eternal Victory; in sum, Life Eternal.[1]

Even worse was the habit of repeating over and over again the name of Christ or of the Lord Jesus in what appears to be a naïve belief that the oftener the Holy Name was uttered, the holier and more affecting the discourse became. This, joined often with a peculiar jargon invented by the Dissenters to describe the union with, acceptance of, and dependence on Christ, produced examples eagerly seized on by their opponents and satirists. John Eachard complained that too often these preachers attempted 'to make people sigh and cry by meer repetition of *Scripture* words' and that 'to repeat the word *Christ* (for that was then, and is still by many called *preaching of Christ*) . . . is still too often that which the *Nonconformists* call *powerful preaching*'.[2] Joseph Glanvil sarcastically offers one good example of this repetition and jargon in 'But if you tell the People that they must roll upon *Christ*, close with *Christ*, get into *Christ*, get a saving interest in the Lord *Christ*; O this is savoury, this is precious, this is spiritual teaching indeed.'[3] Such empty rhetoric is not to be found in Bunyan. True, the name of Christ was often on his lips, but never as an empty refrain, and his moving rhetoric is too firmly underpinned with strenuous thought and argument to fall into the jargon which conceals lack of thought or clarity of idea.

---

[1] Zachary Gray, *English Presbyterian Eloquence* (1736), p. 5.
[2] John Eachard, *The Grounds and Occasions*, pp. 113 and 111.
[3] Joseph Glanvil, *An Essay concerning Preaching*, p. 26.

This ability of Bunyan to use the accepted forms and style of his co-religionists, to exploit their strength, and avoid their pitfalls of excess and crudity, is demonstrated finally in his handling of another figure of speech which received wide discussion in the preaching manuals and provided equally extensive material for the satirists—the use of metaphor and simile or, as these writers preferred, 'similitudes'. Their value to the preacher was never questioned, nor their power to add delight to instruction and to bring home more powerfully and understandably to the congregation the abstract truths of faith and salvation. 'Similes', wrote Richard Bernard, 'are of excellent use even to teach, move, and delight the hearer, and their ministrie most powerful which most use them.'[1] Bunyan closely echoes this in *The Holy City*: 'Indeed similitudes, if fitly spoke and applied, do much set off and out any point that either in the doctrines of faith or manners, is handled in the churches.'[2] The same advice governed the choice of similitudes as the choice of words. The plain style was to be made of the everyday language of the people, avoiding swellings, archaisms, and learned vocabulary: the similitudes, to match this diction, were to be drawn from the everyday objects, experience, work, and trade of the congregation. The same strengths were possible and the same pitfalls lay in the way, a robust and telling immediacy, or 'a groveling stoop to clownish phrases'.[3] The search for similitudes could, in some preachers, become almost frantic, in its wide-ranging and continuous activity. John Eachard considered this 'inconsiderate use of frightful Metaphors' to be one of the main grounds for the contempt of these preachers, and pilloried them as, in their search for metaphors, they rushed 'away presently to both the *Indies*, rake Heaven and Earth, down to the bottom of the Sea, then tumble over all the Arts and Sciences, ransack all Shops and Ware-houses, spare neither Camp nor City, but that they will have them'.[4] Certainly the collections of examples made by their opponents would justify the violence of these attacks. The *Quaint Sermons of Samuel Rutherford* show the possible

[1] Richard Bernard, *The Faithful Shepherd* (1607), pp. 65–6.
[2] *The Holy City*, Offor, iii. 409.
[3] James Arderne, *Directions concerning the Matter and Stile of Sermons* (1671), p. 50.
[4] John Eachard. *The Grounds and Occasions*, pp. 45 and 46.

range, from images taken, with some effectiveness, from commonplace
events and objects:

Prayer is like God's file to stir a rusty heart.

And little thanks to you to swim when Christ holds up your chin.

. . . there is no more strength in him to stand against Him than in an old moth-
eaten clout that falls out all in holes when any hand touches it.

moving towards oddity in such an extended image as:

. . . silly, tempted, wounded, crossed soldier, look up to the standard-bearer,
Ensigner Jesus, in red and white! Take courage and buy a heart from Christ
. . . His colours slapped with cannon bullets . . . but God sews the holes in
Christ's standard again.

and degenerating into the tasteless crudity of physical detail which
these preachers obviously thought powerfully affecting:

swell not in pride . . . If you do, look for a temptation, as God's lance to make a
hole and let out the wind.

No man owes his tongue to lick his neighbours running boils.

We are like the fly that cannot sit down upon the whole skin, but with eyes,
smell and tongue, we fall upon the sore boil at the first.[1]

Zachary Grey, with more direct satirical intent in his selection of these
'remarkable Flowers of Rhetorick' provides further fascinating speci-
mens. Andrewe Perne asked the House of Commons in a Fast Sermon
of 1643, 'Shall we, like tame fools, suffer everyone to wipe our Noses
of God?' Simeon Ashe in a funeral sermon of 1654 built carefully up to
his bathetic climax in 'Some though they smile upon Christ's Face
with a Salute, yet they stab his Body; they kiss his Mouth, and tread
upon his Toes.' Spurstow told both Houses of Parliament in 1643 that
'The Fresh Rememberance of Sin is like a Pea in an Issue, that keeps it
open, and makes it run', and no doubt the House of Lords was
contented to be informed by Edmund Calamy in that same year that
'There is nothing done in the Lower House of Parliament upon Earth,
but what is decread in the Higher House of Parliament in Heaven.'[2]

---

[1] *Quaint Sermons of Samuel Rutherford, hitherto unpublished* (1885), pp. 134, 113, 37,
151, 86, 140.
[2] Zachary Grey: *English Presbyterian Eloquence*, pp. 5, 12, 6, 4.

Bunyan again avoids, on the whole, the excesses of his fellow preachers and achieves in his image-making, much effective strength and often beauty. Certainly he is not free from such occasional oddities as 'Oh Sinner! What saist thou! Doth not thy Mouth water? Doth not thy Heart twitter at being saved?'[1] Or, '. . . for if you do, hope will stay below, and creak in the wheels as it goes, because it will want the oil of faith'.[2] These three treatises are seldom marred in this way, although he can undeniably seem tasteless and crude to the delicate ear with such images as 'if thou shalt after a gracious manner suck in the Gospel-dung';[3] or, at greater length: 'A loathing of sin, *because* it is sin, that he cannot have, but a loathing of sin because it is offensive to him, that he may have: the dog doth not loath that which troubleth his stomach because it is there, but because it troubleth him; when it has done troubling of him, he can turn to it again, and lick it up as before it troubled him.'[4] Elsewhere his images work, drawing on a wide range of homely and vivid objects and acts which a few examples will illustrate:

This word lies in the Bible, as excellent salves lie in some mens houses, thrust into a hole, and not thought on for many moneths, because the houshold people have no wounds nor sores: In time of sickness, what so set by, as the Doctors glasses, and gally-pots full of his excellent things; but when the person is grown well, the rest is thrown to the dunghil.[5]

. . . some professors do with religion, just as people do with their best apparrel, hang it against the wall all the week, and put them on on Sundays . . .[6]

. . . then dost thou think that thou art a Wise Man to let thy Immortal Soul hang over Hell by a Thread of uncertain time, which may soon be cut asunder by Death.[7]

. . . some Professors, do not go on so fast in the way of God, as a Snail doth go on the Wall.[8]

Also the *Law*, that *can shoot a great way*, have a care thou keep out of the reach of those great Guns, the Ten Commandments.[9]

---

[1] *Light for them that sit in Darkness*, Oxford Bunyan, viii. 182.
[2] *Israel's Hope Encouraged*, Offor, i. 577.
[3] *The Barren Fig-Tree*, p. 43, l. 4.   [4] *The Strait Gate*, p. 116, ll. 7–11.
[5] *The Strait Gate*, p. 72, ll. 12–17.   [6] *The Strait Gate*, p. 99, ll. 24–26.
[7] *The Heavenly Foot-man*, p. 140, ll. 23–25.
[8] *The Heavenly Foot-man*, p. 149, ll. 27–28.
[9] *The Heavenly Foot-man*, p. 151, ll. 5–7.

The Heavenly Foot-man seemed inevitably to produce a wide range of images from journeying and the dangers and privations of the road 'Because', writes Bunyan, 'the *way is long*, (I speak Metaphorically) and there is many a dirty step, many a high Hill, much Work to do, a wicked Heart, World and Devil to overcome.'[1] The outline plan of a different work is already starting to emerge in these scattered images in which the reader cannot fail to recognize the new form of the larger and all-embracing allegory of *The Pilgrim's Progress*.

(iv)

The development to that form depends essentially upon the use of such metaphors or similitudes as we have been discussing, and the pattern of the development is of a change in the nature of metaphor, from an incidental to a continuous use, the movement of metaphor from a peripheral to a central position, from a mass of metaphors drawn from varied objects and actions to a body of metaphors all springing from one dominant metaphor, and in the use of the metaphor from an illustrative to an organizing and structural purpose. The obvious stages in Bunyan's works are threefold: many sermons and sermon treatises with little or no metaphorical content; a group where the metaphorical usage is on the increase and where some of his favourite metaphors are being tentatively and occasionally explored; treatises, such as the three in this volume, where a single controlling metaphor has become the instrument to structure and develop the work; and finally, the move beyond these three, where the single metaphor, elaborated and extended into a narrative, has become the vehicle for the fully developed allegory of *The Holy War* and *The Pilgrim's Progress*. This development is not necessarily one which can be charted chronologically through Bunyan's works. Rather it is a matter of stylistic discovery as he moved towards the way in which he thought and wrote most powerfully and memorably, even though he sometimes had, through necessity or choice, to revert to plainer and often less successful modes of argument and exhortation.

---

[1] *The Heavenly Foot-man*, p. 150, ll. 15–17.

Many treatises provide examples of a style which has a minimal use ˄ven of illustrative metaphor. *The Saints Knowledge of Christ's Love*, suffering from excessive sermon subdivision and wearisome repetitiveness, shows the style which is, perhaps, the farthest from allegory, with a word-by-word analysis for its structure rather than the verse-by-verse method which can more easily produce narrative interest, and with hardly any movement from statement into metaphor. *Light for them that sit in Darkness, Justification by Imputed Righteousness*, and *Come and Welcome to Jesus Christ* have a similar barrenness of figurative interest.

But the similitude was a figure which, in its dangers and its possibilities, fascinated Bunyan, and one on which he often commented. 'I choose to follow the similitude', he writes, '. . . because the Scripture seems to smile upon such a way of discourse . . .';[1] and towards the end of his life after the great works were written, 'These words are metaphorical, a word by which a thing most excellent is presented to and amplified before our faces.'[2] His fullest discussion and defence is, of course, in the verses prefaced to the two parts of *The Pilgrim's Progress*. With this interest, and perhaps the discovery that he had a natural talent in the finding and elaborating of similitudes, it is not surprising that they start to appear more frequently with a consequent enrichment of his writing.

The incidental use of the metaphors which, centrally used, lie behind the three treatises of this volume, illustrate this second stage of development. The imagery of *The Heavenly Foot-man* and *The Strait Gate*, of the journey to salvation, the temptations and difficulties, and the strengthenings of Grace which accompany the Footman, the severity of the final test at the end of the journey, often appear to illustrate and strengthen a point, and obviously are parts of two main allegorical images which were constant ones in Bunyan's imaginative theological thinking. In *Law and Grace*, 'Many go in at the broad gate'.[3] *Israel's Hope Encouraged* is, for some reason, particularly frequent in its use of both these metaphors, as it speaks of 'those difficulties that men, by frights and terrors, may lay in our way', and how Hope 'is one piece

---

[1] *The Work of Jesus Christ as an Advocate*, Offor, i. 171.
[2] *The Water of Life*, Offor, iii. 540.
[3] *Law and Grace*, Oxford Bunyan, ii. 176.

of armour with which the Son of God was clothed when he came into the world', which 'will point and show . . . the gate afar off',[1] and there is quite an extended treatment of the image when Mercy 'shall follow us to guide us in the way . . . by the same he will uphold our goings in his paths . . . though the path we go in were never so plain, yet we are apt to stumble and fall . . . Mercy shall follow to carry thee when thou art faint . . . Mercy shall follow us, to take us up when we are fallen, and to heal us of those wounds that we have caught by our falls.'[2] The pilgrim is exhorted to 'Look behind thee, take a view of the path thou hast trodden these many years. Dost thou think that the way that thou art in will lead thee to the strait gate, sinner?'[3] *A Treatise of the Fear of God* provides a further example of the incidental use of this image, to be exploited centrally and continuously in these two treatises and ultimately in *The Pilgrim's Progress*. 'Thou hast chosen the way to life, Gods way', the listener is told,

but perhaps thy ignorance about it is so great, and those that tempt thee to turn aside, so many, and so subtil, that they seem to outwit thee, and confound thee with their guile. Well, but the Lord whom thou fearest will not leave thee to thy ignorance, nor yet to thine enemies power or subtilty, but will take it upon himself to be thy teacher and thy guide, and that in the way that thou hast chosen . . . and whoever wanders, turns aside, and swerveth from the way of Salvation: whoever is benighted, and lost in the midst of darkness, thou shalt find the way to the Heaven and the glory that thou hast chosen . . . he hath the heart and mind of God still discovered to him in the way that he hath chosen even all the way from this world, to that which is to come, even until he shall come to the very gate and door of Heaven.[4]

Even more frequent are the incidental occurrences of the Barren Fig-tree image. *A Holy Life the Beauty of Christianity* often uses it, as might be expected, in its attacks on the fruitless professors of the faith. *The Acceptable Sacrifice* laments how, with some sinners, '. . . their hard heart, their stupified heart, has no sense of such kindness as this, and therefore they take no notice of it. How many times has God said to this dresser of his vineyard, "Cut down the barren fig-tree," while he yet, by his intercession, has prevailed for a reprieve for another year!'[5]

---

[1] *Israel's Hope Encouraged*, Offor, i. 582–90.
[2] Ibid., i. 598.   [3] Ibid., i. 620.
[4] *A Treatise of the Fear of God*, Oxford Bunyan, ix. 77–8.
[5] *The Acceptable Sacrifice*, Offor, i. 711.

The image receives more extended treatment in a passage from *Of The Resurrection of the Dead*, with more hint of narrative action and drama:

if thou hast but a tree in thy orchard, that neither beareth fruit, nor ought else that is good, why thou art for hewing it down, and for appointing it, as fuel for the fire. Now thou little thinkest that by thy thus judging thou shouldest pass sentence upon thy own fruitless soul; but it is so . . . For as truly as thou sayest of thy fruitless tree, Cut it down, why doth it cumber the ground, so truly doth thy voice cause heaven to echo again upon thy head, Cut him down; why doth he cumber the ground?[1]

Small wonder that when Bunyan came to write the sermons to be inset as part of the complex allegory of *The Holy War*, he should take up this image again. Captain Execution bears on his escutcheon 'a fruitless tree, with an axe lying at the root thereof', and his sermon to Mansoul is a miniature *Barren Fig-Tree*. When Captain Boanerges, at the request of the subordinate Preacher, preaches to the afflicted inhabitants of Mansoul, '. . . his text was this, "Cut it down, why cumbereth it the ground?" and a very smart sermon he made upon the place . . . For this sermon, as well as the former, wrought much upon the hearts of the men of Mansoul; yea it greatly helped to keep awake those that were roused by the preaching that went before.'[2] Nine years before the Captain's Sermon, Bunyan himself preached and published a smart sermon, with the image of the barren fig-tree and the drama of its reprieves and final doom no longer incidentally illustrative, but now the single organizing metaphor of the work.

Such sermons as these with this single metaphor at their centre are not unique to Bunyan. He was, as often, working in an accepted seventeenth-century mode although, as often again, producing something far more exciting and alive than his models. To read some of these almost forgotten productions is to realize that the use of the single metaphor by no means guaranteed the successful shaping of a lively homily. Faithful Teate, in 1655, pursued the metaphor of the map and pathfinding at an interminable length through his *A Scripture-map of the Wildernesse of Sin*, an example of metaphor expansion or complication completely lacking in narrative interest or progression. A similar example is William Gurnall's *The Christian in Compleat Armour*,

[1] *Of The Resurrection of the Dead*, Offor, ii. 112.
[2] *The Holy War*, ed. Sharrock and Forrest (Oxford, 1980), pp. 158–9.

Or, a Treatise of the Saints War against the Devil . . . *A Magazin open'd: from Whence the Christian is furnish'd with Spiritual Armes for the battel, help't on with his Armour, and taught the use of his Weapon,* which manages to keep up the martial metaphor through 396 pages. Thomas Porter's appallingly dull sermon *Spiritual Salt,* preached in 1649, riddled with text-crumbling and concordance-disease, exploits the image of salt and all its properties, and reaches its conclusion with: 'Providence hath pitcht my thoughts on this Subject, that whensoever you see Salt on a table, whether Minister or people, you may remember your duty respectively. And let me beseech you to take what I have said, *cum grano salis,* with a grain of Salt, and then all will relish well, which that you may do, let us pray—'. There are examples too of such sermons centred on the same metaphors used by Bunyan in these three treatises. The strait gate was used by the Reverend William Payne in 1698,[1] and the Bishop of Exeter, the Right Reverend Ofspring Blackall, had preached on the same text.[2] More interesting and more thoroughgoing in its use of the metaphor are the Reverend Dr. Mark Frank's sermons for the fourth and fifth Sundays in Lent on the same texts as those of *The Heavenly Foot-man.*[3] The first, on 'So run that you may obtain', declares 'That Christianity is a Race, and Heaven the Goal, and we, all of us, they that are to run, is an Ordinary *Allegory* in *Scripture* and *Sermons,* which you have none of you but heard,' and it uses the terms of the race, running, how to run, the end in sight, while the related metaphors of training, exercise, exhaustion, and endurance hold the sermon together. The sermon for the 5th Sunday in Lent employs the imagery of wrestling, following through the parallel between the Olympic and the heavenly struggle, and the corruptible and incorruptible crowns of victory. It was in the context of such works as these, of varying degrees of complexity and success, that Bunyan worked with a similar range of worthwhile achievement.

The use of this central organizing metaphor is not, as we have seen in these sermons of other divines, a sure way to greatness. The variations in liveliness and ability to hold our attention seem to vary in the same proportion as another element—narrative or dramatic development, between a static metaphor which can be turned round

---

[1] William Payne, *Discourses upon Several Practical Subjects* (1698), p. 71.
[2] *The Works* (1723), ii. 852.   [3] *LI Sermons* (1672).

and round and seen from different angles but which never moves, and a metaphor which has in it the potential for action, movement, change, and dramatic tensions. An example of the static metaphor-elaboration would be Teate's *A Scripture-map of the Wildernesse of Sin*, and, in Bunyan's writings, *The Work of Jesus Christ as an Advocate* where he uses the central similitude of the Advocate with its related terminology of law and court-room procedure, but in a static way without narrative progression or interest, producing a treatise which is in no way one of his more memorable performances.

When the main metaphor has this inbuilt narrative possibility, Bunyan's writing gathers impetus and excitement, his language becomes more intense and personal. In other words, he shows his real power the nearer he moves towards a metaphor in action, where metaphor and fable combine to lead him to allegory. It was his good fortune that the central spiritual patterns of the preaching of his time and of his religious persuasion provided him with the two great metaphors of action which were to be the foundation of his greatest works. Spiritual biography in one way, and sermons in another, were largely occupied in tracing step by step the progress of the soul from sin and hardness of heart, to an acknowledgement of sin and the struggle onwards, through the darkness of the resultant sorrow and despair, to faith in salvation and confidence in final glory. Parallel to this was the vivid presentation of the dangers and temptations which threatened the soul in its progress, the machinations of the Devil as he struggled to hinder the movement to salvation, which must be fought against and conquered. Clearly and inevitably, from these two concerns came the great metaphors of the life of the spirit, as a journey or pilgrimage, and as a warfare. At one extreme these images could appear incidentally and illustrative of moral and theological statements: at the other they could become the central and predominant vehicle from which a moral and a theology had to be inferred and understood. At this point of highest development stand Bunyan's masterpieces shaped by these two predominant metaphors, *The Holy War* and *The Pilgrim's Progress*. In the treatises of this volume we are, as we have seen, at a half-way stage in this development, where a single metaphor is held and elaborated, the related scenery, equipment, and vocabulary connected with that metaphor consistently used, and where the form moves towards greater life and nearer to allegory when the scene is realized with more vivid imaginative presentation, and when the excitement of narrative action is created. The extent of this narrative and dramatic content varies, and accounts partly for the unequal success of the treatises, although other features—rhetorical structures, the mode of analysing the chosen text, the tone of voice, and the varying rapport which Bunyan can achieve with his reader/congregation—must be taken into consideration to explain the different impression each of them makes.

(v)

The Strait Gate is perhaps the least powerful, and makes the most clogged and least exciting reading, only occasionally coming to life. One reason is quite clearly that the text itself has little narrative potential, but offers itself rather to close examination and explication of its separate words, a course which Bunyan takes here, consciously and unashamedly. Having dwelt for some time on the word 'in', he adds, 'This should teach us, not only to reade but to attend in reading, not only to read, but to lift up our hearts to God in reading, for if we be not heedful, if he give us not light and understanding; we may easily pass over without any great regard, such a word as may have a glorious kingdom and eternal salvation in the bowels of it ...'.[1] We are not allowed to pass easily over any fragment of the text, and the bowels of each word are diligently searched, often producing such constipated crumbling as '... for when he saith, *strive to enter in*; and in such phrases there is supposed a place or state or both to be enjoyed; enter *in*, enter into what, or whether but into a state or place or both ...',[2] and sometimes approaching that solemn presentation of the obvious which the satirists of dissenting sermons so often parodied: 'It is set forth by the similitude of a *gate*. A *gate*, you know, is of a double use, it is to *open* and *shut*, and so consequently, to let in, or to keep out; and to do both these *at the season* ...'.[3]

The main rhetorical colouring of the treatise is, correspondingly,

---

[1] *The Strait Gate*, p. 73, ll. 36.   [2] *The Strait Gate*, p. 73, ll. 2–5.
[3] *The Strait Gate*, p. 74, ll. 14–16.

one of verbal patterning, in word-play, word listing, word repetition and phrasal repetition and so on. Triplets are a favourite device and throughout the treatise he naturally falls into the rhythm of 'a little honour, a little profit, a little pleasure', 'watchful, diligent, unwearied', 'mighty, subtle and malicious', 'his word, and his name, and his ways'. This is frequently extended to multiple listings such as 'The world will seek to keep thee out of heaven, with mocks, flouts, taunts, threatnings, goals, gibbits, halters, burnings, and a thousand deaths, *therefore strive*. Again, if it cannot overcome thee with these, it will flatter, promise, allure, intice, intreat, and use a thousand tricks on this hand to destroy thee . . .';[1] or 'without are also the devils, and hell, and death, and all damned souls; without is houling, weeping, wailing, and gnashing of teeth; yea without are all the miseries, sorrows, and plagues . . .'.[2] At its most effective, this achieves a pulpit urgency: at its worst it is an empty and wearisome habit, producing such inanity as 'A remnant, a small remnant, a very small remnant: O how doth the holy Ghost word it, and all to shew you, how few shall be saved: everyone knows, what a remnant is, but this is a *small* remnant, a *very* small remnant,'[3] or the pointless marking-time-on-the-spot of '. . . poor sinner, thou readest here, that but a few will be saved, that many that expect heaven, will go without heaven; what saist thou to this, poor sinner? Let me say it over again: There are but few to be saved, but very few, let me add, but few professors; but few eminent professors; what saist thou now sinner?'[4] Phrasal repetition, developing out of verbal repetition, is his other predominant device, the repetition occurring at varying distances, closely, to give a mere equivalent of verbal repetition for effects of urgency, or at greater intervals as a refrain to mark off sections of a larger rhetorical arrangement. The first type can be seen in such lines as 'The heaven is within, *strive therefore to enter in*; the glory is within, *strive therefore to enter in*; the *Mount Sion* is within, *strive therefore to enter in*; the *heavenly Jerusalem* is within, *strive therefore to enter in; Angels, and Saints are within, strive therefore to enter in*; and to make up all, the God and father of our Lord Jesus Christ, and that glorious redeemer is within, *strive therefore to enter in*.'[5] The more extended repeat patterns

---

[1] *The Strait Gate*, p. 83, ll. 35. [2] *The Strait Gate*, p. 87, ll. 36.
[3] *The Strait Gate*, p. 108, ll. 5–8. [4] *The Strait Gate*, p. 119, ll. 17–22.
[5] *The Strait Gate*, p. 87, ll. 28–31.

have greater variety. Paragraphs are held in a larger group by the use of a repeated opening phrase such as

Now they will see what a kingdom it is . . .
They will now see what hell is . . .
Now they will see what the meaning . . .
Now they will see what glory . . .

or 'the poor ignorant world miss of heaven, because . . .'[1] used in a sixfold build-up.[2] It admits of variations within the repeat as in the extended exhortation to erring professors where each paragraph of warning closes with

. . . therefore let professors look to it.
. . . look to it professors.
. . . look to it professors.
. . . Look to it professors.
. . . Tremble professors, pray professors.
. . . watch and be sober, professors.[3]

It can exploit an opposition or contrast within the sevenfold contrast between 'Saving repentance' and 'the other repentance', and the tenfold contrast between 'Saving faith' and 'a faith that is not saving', which follows it.[4]

In the midst of all this, there are moments which remind us of Bunyan at his more compelling and which, when they occur, emphasize what is lacking elsewhere in *The Strait Gate*. When he ceases to preach in his own voice and, entering into the characters of his examples, speaks through them, we sense something of the strength of the dialogues of the greater allegories, as when latter-day Esaus ask '. . . *what good will this birth-right do me?* . . . tush (say they,) they talk of being born again, what good shall a man get by that? . . . no going to heaven without being born again, but God is merciful, Christ died for sinners, and we will turn when we can tend it, and doubt not but all will be well at last.'[5] Or again: 'God forbid that we should have been such sinners, but Lord, give an instance; when was it, or where? true, there

---

[1] *The Strait Gate*, p. 95, ll. 16–37.
[2] *The Strait Gate*, pp. 114–115.   [3] *The Strait Gate*, pp. 111–112.
[4] *The Strait Gate*, pp. 115–117.   [5] *The Strait Gate*, p. 100, ll. 23–28.

was a company of poor sorry people in the world very inconsiderable, set by with no body, but for thy self we professed thee, we loved thee, and hadst thou been with us in the world, wouldest thou have worn gold, wouldest thou have eaten the sweetest of the world, we would have provided it for thee . . .'.[1] Or in the fearful repetitions, dramatic now and not merely word patterns, of: 'Lord, Lord, *open unto us*. The devils are coming; Lord, Lord, the pit opens her mouth upon us: Lord, Lord there is nothing but hell and damnation left us, if Lord, Lord thou has not mercy upon *us*; *Lord, Lord open to us*.'[2] It is the infrequency of this sort of writing, the verbal anatomizing of the text and the verbal organizing of the rhetoric, rather than the exclusive severity of its message, which makes *The Strait Gate* the least attractive reading of these three.

The Barren Fig-Tree, on the other hand, is built around a text which, though quite brief, is a little narrative in itself and provokes a more narrative and dramatic treatment, a building up of tension with a progress of incidents, until the climax and expected catastrophe are reached. Not that the verbal rhetoric of *The Strait Gate* is absent. Repetition of questions and exclamations, repetition of words and phrases, and more complex patterned and choric repetitions are to be found in abundance. But the final impression of the treatise is stronger and more memorable for other reasons. The fable or parable has been grasped more imaginatively, and fleshed out with realistic detail. The phrase 'I come seeking fruit', instead of producing prose where 'every Word affords a distinct material Observation', expands into realized moments such as '. . . he goes round it, and round it, now looking into this bough, and then into that, he peeks into the inmost boughs, and the lowermost boughs, if perhaps fruit may be thereon,'[3] and the words 'Cut it down' are given a lively immediacy in a realistic garden scene:

Suppose such a *slip* as I told you of before, should be in your garden, and there die: *Would you let it abide in your Garden?* No! away with it, away with it. The woman comes into her garden towards the Spring, Where first she gives it a *slight* cast with her eye; then she sets to gathering out the *weeds*, and *nettles*, and *stones*; takes a *beesom* and *sweeps* the *walks*: this done, she falls to *prying* into her

---

[1] *The Strait Gate*, p. 98, ll. 2–8.   [2] *The Strait Gate*, p. 98, ll. 25–29.
[3] *The Barren Fig-Tree*, p. 31, ll. 17–19.

herbs and *slips*, to see if *they* live, to see if they are likely to grow: Now, *if she comes to one that is dead*, that she is confident will not grow, up she pulls that, and makes to the heap of rubbish with it, where she despisingly casts it down, and valueth it *no more* than a *nettle*, or a *weed*, or than the *dust* she hath swept out of her *walks*. Yea, if any that see her should say, Why do you so? The answer is ready, 'Tis dead, 'tis dead at root: If I had let it stand, 'twould but have cumbered the ground.'[1]

The approach to the climax is marked by similarly vividly realized scenes as the entrance of Death: 'At this, Death comes with *grim* looks into the Chamber, yea and Hell follows with him to the Bed-side, and both stare this Professor in the face, yea, begin to lay hands upon him';[2] while the execution itself is depicted with dramatically realistic horror, fusing and shifting between the tree-woodman vehicle of the metaphor and its sinner-death tenor:

Death is at his work, *Cutting of him down*, hewing both bark and heart, both Body and Soul asunder; The man groans, but Death hears him not: He looks gastly, carefully, dejectedly; he sighs, he sweats, he trembles, but Death matters nothing. . . . He that cuts him down, swaies him, as the Feller of wood, *swaies the tottering tree*; now this way, then that, at last a root breaks: an heart-string, an eye-string snaps asunder. . . . *Life* is going, the *Blood* settles in the *Flesh*, and the *Lungs* being now no more able to draw breath through the Nostrils, at last out goes the weary trembling Soul, who is immediately seized by Devils, who lay lurking in every hole in the Chamber, for that very purpose . . . .[3]

This more narrative, dramatic approach naturally offers opportunity for more realistic speech and dialogue, which only very occasionally enlivened *The Strait Gate*. Here Bunyan captures the real speaking voice, in monologue and dialogue, and makes it a much more staple ingredient of this treatise's method of driving home its message. He can fill out the character of the intercessor in his parable and, taking the plea, 'Lord, let it alone this year also', give him the real speech of 'Lord, a little longer, lets not lose a Soul for want of means; *I will try*, I will see if I can make it fruitful, *I will not beg a long life*, nor that it might still be *barren*, and so provoke thee. I beg for the sake of the Soul, the immortal Soul, Lord spare it *one year only, one year longer, this year also*; if I do any good to it, it will be *in little time*. Thou shalt not be over-

---

[1] *The Barren Fig-Tree*, p. 34, ll. 21–33.   [2] *The Barren Fig-Tree*, p. 51, ll. 33.
[3] *The Barren Fig-Tree*, p. 64, ll. 9–28.

wearied with waiting, *one year and then*.'[1] In a similar way the text's words 'After that, thou shalt cut it down' are expanded into an imagined speech of the disappointed intercessor: 'Father, I begg'd for *more time* for this barren Professor. I begged until I should *dig about it, and dung it*; But now, Father, the *time is out*, the year is ended, *the Summer is ended*, and no good done; I have also tried with my *means*, with the *Gospel*, I have digged about it; I have laid also the *fat* and *hearty* dung of the Gospel to it; *but all comes to nothing*.'[2] For the voice of the backsliding sinner, released from what had seemed his death-bed, he can lower the tone to the more colloquial directness of 'But by that he hath put on his cloaths, is come down from his bed, and ventured into the Yard, or Shop, and there sees how all things are gone to *Sixes* and *Sevens*, he begins to have *Second* thoughts: and saies to his folks, What have you all been doing? How are all things out of order? I am I cannot tell what behind-hand; one may see if a man be but a little a to-side, that you have neither wisdome, nor prudence to order things.'[3] Dialogue, too, adds dramatic urgency to the moments of fear and pleading and repentance, and it only needs a small alteration, removing the inset speaker-indications, to move from narrative to the drama of:

SINNER. *Lord, spare me, Lord, spare me.*

GOD. Nay . . . you have been a Provocation to me, *these three years*. How many times have you disappointed me? How many seasons have you spent in vain? How many Sermons and other Mercies did I of my patience afford you? but *all* to no purpose at all. *Take him Death.*

SINNER. O good Lord . . . Spare me but *this once*. Raise me but *this once*. Indeed I have been a barren Professor, and have stood to no purpose at all in thy Vine-yard: But spare! O spare, *this one time*, I beseech thee, and I will be better.

GOD. *Away, away*, you will not. I have tried you *these three years* already, you are nought; If I should recover you again, you would be as bad as you was before . . .

SINNER. Good Lord, try me *this once*, let me get up again *this once*, and *see* if I do not mend.

GOD. But will you promise me to mend?

SINNER. Yes indeed, Lord, and vow it too; I will never be so bad again, *I will be better.*

---

[1] *The Barren Fig-Tree*, p. 40, ll. 6–11.
[2] *The Barren Fig-Tree*, p. 44, ll. 26–30.
[3] *The Barren Fig-Tree*, p. 52, ll. 30–36.

GOD. Well . . . *Death*, let this Professor alone *for this time*. I will try him a while
   longer . . .¹

The Heavenly Foot-man once more varies the method and differs in
final effect. The text, while lacking the narrative potential of the fig-
tree and the husbandman, offers a metaphor with more possible
elaboration than that of the narrow gate, and a glance at the plan which
prefaces the treatise shows how the image and vocabulary of the race is
maintained in the structure of the piece. Running, stripping for a race,
keeping to the track, fixing one's eye on the path, refusing to be
distracted by the cries of those behind, the dangers, the stumbling, the
temptation to give in through exhaustion, to turn back—all these form
the separate images around which the sections of the treatise are built,
and are, at the same time, part of the greater image which gives the
treatise its unity. It stands, in its mode, between *The Strait Gate* and
The Barren Fig-Tree, lacking the dramatic progression and sense of
approaching catastrophe of the latter, but with greater imaginative
interest and complexity than the former, in its exploiting of the central
similitude.

It is not without the same verbal rhetoric of persuasion and
exhortation which the other treatises employ, but it is not so
elaborately contrived and consequently not so obvious. The constant
return to 'Run', 'so run', 'so run, that you may obtain', in the first
section, used as an urgent chorus, is typical of this simpler manner.
The repetition captures much more the speaking voice of the preacher
than the shaping hand of the writer:

Methinks I have seen sometimes, how these poor Wretches that get but almost
to Heaven, how fearfully their *almost*, and their but *almost* will torment them in
Hell. When they shall cry out in the bitterness of their Souls, saying, *I was
almost a Christian*, I was *almost* got into the Kingdom, *almost* out of the Hands
of the Devil, *almost* out of my Sins, *almost* from under the Curse of God,
Almost, and that was all, *almost, but not all together*. O that I should be *almost* at
Heaven, and should not go quite thorow!'²

The whole treatise has a much more personally involved urgency
and a tone of emotional caring than the other two, which this more
natural speaking-voice style helps largely to create. Much of the

---

¹ *The Barren Fig-Tree*, p. 52, ll. 9–24.
² *The Heavenly Foot-man*, p. 172, ll. 3–10.

exclamatory repetition is made up of affectionate addresses, 'Friend', 'Why Man', and the much more extensive use of the first person singular and personal reference further increase the impression of a closer personal relationship between writer and reader. 'I tell thee,' he writes in this intimate confessional manner, 'this is such a serious matter, and I fear thou wilt so little regard it, that the thoughts of the worth of the thing, and of thy too light regarding of it, doth even make my Heart ake whilst I am writing to thee.'[1] And again:

Sometimes, when my base Heart hath been inclining to this World, and to loiter in my Journey towards Heaven, the very consideration of the glorious Saints and Angels in Heaven, what they enjoy, and what *low thoughts they have of the things of this World* together, how they would befool me, if they did but know that my heart was drawing back, hath caused me to rush forward, to disdain these poor, low, empty beggarly things, and to say to my Soul, *come Soul let us not be weary*, let us see what this Heaven is, let us even venture all for it, and try if that will quit for cost.[2]

Exhortation, too, has this man-to-man intimacy, not the loftier denunciation of *The Barren Fig-Tree* or the systematized exposure of unworthiness of *The Strait Gate*, but rather an invitation to join the writer in a race he too is running: 'O therefore, *throw away stinking lusts*, follow after Righteousness, love the Lord Jesus, devote thy self unto his fear, I'll warrant thee he will give thee a goodly recompence. Reader, what sayest thou to this? Art resolv'd to follow me, nay, resolve if thou canst to get before me. *So Run, that ye may obtain.*'[3]

It was in this mood that the momentous notion came to Bunyan, and in his manipulating of the central similitude of this piece that the way forward suggested itself:

And thus it was: I writing of the Way
And Race of Saints in this our Gospel-Day,
Fell suddenly into an Allegory
About their Journey, and the way to Glory,
In more than twenty things, which I set down;
This done, I twenty more had in my Crown,

---

[1] *The Heavenly Foot-man*, p. 153, ll. 16–19.
[2] *The Heavenly Foot-man*, p. 168, ll. 23–31.
[3] *The Heavenly Foot-man*, p. 168, ll. 33.

And they again began to multipy,
Like sparks that from the coals of Fire do flie.
Nay then, thought I, if that you breed so fast,
I'll put you by your selves, lest you at last
Should prove *ad infinitum*, and eat out
The Book that I already am about.[1]

The excitement of the artist and the release of easy creative power in the new method of full allegory can be felt through the lines describing the creation of his masterpiece:

Thus I set Pen to Paper with delight,
And quickly had my thoughts in black and white.
For having now my Method by the end;
Still as I pull'd, it came: and so I penn'd
It down . . .[2]

If we value *The Heavenly Foot-man* for nothing else, we value it for this, that its map of the way and race of saints led Bunyan to the greater progress of pilgrims, and to an assured and consistent literary mastery of which the works in this volume give only occasional and exciting glimpses.

[1] *The Author's Apology for his Book*, Oxford Bunyan, vi. 136, ll. 7–18.
[2] Ibid., vi. 137, ll. 30–4.

THE
BARREN FIG-TREE

THE
Barren Fig-tree:
OR,
The Doom and Downfal of the Fruitless Professor.

Shewing,

That the Day of Grace may be past with him long before his Life is ended.
The Signs also by which such miserable Mortals may be known.

By *John Bunyan.*

And now also the Ax is laid unto the root of the trees: therefore every tree that bringeth not forth good fruit, is hewen down, and cast into the fire; Matth. 3. 10.

London, Printed for *Jonathan Robinson* at the Golden Lion in *Paul's* Church-yard, 1673.

Title-page of the 1673 first edition of *The Barren Fig-Tree*, from the Bruce Peel Special Collections Library in the University of Alberta.

THE BARREN FIG-TREE

Note on the Text

ONLY one edition of *The Barren Fig-tree*, that of 1673, was published during Bunyan's lifetime. The Term Catalogue for Michaelmas 1673 (Arber, i. 148) advertises 'The barren Fig tree, Or The doom and downfall of the fruitless Professor; Shewing that the day of grace may be past with him, long before his life is ended. In Twelves. Price, 1s.' There is no attribution to Bunyan or any other author. The book is advertised with two others, 'All three printed for Jonathan Robinson at the Golden Lion in St. *Paul's* Churchyard.'

This edition appears to have been unknown to Charles Doe, who lists the work as published in 1682, and both Offor and Brown followed Doe in accepting this as the date of the first publication of what Offor calls 'this solemn, searching, awful treatise'. F. M. Harrison in 1924 quoted the 1673 advertisement in the Term Catalogue, but noted, 'no copy of the 1st. ed. (1673) is known.'

The book, indeed, is exceedingly rare, one being in the possession of the Library of the University of Alberta, and another in the Newberry Library, Chicago. The Alberta copy was added to the Ralph Ford Collection of that University on acquisition by auction from Sotheby's, April 22, 1969 (Cat. Item 387, described as 'The Property of a Gentleman', p. 90).

THE FIRST EDITION, 1673

Title-page: [within rules] THE | **Barren Fig-tree:** | OR, | The Doom and Downfal of | the Fruitless Professor. | *Shewing,* | That the Day of Grace may be | past with him long before his Life | is ended. | The Signs also by which such mi- | serable Mortals may be known. | [rule] | By *John Bunyan.* | [rule] | *And now also the Ax is laid unto the* | *root of the trees: therefore every tree* | *that bringeth not forth good fruit, is* | *hewen down, and cast into the fire;* | Matth. 3. 10. | [rule] | *London,* Printed for *Jonathan Robinson* | at the Golden Lion in *Paul's* | Church-yard, 1673.

Collation: 12°: A⁶, B–I¹² [$ 5 – A, A2, A5, D5, G4, G5, H3; A5 is missigned A4.] Pages: [i–xii] + 192. Page 187 is misnumbered 163, and page 191 is misnumbered 161. The Alberta copy is deficient pages 57–64 (D9 – D12) inclusive.

Contents: [Binder's paper of Alberta copy inscribed in ink, 'Benedictus Winch 1696'.] A1ʳ blank [Alberta copy inscribed in ink 'Dan; Negus 1746/7]. A1ᵛ: [rule] | *ERRATA.* | Pag. 12. line 13. Leave out *in* | *appearance.* Pag. 35. lin. 17. for | *desire*, read *defer.* | *'Tis probable other faults (the | Author being absent) have escaped,* | *which the Reader is desired to par-|don.* | [rule]. A2ʳ title-page [the Alberta copy is inscribed in ink 'B. Davies 1857']. A2ᵛ blank. A3ʳ [double row of ornaments] | TO THE| READER. | [rule] — A6ʳ: (signed) J. Bunyan. | [rule]. A6ᵛ [rule]. | *Books lately printed for* Jo- | nathan Robinson. | An Exposition upon the *Eighth* Chapter | to the *Romans*, By *Tho. Jacomb*, D.D. | In quarto. | The Anatomy of Infidelity, *Etc. large* | *Octav.* by *Theoph. Gale.* | The Virgin Saint, *or* the pious Life and | Christian Death of *Mary Wilson*, in | small *Octav.* | Correction, Instruction; *or*, a Treatise | of Affliction, By *Tho. Case.* | *Quakerism* no Christianity, *Etc.* by | *J. Faldo.* | The great Concern: *or*, A serious | Warning for a timely and through- | Preparation for Death. The *Second* | Edition, now in the Press, by *Ed-* | *ward Pearse.* | [Rule]. B1ʳ: [single row of ornaments] THE **Barren Fig-tree:** | Or, | The Doom and Down- | fall of the fruitless | Professor. | [rule] — I12ᵛ: [rule] FINIS | [rule], text. [The back cover of the Alberta copy is inscribed in ink 'I thank you very kindly for yᵉ use of this Book And god grant yᵗ neither you nor I may be barren nor unfruitfull.']

Running titles: Running title of the address to the reader, 'To the Reader'. Running title to the text, 'The barren Fig-tree.' Page 6 **The barren Fig-tree,** pages 34, 63, 89, 109, 133, 157, 181 use u.c. 'T' from a different fount.

Catchwords: (incorrect) B1ᵛ Malice, [Malice] G5ʳ truly [true] G10ʳ by (type misset) [by] 19ʳ strength, [strength:]

THE SECOND EDITION, 1688

The second edition was published in the year of Bunyan's death and, as the title-page indicates, after his death.

Title-page: [within black border] | **The Barren Fig-tree:** | OR, | The Doom & Downfal | of the *Fruitless Professor.* | *Shewing, That the Day of Grace* | *may be past with him long* | *before his Life is ended.* | *The Signs also by which such mise-* | *rable Mortals may be known.* | *[rule]* | *By JOHN BUNYAN.* | *— who being dead, yet speaketh*, Heb. 11. 4. | [rule] | *To which is added,* | His Exhortation to **Peace** and | **Unity** among all that fear God. | [rule] | LONDON; | Printed for *J. Robinson*, at the Golden | Lion in St *Paul*'s Churchyard, 1688.

Collation: 12⁰: A–H¹² [$5–A1; H4 is missigned G4; A7ʳ, A11ᵛ, B12ʳ, B12ᵛ, C11ʳ, F6ᵛ, F7ᵛ, G8ᵛ are signed †]. Pages: i–vi + 118 + (64 + 4) = 192. Page 8 missing figure.

Contents: A1ʳ title-page. A1ᵛ blank, A2ʳ [double row of ornaments] | 'To the Reader', | [rule] — A3ᵛ (signed) 'J. Bunyan'. | [rule] A4ʳ [double rule] | 'The **Barren Fig-tree**' (&c) | [rule] — F2ᵛ [rule] | 'FINIS', text. F3ʳ [single row of ornaments] | 'AN | EXHORTATION | TO | PEACE and UNITY' | [rule] — H9ᵛ [rule], text. H10ʳ [double rule] | 'POSTSCRIPT' — H10ᵛ (five lines of text) | VALE. | [rule] | FINIS, H11ʳ [rule] '*Some Books printed for* Jonathan Robinson — H12ᵛ.

The Bodleian copy has, pasted onto the binder's paper, facing the title-page, a plate of a sleeping Professor, his left elbow resting on a skull, an open and flaming hell-mouth beneath him, and a barren fig-tree behind him. This plate is from a third edition, printed for R. Robinson in 1692. On the verso of the plate, now pasted to the binder's paper, is inscribed in ink, faded and confused with the lines of the print: 'Mr. John Do' | John Adlum | (?) Thania Street | Purchased April | the 13 1777 | Seventy Seven.

Running titles: **The Barren Fig-tree.** | **An Exhortation** | to | **Peace and Unity.** Pages 22, 24, 46, 48 of *An Exhortation* have **An Exhortation.** | to **Peace and Unity.**

Catchwords: B10ᵛ demon- *[demonstrate]* C2ᵛ in *[insignificant]* D11ᶜ Profes- *[Profession]* E1ᶜ Death *[Death,]* F6ᶜ skil- *[skilful]* H5ʳ 2.Con- *[2. Consider]* H7ʳ Seventhly, *[Seventhly;]*

The first edition of 1673 is the only edition published during Bunyan's lifetime. We must, however, consider the possibility of the second edition, appearing so soon after Bunyan's death in 1688, having been revised by Bunyan and posthumously published.

A collation of the two editions shows extensive variations, resulting from a thorough going-over of the text. The most obvious of these is the fondness of the revision for upper case, well over a thousand words being given upper case initial letters which had only lower case in the first edition, while only some seventy or so words are demoted to lower case initial letters. There is a corresponding distaste for the first edition's distinctive use of black letter for emphasis, over fifty such black letter words being changed to roman. A similar distaste for italic results in over seventy italicized words in the first edition being changed to roman for no apparent reason. Conversely a few words in roman type in the 1673 edition have been italicized where the reviser is rightly correcting obvious errors.

Punctuation has also been extensively changed, but it is difficult to see any clear principles behind many of the alterations. Some sixty commas are removed, all, except one, performing a perfectly sound job in pointing sense, phrase, or rhythm: a similar number of commas have been strengthened into semi-colons, colons, or full-stops, in what appears to be a movement away from the looser and swifter rhetorical punctuation of 1673 to a more 'written' or grammatical punctuation. An apparent reverse process of similar magnitude is mainly the result of bringing scriptural references into the text from the margin with consequent repunctuation. The revision of question marks is less extensive and, on the whole, justified, two being removed to give much better sense, and some ten replacing other punctuation with a similar improvement in sense.

There has been a consistent modernization of spelling. The —ie ending is altered to —y, the —aies ending is altered throughout to —ays, mostly final —e is removed, and many spellings are updated, for instance: crouded > crowded, hoast > host, cloaths > clothes, suckering > succouring, rejoyced > rejoiced, houshold > household, conveigh > convey, streights > straits. 'Tho' and 'Thro' are altered fairly consistently to 'though' and 'through'.

Many other variations are the result of a typographical rearrangement of parts of the text. The removal of the scriptural references from margin into the body of the text has been done with some degree of carelessness, twenty-eight having been omitted in the process. In addition, a general clearing of the margin has been undertaken, eight marginal notes 'Observe' being moved safely into the text, but many overlooked or purposelessly cleared away, among them 'The first Proposition' (p. 47. l. 19), 'the 2 Sign of' (p. 55. l. 12), 'He is left in hearing' (p. 56. l. 36), 'He is left in his Affliction' (p. 57. l. 12), 'He is left to do what he will, or go where he will' (p. 57. l. 25). There has also been an attempt to reorganize some of Bunyan's indications of his admittedly complicated subdivisions of his treatise. To make all doubly clear, 'First' has been altered to 'Prop. 1' (p. 47. l. 22) and 'Secondly' to 'Prop. 2.' (p. 47. l. 13) but clear headings such as 'A Second Sign' (p. 55. l. 11), 'A Third Sign' (p. 58. l. 1), 'A Fourth Sign' (p. 59. l. 29), and 'A Fifth Sign' (p. 61. l. 26) have been removed and incorporated in the text, avoiding what is, in the 1673 text, a rather tedious repetition of the numerical indicators.

Many of the 1673/1688 alterations, however, indicate careless and even incomprehending revision, as in 'ever a barren Fig-tree' > 'even a barren Fig-tree' (p. 13. l. 11), '*Christ*' > 'God' (p. 40. l. 4), 'defers' | 'desires' (p. 20. l. 35), '*whose ruine God* contriveth' > 'whose *Ruine contriveth*' (61. 1), 'but *all* to no purpose' > 'but to no purpose' (p. 52. l. 13), 'When after a Profession' > 'when a Profession' (59. 33). There are especially careless omissions where rhetorical repetition has confused the reviser's eye, such as 'to mourn for sin, too late' (p.23. l. 25), 'what fruit' (p. 26. l. 17), 'seriously' (p.32. l. 37) and 'a *little more* Time, and' (p. 45. l. 14).

None of these revisions of the 1688 text suggests the presence of Bunyan's hand, but rather that of a printing-house editor, possibly working under some pressure to produce the volume quickly after Bunyan's death. I have therefore taken the 1673 first edition as the copy-text for this edition, emending only obvious errors of typography, and emending the punctuation only where it is obviously faulty, or where the sense is badly obscured. All substantive alterations, and major alterations to accidentals appear in the footnotes. I have noted the correction of the fairly frequently inaccurate scriptural references, but not the movement of these scriptural references to a more suitable place in the margin. Where the emendations are supported by the edition of 1688, this has been noted.

The black letter type, extensively used for emphasis in the 1673 edition, is represented here by bold type, both in the body of the text, and in the bibliographical descriptions of the note on the text.

TO THE READER

COURTEOUS Reader,
I Have Written to thee now about the Barren Fig-tree, *or how it will fare with the* Fruitless Professor, *that standeth in the* Vineyard *of God.*
Of what Complexion thou art, I cannot certainly divine, but the Parable *tells thee, that the* Cumber-ground *must be cut down.*

A Cumber-ground *Professor, is not only a provocation to* God, *a stumbling-block to the* World, *and a blemish to* Religion, *but a snare to his own Soul also. Though his* excellency *mount up to the Heavens, and his Head reach unto the* Clouds, *yet he shall perish for ever, like his own dung, they that have seen him, shall say, where is he?*   Job 20. 6.

Now they count it pleasure to riot in the daytime, but what will they do when the Ax is fetcht out?   2 Pet. 2. 13, 14.

The Tree whose Fruit withereth, is reckoned a tree without fruit, a tree twice *dead, one that must be pluckt up by the roots.*   Jude 12

O thou Cumber-ground, *God expects fruit, God will come seeking fruit shortly.*

My Exhortation therefore is to Professors, that they look to it, that they take heed.

The Barren Fig-tree *in the* Vineyard, *and the* Bramble *in the* Wood, *are both prepared for the* Fire.

Profession is not a Covert *to hide from the eye of God, nor will it palliate the revengeful threatning of his* Justice, *he will command to cut it down shortly.*

The Church *and a* Profession, *are the best of places for the* Upright; *but the worst in the world for the* Cumber-ground: *He must be cast, as profane, out of the* Mount of God; *Cast, I say, over the wall of the* Vineyard, *there to wither; thence to be gathered and burned.* It had been better for them that they had not known the way of Righteousness; *And yet if they had not, they had been damned; but it is better to go to Hell without, than in, or from under a* Profession; These shall receive greater Damnation.   Ezek. 28. 16. Joh. 15. 16. 2 Pet. 2. 21.

Luk. 20. 47.

If thou be a Professor, *read and tremble; If thou be* Profane, *do so likewise.* For if the righteous scarcely be saved, where shall the Ungodly and Sinners appear? Cumber-ground, *Take heed of the* Ax; Barren Fig-tree, *beware of the Fire.*

But I will keep thee no longer out of the Book; Christ Jesus, *the Dresser of the* Vine-yard, *take care of thee, dig about thee, and dung thee, that thou* 5 *maist bear* Fruit: *That when the Lord of the* Vineyard *cometh with his* Ax *to seek for* Fruit, *or pronounce the Sentence of Damnation on the* Barren Fig-tree, *thou maist escape that judgment. The* Cumber-ground *must to the* Wood-pile, *and thence to the* Fire.

Farewel,   10

Grace be with all them that love our Lord
Jesus in Sincerity,
Amen.

J. Bunyan.

THE BARREN FIG-TREE:
OR,
THE DOOM AND DOWNFALL OF THE FRUITLESS PROFESSOR.

---

5   Luke 13. 6, 7, 8, 9.

A certain man had a Fig-tree planted in his Vine-yard, and he came and sought fruit thereon, and found none. Then said he to the Dresser of his Vineyard, Behold, these three years I come seeking fruit on this Fig-tree, and find none: cut it down, why cumbreth it the ground. And he answering, said,
10 *Lord, let it alone this year also, until I shall dig about it, and dung it: And if it bear Fruit, well: And if not, then after that thou shalt cut it down.*

A T the beginning of this Chapter, we read, how some of the *Jews* came to *Jesus Christ*, to tell him of the cruelty of *Pontius Pilate*, in mingling the blood of the *Galileans* with
15 their Sacrifices. An Heathenish and prodigious Act. For therein he shewed, not only his Malice against the *Jewish* Nation, but also against their Worship, and consequently, their God. An action, I say, not only Heathenish, but prodigious also; for the Lord *Jesus* *paraphrasing* upon this fact of his, teacheth the *Jews*, that without
20 Repentance, *they should all* **likewise** *perish. Likewise*, that is, by the hand and rage of the *Roman* Empire: Neither should they be more able to avoid the stroke, then were those *eighteen upon whom the Tower of* Siloam *fell, and slew them*: the fulfilling of which *Prophecy*, for their Luke 13. hardness of Heart, and impenitency, was in the days of *Titus* Son of 3, 4, 5.
25 *Vespasian*, about *forty* years after the Death of Christ. Then, I say, were these *Jews*, and their City both, environed round on every side, wherein both they and it, to amazement, were miserably overthrown. God gave them Sword, and Famine, Pestilence, and Blood, for their

23 marg. Luke 13. 3, 4, 5.] Luke 19. 32, 33, 34.

outrage against the Son of his Love: So *wrath came on them to the uttermost.*

Now to prevent their old and foolish *Salvo*, which they alwaies had in readiness against such *Prophecies* and Denunciations of Judgment, the Lord *Jesus* presents them with this *Parable*, in which he *emphatically* 5 shews them, that their cry of being the *Temple of the Lord*, and of their being the Children of *Abraham* &c. and their being the Church of God, would not stand them in any stead. As who should say, It may be you think to help your selves against this my *Prophecy*, of your utter and unavoidable overthrow, by the interest which you have in your outward 10 Priviledges; *But all these will fail you*; for what think you, *A certain man had a* Fig-tree *planted in his Vineyard, and he came and sought fruit thereon, and found none.* This is your case, the *Jewish* Land is Gods Vineyard, I know it; and I know also, that *you are the Fig-trees.* But behold, there wanteth the main thing *fruit*, for the sake and in 15 expectation of which, he set this Vineyard with trees. Now, seeing the *fruit* is not found amongst you; the fruit, I say, for the sake of which he at first did plant this Vineyard; what remains, but that in Justice he command to cut you down, *as those that cumber the ground*, that he may plant himself another Vineyard. *Then said he to the Dresser of his* 20 *Vineyard, Behold, these* three *years I come seeking fruit on this Fig-tree, and finde none; cut it down, why cumbreth it the ground?* This therefore must be your end, although you are planted in the Garden of God, for the barrenness and unfruitfulness of your Hearts and Lives, you must be cut off, yea rooted up, and cast out of the Vineyard. 25

In *Parables* there are *two things* to be taken notice of, and to be enquired into of them that read;

First, The *Metaphors* made use of.

Secondly, The Doctrine, or *Mysteries* couched under such *Metaphors.*

The *Metaphors* in this *Parable* are; (1.) A certain man. (2.) A 30 Vineyard. (3.) A Fig-tree, barren or fruitless. (4.) A Dresser. (5.) Three years. (6.) Digging and Dunging, *&c.*

The *Doctrine*, or Mystery, couched under these words, is to shew us, *What is like to become of a fruitless*, or *Formal Professor*; for

1. By the *Man* in the *Parable*, is meant *God* * the *Father.* 35

2. By the *Vineyard*, his †*Church.*

3. By the *Fig-tree*, a *Professor.*

1.

2.

* Luk. 15.
11.
† Isa. 5. 7.

4. By the *Dresser*, *The Lord Jesus*.

5. By the Fig-trees Barrenness, *The Professors fruitlesness*.

6. By the *three* years, *the patience of God, that for a time he extendeth to barren Professors*.

5   7. This calling to the Dresser of the Vineyard *to cut it down*, is to shew, *the outcries of Justice against fruitless Professors*.

8. The *Dressers* interceding, is to shew, *how the Lord Jesus steps in,*   Isa. 53. 12. *and takes hold of the head of his Father's Ax*, to stop, or at least to defer present execution against a barren *Fig-tree*.

10   9. The *Dressers* desire to try to make the *Fig-tree* fruitful, is to shew you, *How unwilling he is that ever a barren Fig-tree, should yet be barren, and perish*.

10. His digging about it, and dunging of it, is to shew *his willingness to apply Gospel-helps to this barren Professor*, if happily he may be fruitful.

15   11. The Supposition that the *Fig-tree* may yet continue fruitless, is to   Mat. 3. 10. shew, that when Christ Jesus hath done all, *There are some Professors will abide barren and fruitless*.

12. The Determination upon this Supposition, at last to cut it down, *Is a certain prediction of such Professors unavoidable and eternal Damnation*.

20   But to take this *Parable* into pieces, and to discourse more particularly, though with all *brevity*, upon all the parts thereof.

A certain man had a Fig-tree planted
in his Vineyard.

The Man, I told you, is to present us with God the Father, by which
25 *Similitude* He is often set out in the *New-Testament*.

Observe then, That it is no new thing, if you find in God's Church, *barren Fig-trees*, fruitless Professors; even as here you see is a *tree*, a fruitless tree, a fruitless *Fig-tree* in the Vineyard. Fruit is not *so easily* brought forth, as a Profession is *got into*; 'tis easie for a man to cloath
30 himself with a fair show in the flesh, to word it, and say, be thou warmed and filled with the best. 'Tis no hard thing to do these with other things; but to be *fruitful*, to bring forth *fruit to God*, this doth not *every* tree; No not every *fig tree*, that stands in the Vine-yard *of God*.

1 *Dresser*] Dresser

Joh. 15. 2.   Them words also, (*Every branch in me that beareth not fruit, he taketh away*,) assert the same thing. There are branches in Christ, in Christ's Body mystical, (which is his Church, his Vine-yard) that beareth not fruit, wherefore the hand of God is to take them away. *I looked for*
Isa. 5. 4.   *Grapes, and it brought forth wild grapes*, that is, no fruit at all that was   5
Hos. 10. 1.   acceptable with God. Again, *Israel is an empty Vine, he bringeth forth fruit unto himself*, none to God; he is without fruit to God. All these, with many more, shew us the truth of the Observation, and that God's Church may be cumbered with fruitless Fig-trees, with barren Professors.   10

Had a (Fig-tree.)

Although there be in God's Church that be barren and fruitless; yet, as I said, *to see to*, they are like the rest of the trees, even a *Fig-tree*:
Ezek. 33. 30, 31.   'Twas not an *oak*, nor a *willow*, nor a *thorn*, nor a *bramble*, but a *Fig-tree.*
Isa. 58. 1, 2, 3, 4.   *They come before thee as the people cometh; they delight to know my ways, as*   15
a nation that did righteousness, and forsook not the Ordinances of their God; they ask of me the ordinances of Justice, they take delight in approaching to God; And yet but barren, fruitless, and unprofitable Professors. *Judas* also was one of the *twelve*, a *Disciple*, an *Apostle*, a *Preacher*, an *Officer*, yea, and *such* an one also, as none of the *eleven* mistrusted, but   20
Mar. 14. 19   preferred before themselves, each one crying out *Is it* I? *Is it* I? none of them, as we read of, mistrusting *Judas*, yet he in Christ's eyes was the
Joh. 6. 70.   *barren Fig-tree*, a Devil, a fruitless Professor. The foolish Virgins also went forth of the world with the other, had Lamps, and Light, and were awakened with the other; yea had boldness to go forth when the   25
Midnight cry was made with the other, and thought that they could have looked Christ in the face, when he sat upon the Throne of Judgment, with the other; and *yet* but *foolish*, but *barren* Fig-trees, but fruitless
Mat. 7. 22, 23.   Professors: *Many*, saith Christ, *will say unto me in that day, this and that*,
Luk. 13. 26, 27.   and will also talk of many wonderful works; yet, behold, he finds   30
nothing in them, but the *fruits* of unrighteousness: they were altogether barren and fruitless Professors.

13 *see to*] *see to in appearance* Corrected in the Errata.

Had a Fig-tree (planted)

This word (*planted*) doth also reach far; It supposeth one taken out of its natural Soil, or removed from the place it grew in once; one that seemed to be called, awakened; and not only so, but by strong hand
5 carried *from the world*, to the Church; *from nature*, to Grace; *from sin*, to Godliness. *Thou broughtest a Vine out of* Egypt, *thou didst cast out the* Psal. 80. 8. *heathen and plant it.* Of some of the Branches of this Vine, were there unfruitful Professors.

It must be concluded therefore, That this Professor (that remaineth
10 notwithstanding fruitless) is, as to the view and judgment of the Church, rightly brought in thither; to wit, by Confession of Faith, of Sin, *and a shew of Repentance* and Regeneration, (thus false Brethren creep in unawares.) All these things this word, *Planted*, intimateth; yea further, that the Church is satisfied with them, consents they should
15 abide in the garden, and counteth them sound as the rest. But before God, in the sight of God, they are graceless Professors, *barren and fruitless Fig-trees.*

Therefore it is one thing to be IN *the Church*, or in a Profession; and another to be OF *the Church*, & to belong to that Kingdom, that is
20 prepared for the Saint, that is so indeed. Otherwise, *being planted, shall* Ezek. 17. 10. *it prosper, shall it not utterly wither, when the East wind toucheth it? It shall wither in the Furrows where it grew.*

Had a Fig-tree planted in (his)
Vine-yard.

25 In (*his*) Vineyard. Hypocrites, with rotten hearts, are not afraid to come before God in *Sion*. These words therefore suggest unto us, a prodigious kind of boldness and hardened Fearlessness: For what presumption higher, and what attempt more desperate, than for a man that wanteth Grace, and the true Knowledg of God, to croud himself
30 (in that condition) into the House, or Church of God; or to make profession of, and desire that the name of God should be called upon him?

For the man that maketh a Profession of the Religion of Jesus

Dan. 9. 19.
Ezek. 36. 20,
21, 22.
Act. 2. 39.

Christ, that man hath, as it were, *put the name of God upon himself*, and is called and reckoned now, (how fruitless soever before God, or men) the man that hath to do with God, the man that God owneth, and will stand for. This man, I say, by his Profession suggesteth this to all that know him, to be such a Professor. Men meerly natural, I mean, men 5 that have not got the *devilish* art of Hypocrisie, are afraid to think of

Act. 5. 13.

doing thus. *And of the rest durst no man join himself to them, but the people magnified them.* And indeed it displeaseth God, *They have brought*, saith

Isa. 1. 12.

he, *men uncircumcised into my Sanctuary*. And again, *When you come to appear before me, who hath required this at your hand, to tread my Courts?* 10

Job 1. 6.

saith God. They have therefore learnt this boldness of none in the visible world, they only took it of the Devil; for he, and he only (with these his Disciples) attempt to present themselves in the Church

Mat. 13.
25–38
& 23. 33.

before God. *The tares are the children of the wicked one*; the *Tares*, that is, the Hypocrites that are Satans brood, the generation of Vipers, that 15 cannot escape the Damnation of Hell.

(Had) *a Fig-tree planted in his Vineyard.*

He doth not say, *He planted a Fig-tree*, but there **was** *a Fig-tree there*, he **had**, or *found*, a Fig-tree planted in his Vine-yard. 20

The great God will *not* acknowledg the *barren Fig-tree*, or barren Professor to be **his** workmanship; or a tree of *his* bringing in; only the

Mat. 15. 13.

Text saith, he **had** one there. This is much like that in *Matthew*, *Every plant which my Heavenly Father hath not planted shall be rooted up.* Here again are Plants in his vineyard, which God will not acknowledg 25 to be of his planting: and he seems to suggest, that in his Vineyard there are many such—*Every plant*, or all those Plants, or Professors that are got into the Assembly of the Saints, or into the Profession of their Religion, without God and his Grace, *shall be rooted up.*

Mat. 22. 11,
12.

And when the King came in to see the Guests, he saw there a man that had 30 *not on a Wedding-garment, and he said unto him, Friend, how camest thou in hither not having on a Wedding-garment?* Here is one so cunning and crafty, that he beguiled all the Guests; he got and kept in the Church,

1 marg. Dan. 9. 19. Ezek. 36. 20, 21, 22, Act. 2. 39.] Dan. 9. 19: *chap* 36. 20, 21, 22 & 2. 39.

even until *the King himself came in to see the Guests*; but his subtilty got him nothing. It did not blind the eyes of the King; it did not *pervert the judgment of the Righteous*. *Friend, how camest thou in hither?* did overtake him at last; even a publick rejection: the King discovered him in the
5 face of all there present. *How camest thou in hither?* My Father did not bring thee hither, I did not bring thee hither, My Spirit did not bring thee hither, thou art not of the Heavenly Father's planting, **how** *camest thou in hither?*

He that cometh not in by the Door, but climbeth up some other way, the Joh. 10. 1.
10 *same is a Thief and a Robber.* This *Text* also is full, and plain to our purpose; for *this* man *came not* in by the *door*, yet got into the *Church*, he got in by climbing; he broke in at the windows, he got something of the light and glory of the Gospel of our Lord *Jesus Christ* in his head; and so (hardy wretch that he was) he presumed to croud himself among the
15 children. But how is this resented? what saith the King of him? Why this is his sign, *The same is a Thief and a Robber.* See ye here also, if all they be owned as the planting of God, that get into his Church, or Profession of his Name.

Had a Fig tree, had one without a Wedding-garment, had a thief in
20 his garden, at his wedding, in his house. These climbed up **some** other way. There are *many* waies to get into the Church of God, and Profession of his Name, besides, and without an entring by the door.

1. There is the way of *lying* and *dissembling*, and at *this gap* the *Gibeonites* * got in. 2. There is sometimes falsness amongst *some*   * Josh. 9. 3,
25 Pastors, either for the sake of carnal Relations, or the like; *at this hole*,   4, 5, 6, 7, 8, 9. *Tobiah* the enemy of God got in. 3. There is sometimes *negligence*, and   Neh. 13. 4, 5, 6. too much uncircumspectness in the whole Church, thus the uncircum- cised got in. * 4. Sometimes again, let the Church be *never so*   * Ezek. 44. *circumspect*, yet *these* have so much help from the Devil, that *they* beguile   7-9.
30 them all, *and so get in.* These are of that sort of Thieves that *Paul* complains of; *false Brethren brought in †* unawares. *Jude* also cries out of   † Gal. 2. 3, these, *certain men* * *crept in unawares. Crept in*, What! were they so   4. * Jude 4 lowly! A voluntary humility, a neglecting of the † body, not in any   † Col. 2. 22, honor. Oh, how seemingly self-denying are some of these creeping   23.
35 things, that yet are to be held, (as we shall know them) an *   * Lev. 11. abomination to *Israel*.   43, 44.

34 honor] humor.

2 Tim. 2.
20.
But in a great house, there are not only vessels of gold, and of silver, but also of wood, and of earth, and some to honour and some to dishonour. By these words the Apostle seems to take it for granted, that as there *hath* been, so there still *will* be, these kind of Fig-trees, *these* barren Professors in the house, when all men have done what they can; *Even* 5 *as in a great house, there are almaies vessels to dishonour,* as well as those to honour and glory; vessels of **wood**, and of **earth**, as well as of *Silver* and *Gold*: So then there must be *wooden* Professors in the Garden of God, there must be *earthy, earthen* Professors in his

Rom. 9. 21,
22.
Vineyard; but that methinks is the biting word, *and some to dishonour.* 10 *That* to the *Romans* is dreadful, but *this* seems to go beyond it; *That* speaks but of the Reprobate in general, but *this* of such and such in particular. *That* speaks of their hardening but in the common way; But *this*, that they must be suffered to creep into the Church; **There** to fit

* Act 1. 25.
themselves for their place, their **own** place, * the place prepared 15 for them of *this sort only.* As the Lord Jesus said once of the *Pharisees,*

† Luke 20.
47.
These shall receive greater damnation. †

Barren Fig-tree, fruitless Professor, Hast thou heard all these things? Hast thou considered that this *Fig-tree* is not acknowledged of God to be his, but is denied to be of his Planting, and of his bringing unto his 20 Wedding? Dost not thou see thou art called a *Thief,* and a *Robber,* that hast either *climbed* up to, or *crept* in at another place than the door? Dost thou not hear, that there will be in God's house, *wooden* and *earthly* Professors, and that no place will serve to fit those for Hell, but the House, *Church,* the Vineyard of God! Barren *Fig-tree,* fruitless 25 Christian, do not thine ears tingle?

And (He) *came and sought fruit thereon.*

When a man hath got a Profession, and is crouded into the Church and House of God; the question is not *now,* hath he life, hath he right 30 Principles, *but hath he fruit,* **he** *came seeking fruit thereon.* It mattereth not who brought thee in hither, whether God or the Devil, or thine own vain-glorious heart; *But hast thou fruit,* dost thou bring forth fruit unto God? *And let every one that nameth the name of the Lord Jesus Christ*

2 Tim. 2.
19.

32 hither, *1688*] hither?   34 marg. 2 Tim. *1688*] 1 Tim.

depart from iniquity. He doth not say, and let every one that hath Grace, or let those that have the Spirit of God; but let *every one* that **nameth** the name of the Lord Jesus Christ, depart from Iniquity.

What do men meddle with Religion for? Why do they call
5 themselves by the name of the Lord Jesus, if they have not the Grace of God; if they have not the †Spirit of Christ. *God therefore expecteth Fruit;* What do they do in the Vineyard? Let them work, or get them out, The Vineyard must have Labourers in it: *Son, Go work to day in my Vineyard.* Wherefore, *want of Grace,* and want of Spirit, will not keep
10 God from seeking fruit; *And* **he** *came and sought fruit* **thereon.** He requireth that which **he** seemeth to have: Every man in the Vineyard, and House of God, promiseth himself, professeth to others, and would have all men take it for granted, that an Heavenly Principle is in him; Why then should not God seek fruit?
15 As for them therefore, that will retain the name of Christians, fearing God; and yet make no conscience of bringing forth fruit to him: He saith to such, **away,** *As for you, go ye, serve every one his Idols, and hereafter also, if ye will not hearken unto me.* Barren *Fig-tree,* dost thou hear, God expecteth fruit, God calls for fruit, yea God will shortly
20 come *seeking* fruit on this barren *Fig-tree.* Barren Fig-tree either bear fruit, or go out of the Vineyard, (and yet then thy case will be unspeakably damnable.) Yea let me adde, if thou shalt neither bear fruit, nor depart, God *will take his name out of thy mouth**: He will have fruit. And I say further, if thou wilt do neither, yet God in Justice and
25 Righteousness will still come for fruit. And it will be in vain for thee to count this *Austerity;* He will * *reap where he hath not sowed, and gather where he hath not strewed.* Barren *Fig-tree* dost thou hear?

Q. *What if a man have no Grace?*
A. Yes, seeing he hath a Profession.

30 *And he came and sought*
fruit (thereon).

A Church then, and a Profession, are not places where the workers of Iniquity may hide themselves, and Sins from God. Some of old thought, that because they could cry, *The Temple of the Lord, the Temple*

Rom. 8. 9.
†Mat. 20. 1,
2, 3, 4, 5.
Mat. 21. 28.

Ezek. 20. 39.

*Jer. 44. 26.

*Matt. 25.
24, 25, 26.

Jer. 7. 4, 5,
6, 7, 8, &c.

13 him; *1688*] him, 14 fruit?] fruit.

of the Lord, that therefore they were delivered, or had a Dispensation to do the abominations which they committed; as some in our days. For, who, say they, have a Right to the creatures if not Christians, if not Professors, if not Church-Members? And from this Conclusion let go the reins of their inordinate Affections after Pride, Ambition, 5 Gluttony, pampering themselves without fear, daubing themselves with the Lust-provoking Fashions of the times; to walk with stretched out Necks, naked Breasts, frizled Fore-tops, wanton Gestures, in gorgeous Apparel, mixt with Gold and Pearl, and costly array. I will not here make inspection into their lives, their carriages at home in their 10 corners, and secret holes; But certainly, persons thus spirited, thus principled, and thus enclined, have but empty Boughs, Boughs that want the fruit that God expects, and that God will come down to seek.

Barren Fig-tree, thou art not licensed by thy Profession, nor by the Lord of the Vineyard, to bear *these* Clusters of *Gomorrah*: neither shall 15 the *vineyard*, nor thy being *crouded* among the *trees there, shelter* thee from the sight of the eye of God. Many make Religion their *cloak*, and Christ their *stalking-horse*, and by that means cover themselves, and hide their own wickedness from men: *But God seeth their hearts*, hath his print upon the heels of their feet, and pondereth all their goings: 20 and at last, when their iniquity is found to be hateful, He will either smite them with hardness of heart, and so leave them, or awaken them to bring forth fruit. Fruit he looks for, seeks and expects, *barren Fig-tree!*

But what! Come into the Presence of God to sin. What! Come into 25 the Presence of God *to hide thy sin*. Alas man! The Church is Gods garden, and Christ Jesus is the great Apostle and High-priest of our Profession. What! come into the House that is called by my Name! into the place where mine Honor dwelleth! where mine eyes and heart are continually! What, come there to sin, to hide thy sin, to cloak thy sin! 30 His *plants* are an *Orchard* with *pleasant fruits*. And *every* time he goeth into his Garden, it is to see the fruits of the Valley; and to see if the Vine flourish, and if the Pomegranates bud.

Yea, saith he, *He came seeking fruit on* **this** *fig-tree.* The Church is the place of Gods delight; where ever he defers to be, there he is night 35 and day. He is there to seek for fruit, to seek for fruit of all, and every

Jude 12.

Luke 16. 15.
Job 13. 27.
Pro. 5. 21.
& 21. 2.

Heb. 3. 1.
Jer. 7. 8, 9,
10.
Psal. 26. 8.
1 Kin. 9. 3.
Song 4. 13,
14, 15. and
6. 11.

19 marg. & 21. 2.] ch. 21. 2.   35 defers] desires. Corrected in the Errata.

tree in the Garden. Wherefore assure thy self, O fruitless one, that thy
waies must needs be open before the eyes of the Lord. *One black sheep*,
is soon espied, although in company with many; *that* is taken with the
first cast of the eye; its different colour still betrays it. I say therefore, A
5 Church and a Profession are not places where the workers of Iniquity
may hide themselves from God, that seeks for fruit, *My vineyard*, saith   Song 8. 12.
God, *which is mine, is before me.*

And he came and sought fruit
thereon (and found none.)

10   *Barren Fig-tree*, hearken, *The continual non-bearing of fruit, is a
dreadful Sign, that thou art to come to a dreadful end*, as the winding up of
this *Parable* concludeth.
    And found none. **None** at all, or *none* to God's liking: for when he
saith, *He came seeking fruit thereon*, He means fruit †*meet for God*,   †Heb. 6.
15 pleasant fruit good and sweet.
    Alas, It is not any fruit will serve; bad fruit is counted none. *Every
tree that bringeth not forth* **good** *fruit, is hewen down, and cast into the*   Mat. 3. 10.
fire.
    1. There is a fruit among Professors that withers, and so never
20 comes to be ripe, a fruit that is *smitten* in the *growth*, and comes not to
maturity, and this is reckoned *no fruit*. This fruit those Professors bear,
that have *many* fair *beginnings*, or blossoms: That make *many* fair *offers*
of Repentance and Amendment; that begin to Pray, to Resolve, and to
break off their Sins by Righteousness; but stop at those beginnings, &
25 bring no *fruit* forth *to perfection*. This mans fruit is withered, wrinkled,
smitten fruit, and is in effect, *no fruit at all.*
    2. There is an *hasty* fruit, such as is the *Corn upon the house-top*, or   Psal. 129.
that which springs up on the *Dung-hil*, that runs up *suddenly*, violently;
with *great stalks*, and big *shew*, and yet at *last* proves *empty* of kernel.
30 *This* fruit is to be found in those Professors, that on a sudden are so
awakened, so convinced, and so affected with their condition, that they
shake the whole Family, the End-ship, the whole Town. *For a while*
they cry hastily, vehemently, dolefully, mournfully, and yet all is but a

6 marg. Song *1688*] Son.

Pang, an Agony, a Fit, they bring not forth fruit with patience. These
are called those hasty fruits, *That shall be as a fading flower.*

Isa. 28. 4.

3. There is a fruit that is *vile, and* **ill** *tasted,* how long soever it be in
growing; the Root is dried, and cannot conveigh a sufficiency of Sap to
the Branches to ripen the Fruit. These are the fruit of such Professors,
whose heart is estranged from Communion with the Holy Ghost,
whose fruit groweth *from themselves,* from their Parts, Gifts, Strength of
wit, natural or moral Principles. These, notwithstanding they bring
forth fruit, are called *empty vines;* such as bring not forth fruit to God.

Jer. 24.
Hos. 9. 16

*Their root is dried up, they shall bear no fruit; yea though they bring forth,
yet will I slay, even the beloved fruit of their womb.*

4. There is a Fruit that is **wild**, *I looked for Grapes, and it brought
forth* wild *grapes.* I observe, That as there are *Trees* and *Herbs* that are
wholly right, and noble; fit *indeed* for the Vineyard. So there are also
their *Semblance,* but *wild;* not right, but ignoble. There is the *grape* and
the *wild-grape,* the *vine* and the *wild-vine,* the *Rose* and the *Canker-rose,*
Flowers and *wild-flowers,* the *Apple* and the *wild-apple,* which we call the
Crab. Now fruit from these *wild* things, however they may please the
Children to play with, yet the *prudent* and *grave* count them of little, or
no value. There are also in the world a generation of Professors, that
notwithstanding their Profession are wild by nature; yea, such as were
never cut *out,* or *off,* from the *wild olive-*tree, nor never yet planted into
the good *Olive-*tree. Now these can bring nothing forth but *wild Olive
berries,* they cannot bring forth fruit *unto God.* Such are all those that
have lightly taken up a Profession, and crept into the Vine-yard,
without a New-birth, and the blessing of Regeneration.

Rev. 6. 13.

5.There is also untimely fruit, *Even as a Fig-tree casteth her untimely-
Figs.* Fruit out of Season, and so no fruit to Gods liking.

There are *two* sorts of Professors subject to bring forth untimely
fruit.

1.

1. They that bring forth (fruit) *too soon.*

2.

2. They that bring forth (fruit) *too late.*

First, They that bring forth *too soon,* They are such as at *present*
receive the Word with *Joy,* and *anon* before they have root downwards,
they thrust forth upwards, but having *not root,* when the *Sun* ariseth
they are *smitten,* and miserably die without fruit. These Professors are
those light and inconsiderate ones, that think nothing but peace will

attend the Gospel; and so anon rejoice at the tidings, without foreseeing the evil: wherefore when the evil comes, being unarmed, and so not able to stand any longer, they die, and are withered, and bring forth no fruit. *He that received the Seed into stony places, the same is*
5 *he that heareth the word, and anon with joy receiveth it, yet hath he not root in himself, but dureth for a * while; for when Tribulation or Persecution ariseth, because of the word, by and by they are offended.* There is in *Isai.* 28. mention made of some, *Whose glorious beauty shall be a fading flower, because it is fruit * before Summer:* both these are untimely fruit.

      * Mat. 13. 20, 21.

      * Isa. 28. 4.

10   *Secondly,* They also bring forth untimely fruit, that stay *till the Season is over.* God will have *his* fruit in **his** Season; I say, he will receive them of such men as shall render them to him in **their** Seasons: the missing of the *season* is dangerous, staying † till the door is shut, is dangerous. Many there be that come not till the floud of Gods anger is
15 raised, and too deep for them to wade through: *Surely in the flouds of great waters, they shall † not come nigh unto him.* Esau's *afterward,* is fearful: *For ye know, how that * afterward, when he would have inherited the Blessing, he was rejected; for he found no place of Repentance, though he sought it carefully with tears.*

      Mat. 21. 41. †Mat. 25. 10, 11.

      †Psal. 32. 6. *Heb. 12. 16, 17.

20   So the Children of *Israel,* they brought to God the fruits of Obedience too late; their * *Lo we be here,* came too late; their *we will go up,* came too late. The Lord had sworn † *before that they should not possess the Land.* All these are such as bring forth *untimely* fruit. It is the hard hap of the Reprobate to do all things too late: to be sensible of his
25 want of Grace, too late: to be sorry for sin, too late: to mourn for sin, too late; to seek Repentance, too late: to ask for mercy, and to desire to go to Glory, too late.

      *Num. 14. 40, 41, 42. †ver. 21, 22, 23. Mat. 25. 10 & 27. 3. Gen. 4. 13, 14. Heb. 12. 17. Luke 13. 25, 26, 27.

    1. Thus you see that fruit *smitten* in the growth, that *withereth,* and that comes not to maturity, *is no † fruit.*
30   2. That *hasty* fruit, such as the * *Corn upon the house top,* withereth also afore it † *groweth up, and is no fruit.*
    3. That the fruit that is *vile* and *ill* tasted, *is no fruit.*
    4. That *wild* fruit, * *wild* grapes, *are no fruit.*
    5. That † *untimely* fruit, such as comes *too soon,* or that comes *too*
35 *late;* Such as come not in *their* Season, *are no fruit.*

      † & ch. 8. 14. *Psal. 129, 6. †Jer. 12. 4.

      *Isa. 5. 4. †Rev. 6. 13.

30 marg. & ch. 8. 14.] c. 8. 14.   32 marg. 12. 4.] 2. 4.

And he came and sought fruit
thereon, and found none.

Mat. 21. 34.

Nothing will do but fruit: *He looked for Grapes; when the time of fruit*
drew near, he sent his servants to the husbandmen that they might receive the
fruit of it.   5

Quest. But what Fruit doth God expect?

Mat. 7. 19.
Luke 6. 43,
44, 45.
Mat. 7. 16,
17, 18, 19,
20.

Answ. Good fruit. *Every tree that bringeth not forth* **good** *fruit, is*
hewn down. Now before the fruit can be good the tree must be good,
for good fruits make not a good tree, *but a good tree bringeth forth good*
fruit; do men gather Grapes of Thorns, or Figs of Thistles? A man must be 10
good, else he can bring forth no good fruit; he must have righteousness
imputed, that he may stand good in God's sight from the curse of his

Gal. 5. 22,
23.

Law. He must have a Principle of Righteousness in his Soul, else how
should he bring forth good fruits; and hence it is, that a Christians

*Phil. 1. 11.

fruits are called, * *The fruits of the Spirit, the fruits of Righteousness, which* 15
are by Jesus Christ. The fruits of the Spirit, therefore the Spirit must be
there: the fruits of righteousness, therefore righteousness must *first* be
there; but to particularize in a few things briefly.

First, God expecteth fruit that will answer, and be worthy of the
Repentance, which thou feignest thy self to have. Every one in a 20
Profession, and that hath crouded into the Vineyard, pretendeth to
Repentance; now of every such Soul, God expecteth that the *fruits* of

Mat. 3. 8.

Repentance be found to attend them. **Bring forth fruits therefore meet for*
Repentance, or answerable to thy profession of the Doctrine of
Repentance. *Barren Fig-tree*, Seing thou art a Professor, and art got 25
into the Vineyard; thou standest before the Lord of the Vineyard, as
one of the trees of the Garden: Wherefore He looketh for *fruit* from

Psal. 5. 14.
& 38. 4.
& 40. 12.

thee, as from the *rest* of the *trees* in the Vineyard; *Fruits*, I say, and *such*
as may declare thee in heart and life, one that hath made sound
Profession of Repentance. By thy profession thou hast said, *I am* 30
sensible of the Evil of Sin; Now then, live such a life, *as* declares that thou
art sensible of the Evil of Sin. By thy Profession thou hast said, *I am*

Psal. 38. 18.
Isa. 59. 20.
Jer. 31. 19.
Act. 26. 18.
1 Thes. 5.
22.

sorry for my Sin: Why then, Live such a life as may declare **this**
Sorrow. By thy Profession thou hast said, *I am ashamed of my Sin*: I but,
live such a life, that men by that may *see thy shame for sin*. By thy 35
Profession thou sayest, *I have turned from, left off, and am become an*

enemy to every appearance of evil: Ah! But doth thy Life and
Conversation declare thee to be such an one! *Take heed, barren Fig-tree,
lest thy life should give thy Profession the lye.* I say again, Take heed, for
God himself will come for fruit; *And he sought fruit thereon.*

5   You have some Professors, that are only Saints before men, *when
they are abroad*; but are Devils and Vipers at *home*; Saints by Profession,
but Devils by Practice; Saints in word, but Sinners in heart and life.
These men may have the Profession, but they want the *fruits that
become Repentance.*

10   *Barren Fig-tree!* Can it be imagined that those that *paint* themselves,
did ever repent of their *Pride*; or that those that *pursue* this world, did
ever repent of their *Covetousness*: or that those that walk with *wanton
eyes*, did ever repent of their *fleshly lusts.* Where, *barren Fig-tree*, is the
fruit of these peoples Repentance? Nay, do they not rather declare to
15   the world, *That they have repented of their Profession?* Their fruits look as
if they had. Their *Pride* saith, they have repented of their *Humility*:
Their *Covetousness* declareth, that they are weary of *depending upon God*;
and doth not thy *wanton* actions declare, that thou *abhorrest Chastity*?
Where is thy *fruit, Barren Fig-tree*? Repentance is not only a sorrow,
20   and a shame for, but *a turning from sin to God*; it is called *Repentance*   Heb. 6.
from dead works. Hast thou that Godly Sorrow, that worketh *Repentance*   2 Cor. 7. 10,
to Salvation, never to be repented of? How dost thou shew thy carefulness,   11.
and clearing of thy self; thy indignation against Sin; thy fear of
offending; thy vehement desire to walk with God; thy zeal for his
25   Name, and Glory in the world: and what revenge hast thou in thy heart
against every thought of Disobedience?

But where is the fruit of this Repentance? Where is thy Watching,
thy Fasting, thy Praying against the remainders of Corruption? Where
is thy Self-abhorrence; thy blushing before God, for the sin that is yet
30   behind? Where is thy tenderness of the Name of God and his waies?
Where is thy Self-denial and Contentment? How dost thou shew
before *men* the truth of thy *turning to God? Hast thou renounced the
hidden things of dishonesty, not walking in craftiness?* Canst thou   2 Cor. 4. 2.
commend thy self *to every means conscience in the sight of God?*

And he sought fruit thereon.

Secondly, *God expecteth fruits that shall answer that Faith which thou makest Profession of.* The Professor that is got into the Vineyard of God, doth feign that he hath *the* Faith, the faith *most holy*, the faith of *Gods* Elect. Ah! But where are thy fruits, Barren Fig-tree? *The faith of the* 5 Romans *was spoken of throughout the whole world, and the* Thessalonians *Faith grew exceedingly.*

Thou professest to *believe* thou hast a share in *another* world; Hast thou let go *this*, barren Fig-tree? Thou professest thou believest in *Christ*; is he thy Joy, and the *Life of thy Soul?* Yea, what conformity unto 10 Him, to his Sorrows and Sufferings? What resemblance hath his Crying, and Groaning, and Bleeding, and dying wrought in thee? dost thou bear about in thy body the dying of the Lord Jesus? *and is also the Life of Jesus made manifest in thy mortal body?* Barren Fig-tree, *Shew me thy Faith by thy works. Shew out of a good Conversation thy Works with* 15 *meekness of wisdome.*

What *fruit*, what *fruit*, barren Figtree, what degree of *heart*-Holiness? for *Faith purifies the heart*: what *love* to the Lord Jesus? *for Faith worketh by love.*

Thirdly, God expecteth Fruits, *according to the Seasons* of Grace thou 20 art under, according to the *rain that cometh upon thee.* Perhaps thou art planted in a good Soil, by great waters, that thou mightest bring forth Branches, and bear Fruit; that thou mightest be a goodly Vine or Fig-tree: Shall he not therefore seek for *fruit*, for *fruit answerable to the means?* Barren Fig-tree, God expects it, and will find it too, if ever He 25 bless thee. *For the earth which drinketh in the rain that comes oft upon it, & bringeth forth herbs meet for him by whom it is dressed, receives blessing from God; but that which beareth thorns and briars is rejected, and is nigh unto cursing, whose end is to be burned.*

Barren Soul, How many showers of Grace, how many dews from 30 Heaven, how many times have the Silver Streams of the City of God, *run gliding by thy roots, to cause thee to bring forth fruit!* These showers, and streams, and the drops that hang upon thy boughs, will all be accounted for; And will they not testifie against thee, that thou oughtest of right *to be burned!* Hear, and tremble, *O thou barren* 35

Rom. 1. 8.

2 Thes. 1. 3.

Phil. 3. 8, 9, 10.
2 Cor. 4. 10, 11.
Jam. 2. 18 & 3. 13.

Act. 15. 9.
Gal. 5. 6.

Heb. 6. 7, 8.

Rom. 1. 13.
Col. 4. 5, 6.

21 art] are.

Professor! Fruits that become thy profession of the Gospel, the God of Heaven expecteth. The Gospel hath in it the Forgiveness of Sins, the Kingdom of Heaven, and Eternal Life; But what fruit hath thy Profession of a belief of these things put forth in thy heart and life? Hast thou given 2 Cor. 8. 5.
5 thy *self* to the Lord, and is all that thou hast, to be ventured for his Acts. 4. 32.
Name in this world? Dost thou walk like one that is bought with a 1 Cor. 6. 20.
price, *Even the price of precious blood?*

Fourthly, The Fruit that God expecteth is such, *As is meet for himself*, fruit that may glorifie God; God's trees *are trees of righteousness, the* Isa. 61. 3.
10 *planting of the Lord, that* **he** *may be glorified*; fruit *that tasteth of Heaven*, abundance of *such* fruit: *For herein*, saith Christ, *is my Father glorified, Joh. 15. 8.*
that ye bring forth much fruit. Fruits of all kinds, *new and old*, the fruits of Song. 7. 13.
the Spirit is in **all** *goodness, and righteousness, and truth. Fruits* before Eph. 5. 9.
the World, *fruits* before the Saints, *fruits* before God, *fruits* before
15 Angels.

O my Brethren, *What manner of persons ought we to be*, who have subscribed to the Lord, and have called our selves by the name of *Israel? One shall say, I am the Lords; and another shall call himself by the* Isa. 44. 5.
name of Jacob; *and another shall subscribe with his hand unto the Lord, and*
20 *sirname himself by the name of* Israel. Barren Fig-tree, hast thou *subscribed*, hast thou *called* thy self by the name of *Jacob*? And *sirnamed* thy self by the name of *Israel?* All this thou pretendest to, who art got 1 Thes. 2.
into the Vineyard, who art placed among the trees of the garden of 1.
God: God doth therefore look for **such** fruit as is worthy of his
25 *Name*, as is meet for *him*; as the Apostle saith, *We should walk worthy of God*; that is, so as that we may shew in every place, that the presence of God is *with* us, his fear *in* us, and his Majesty and Authority upon *our* actions. Fruits *meet* for him, *such* a dependance upon him, *such* trust in his word, *such* satisfaction in his presence, *such* a trusting of him with
30 all my concerns, and *such* delight in the enjoyment of him, *that may demonstrate that his fear is in my heart*, that my Soul is wrapt up in his things, and that my Body, and Soul, and Estate, and all, are in truth, through his Grace, at his dispose, *fruit meet for him.* Hearty thanks, and blessing God for Jesus Christ, for his good Word, for his Free-Grace,
35 for the discovery of himself in Christ to the Soul, secret longing after another world, fruit *meet* for him. Liberality to the poor Saints, to the poor world; a life, in word and deed exemplary, a patient, and quiet

enduring of all things, till I have done and suffered the whole will of
God, which he hath appointed for me. *That on the good ground are they,*
which in an honest and good heart, having heard the word, keep it, and bring
forth fruit with patience. This is bringing forth fruit unto God. *Having*
our fruit unto Holiness, and our end everlasting life. 5

Luke 8. 15.

Rom. 7. 4. &
6. 22. & 14.
8.

Fifthly, The Lord expects fruit *becoming the Vineyard of God.* The
Vineyard, saith he, *is a very fruitful Hill*; witness the fruit brought forth
in *all ages*: The most barren trees that ever grew in the wood of this
world, when planted in this Vine-yard, *by the God of Heaven*, what fruit
to Godward have they brought forth? *Abel* offered the *more* excellent 10
Sacrifice. *Enoch walked with God three hundred years*; *Noah*, by his life
of Faith, *condemned the world, and became heir of the Righteousness which is*
by Faith. Abraham *left his Countrey, and went out after God, not knowing*
whither he went. *Moses* left a Kingdom, *and run the hazard of the wrath of*
the King, for the love he had to God and Christ. What shall I say of 15
them who had tryals, not accepting Deliverance, that they might obtain
a better Resurrection? *They were stoned, they were sawn asunder, were*
tempted, were slain with the sword: They wandered about in sheep-skins and
goat-skins, being destitute, afflicted, tormented. *Peter* left his father, ships
and nets. *Paul* turned off from the feet of *Gamaliel.* Men brought their 20
Goods and Possessions (the price of them) and cast it down at the
Apostles feet; and others brought their Books together, and burnt
them, *curious Books*, though they were worth *fifty thousand* Pieces of
Silver. I could add, how many willingly offered themselves in all Ages,
and their *all*, for the worthy name of the Lord Jesus: to be wrackt, 25
starved, hanged, burned, drowned, pulled in pieces, and a thousand
calamities. Barren Figtree, the Vineyard of God hath been a fruitful
place, What dost thou there? What dost thou bear? God expects fruit
according to, or becoming the Soil of the Vineyard.

Isa. 5. 1.

Heb. 11. 4.
vers. 5.
vers. 7.

vers. 8.

Heb. 11. 35,
36, 37.

Mat. 4. 18,
19.

Acts 19. 18,
19, 20.

Sixthly, The fruit which God expecteth is such as becometh God's 30
Husbandry and Labour. The Vineyard is *God's Husbandry, or Tillage. I*
am the Vine, saith Christ, *and my Father is the Husbandman.* And again,
Ye are Gods husbandry, ye are Gods building. The Vineyard, God fences
it, God gathereth out the stones, God builds the Tower, and the Wine-
press in the midst thereof. Here is labour, here is protection, here is 35
removing of hindrances, here is convenient Purgation, and **all** *that*
there might be fruit.

Joh. 15. 1.
1 Cor. 3. 9.
Isa. 5.

Barren Figtree, What fruit hast thou? hast thou fruit becoming the care of God, the protection of God, the wisdom of God, the patience *and husbandry of God?* It is the fruit of the Vineyard, that is either the shame or the praise of the Husbandman. *I went by the field of the slothful,* Prov. 24. 30,
5 saith *Solomon, and by the vineyard of the man void of understanding. And* 31, 32. *lo, it was grown over with thorns, and nettles had covered the face thereof.*

Barren Figtree, If men should make a judgment of the care, and pains, and labour of God in his Church by the fruit that thou bringest forth, what might they say, is he not slothful, is not he careless, is he
10 not without discretion! O thy *thorns,* thy *nettles,* thy *barren heart,* and *barren life,* is a continual provocation to the eyes of his Glory, as likewise a dishonour to the glory of his Grace.

Barren Fig-tree, hast thou heard all these things, I will adde yet one more.

15   *And he came and sought*
                                     fruit thereon.

The question is not now, what thou thinkest of thy self, nor what all the people of God think of thee; but what thou shalt be found in that day, when God shall search thy boughs for fruit. When *Sodom* was to
20 be searched for righteous men, God would not, in that matter, trust his faithful servant *Abraham,* but still as *Abraham* interceded, God Gen. 18. 20, answered, *If I find fifty, or forty and five there, I will not destroy the city.* 21, 26, 27. Barren Fig-tree, what saiest thou? God will come down to see, God will make search for fruit himself.

25 *And he came and sought fruit thereon, and found* (none.) *Then said he to the Dresser of the Vineyard, Behold, these* three *years I come seeking fruit on this Fig-tree, and find none; cut it down, why cumbereth it the ground?*

These words are the effect of Gods search into the boughs of a *barren fig-tree*; He sought fruit, and found *none, none* to his liking, *none* pleasant
30 and good. Therefore, *first,* he complains of the want thereof to the Dresser, calls him to come, and see, and take notice of the tree; then signifieth his pleasure, he will have it removed, taken away, cut down from cumbering the ground.

The *barren Fig-tree* is the Object of God's displeasure, God cannot *Observ.*
35 bear with a fruitless Professor.

(Then) *said he, &c.*

Then, after this provocation; *then*, after he had sought and found no fruit; *then*, this word (then) doth shew us a kind of an inward disquietness: as he saith also in another place, upon a like provocation. *Then the anger of the Lord, and his jealousie, shall smoke against that* 5 *man, and all the curses that are written in this Book shall lye upon him, and the Lord shall blot out his name from under Heaven.*

Then; It intimateth that he was *now* come to a point, to a resolution what to do with this Fig-tree. *Then said he to the Dresser of this Vineyard,* that is, to Jesus Christ; *Behold,* as much as to say, come hither, here is a 10 Fig-tree in my Vineyard, here is a Professor in my Church, that is barren, that beareth no fruit.

Observe, However the barren Professor thinks of himself on Earth, the Lord cries out in Heaven against him. *And now go to, I will tell you what I will do to my Vineyard. I will take away the hedg thereof, and it shall* 15 *be eaten up; and I will break down the walls thereof, and it shall be troden down.*

Observ. (margin)
Deut. 29. (margin)
18. 19, 20. (margin)
Isa. 5. 5. (margin)

Behold, these three years I come seeking fruit, &c.

These three years. God cries out that his patience is abused, that his forbearance is abused: Behold, these three years I have waited, 20 forborn; these three years I have deferred mine anger; *Therefore will I stretch out mine hand against thee, and destroy thee, I am weary with repenting.*

These three years. God layeth up *all* the *time*; I say a remembrance of all the time, that a *barren Fig-tree*, or a fruitless Professor, *mis-spendeth* 25 *in this world.* As he saith also of *Israel* of old, *Forty years long was I grieved with this generation.*

These three years, &c.

These *three* Seasons; God remembers how many *Seasons* thou hast mis-spent. For these *three years* signifie so many *Seasons. And when the* 30 *time of fruit drew nigh,* that is, about the Season, by that they begin to be ripe, or that according to the Season, might so have been. *Barren Fig-tree,* thou hast had time, Seasons, Sermons, Ministers, Afflictions, Judgments, Mercies, and what not? and *yet hast not been fruitful*: thou

Observ. (margin)
Jer. 15. 6. (margin)
Observ. (margin)
Psal. 95. 10. (margin)
Observ. (margin)

hast had awakenings, reproofs, threatnings, comforts, *and yet hast not been fruitful*: thou hast had Patterns, Examples, Citations, Provocations; *and yet hast not been fruitfull*. Well, God hath laid up *thy three years* with himself. He remembers *every* time, *every* season, *every* Sermon, *every*
5 Minister, Affliction, Judgment, Mercy, awakening Pattern, Example, Citation, Provocation; He remembers *all*, as he said of *Israel* of old: *They have tempted me these* ten *times, and have not hearkened to my voice.* Num. 14. And again, *I remember all their wickedness.* 22.
  These three *years*, &c. Hos. 7.2.
10 He seeks for the fruit of **every** Season; He will not that any of his Sermons, Ministers, Afflictions, Judgments, or Mercies *should be lost*, or stand for insignificant things; he will have *according to the benefit* 2 Chro. 32. *bestowed*; He hath not done without a cause all that he hath done, and 24, 25. therefore he looketh for fruit, Look to it *barren Fig-tree*. Ezek. 14. 23.
15 *I came* (seeking) *fruit.*
  This word (*seeking.*) signifies *a narrow search*: for when a man Observ. seeks for fruit on a tree, he goes round it, and round it, now looking into this bough, and then into that, he peeks into the inmost boughs, and the lowermost boughs, if perhaps fruit may be thereon.
20 *Barren Figtree*, God will look into *all thy boughs*, he will be with thee in thy bed fruits, thy Midnight fruits, thy Closet fruits, thy Family Fruits, thy Conversation Fruits, to see if there be any among all these, that are fit for, or worthy of the Name of the God of Heaven. *He sees* Ezek. 8. 12. *what the Children of* Israel *do in the dark. All things are open unto the eyes* Heb. 4. 12, 25 *of him, with whom we have to do.* 13.

Seeking fruit on (this)
Fig-tree.

  I told you before, that he keeps in remembrance the Times and Observ. Seasons that the barren Professor had wickedly mispent. Now,
30 forasmuch as he also *pointeth out the Fig-tree*. **This** *Fig-tree*. It sheweth that the barren Professor, above all Professors, is a continual *odium* in the eyes of God. **This** *Figtree*, **This** man *Coniah*, **This** People draw Jer. 22. 28. nigh me with their Mouth, but have removed their Hearts far from me. Isa. 29. 11. God knows *who they are* among all the *thousands* of *Israel*, that are the Mat. 15. 8.
35 barren and fruitless Professors, his lot will fall upon the head of *Achan*,

Josh. 7.
17, 18.

though he be hid among *six hundred thousand* men. *And he brought his houshold, man by man, and* Achan, *the Son of* Carmi, *the Son of* Zabdi, *the Son of* Zerah, *of the Tribe of* Judah, *was taken.* This is the *Achan,* this is the Fig-tree, **this** is the barren Professor.

There is a man hath an 100. *trees* in his Vineyard, and at the time of   5
the season, he walketh into his Vineyard to see how the trees flourish, and as he goes, and views, and pries, and observes how they are hanged with fruit: Behold, he comes to one where he findeth naught but leaves. Now he makes a stand, looks upon it again and again, he looks also here and there, above and below, and if after all this seeking,   10

Simile

he finds nothing but leaves thereon: Then he begins to cast in his mind, how he may know this tree next year, what stands next it, or how far 'tis off the hedg; but if there be nothing there that may be as a mark to

Gen. 4.

know it by, then he takes his *hook,* and giveth it a private mark, (*And the Lord set a mark upon* Cain) saying, Go thy waies, fruitless Fig-tree,   15
Thou hast spent this Season in vain.

Yet doth he not cut it down, I will try it another year; may be this was not a *hitting* Season. Therefore he comes again *next* year to see if now it have fruit, but as he found it *before,* so he finds it *now barren, barren,* every year *barren*; he looks again, *but finds no Fruit.* Now he begins to   20
have *second* thoughts: How! Neither hit *last* year, nor *this.* Surely the Barrenness is not in the Season; sure the fault is in the Tree. However I will spare it this year also, but will give it a *second* mark: and it may be,

1 Tim. 4. 2.

he toucheth it with his hot iron, because he begins to be angry.

Well, at the *third* season He comes again *for fruit,* but the *third* year is   25
like the *first* and *second, no fruit yet; it only cumbreth the ground*: What

Isa. 10. 33,
34.

now must be done with this Fig-tree? Why, *The Lord will lop its boughs with terrour;* yea, the thickets of those Professors *with iron. I have waited, saith God, these three years,* I have missed of fruit *these three years*;

Isa. 28. 10.

It hath been a cumber-ground *these three years; cut it down.* Precept hath   30
been upon Precept, and Line upon Line, one year after another, for *these three years,* but no fruit can be seen, I find none, fetch out the Ax. I am sure **this** is the Fig-tree, I know it from the first year, *Barrenness* was its sign then, *barrenness* is its sign now, make it fit for the·fire.

Mat. 3. 10.

Behold the Ax is laid to the root of the trees, every tree therefore that bringeth   35
not forth good fruit, is hewn down, and cast into the fire.

Obs.

My Brethren, seriously, *Gods heart cannot stand towards a barren Fig-*

tree. You know thus it is with your selves: If *you* have a tree in *your* Orchard, or Vineyard, that doth *only cumber the ground, you* cannot look upon that tree with pleasure, with complacency and delight: No, if *you* do but go by it, if *you* do but cast *your* eye· upon it; yea, if *you* do but
5 think of that tree, *you* threaten it in *your* heart, saying, *I will hew thee down shortly; I will to the fire with thee shortly.* And it is in vain for any to think of perswading of *you* to shew favour to the *barren Fig-tree,* and if they should persuade, your answer is irresistible, *It yields me no profit,* it takes up room, and doth no good, a better may grow in its room.

10   *Cut it down.*

Thus when the Godly among the *Jews made Prayers, that rebellious *Israel* might not be cast out of the Vineyard, what saith the answer of God. *Though* Moses *and* Samuel *stood before me, yet could not my mind be toward this people: wherefore cast them out of my presence, and*
15 *let them go forth.* What a resolution is here, *Moses* and *Samuel* could do almost any thing with God in prayer. How many times did *Moses* by Prayer turn away Gods Judgments from *even* Pharoah *himself!* yea, how many times did he by Prayer preserve *Israel,* when in the * Wilderness, from the anger and wrath of God? *Samuel* is reckoned excellent this
20 way, yea so excellent, that when *Israel* had done that fearful thing, as to reject the Lord, and chuse them another King; he prayed, and the Lord spared, and forgave them: but yet neither *Moses* nor *Samuel can save a barren Fig-tree.* No though *Moses* and *Samuel* **stood** before me, that is pleading, arguing, interceding, supplicating, and beseeching,
25 yet could they not incline mine heart to this People.

Jer. 14. 17, 18, 19, 20.

Jer. 15. 1.

*Psal. 106. 23 & 99. 6.

                    Cut it down.

Ay, but Lord it is a *Fig-tree,* a Fig-tree! if it was a *Thorn,* or a *Bramble,* or a *Thistle,* the matter would not be much; but it is a *Fig-tree,* or a Vine: well, but mark the answer of God; *Son of man, what is the vine*
30 *tree, more than any tree, or than a branch that is among the trees of the Forrest, shall wood be taken thereof to do any work? or will men take a pin thereof, to hang any vessel thereon?* If trees that are set, or planted for fruit, *bring not forth that fruit,* there is betwixt them and the trees of the

Ezek. 15. 2, 3.

Forrest, *no betterment at all,* unless the betterment lieth in the trees of the Wood, for they are fit to build withal; but a *Fig-tree,* or a *Vine, if they bring not forth fruit,* yea good fruit, they are fit for nothing at all, but to be cut down, and prepared for the fire; and so the Prophet goes on, *Behold, it is cast into the fire for fuel, if it serve not for fruit, it will serve for fewel, and so the fire devoureth both the ends of it, and the middle of it is burnt.*

er. 4.

Ay but, these *Fig-trees* and *Vines* are Church-Members, Inhabiters of *Jerusalem.* So was the *Fig-tree* mentioned in the *Text;* But what answer hath God prepared for these *Objections?* Why, *Thus saith the Lord God, as the vine-tree among the trees of the forrest, which I have given to the fire for fuel, so will I give the Inhabitants of* Jerusalem. *And I will set my face against them, they shall go from one fire, and another fire shall devour them.*

Ver. 6. 7.

Cut it down.

The woman that delighteth in her Garden, if she have a *slip* there, suppose (if it was fruitful) she would not take *five* Pounds for it. *Yet if it bear no fruit,* if it wither, and dwindle, and die, and turn cumber-ground only, *it may not stand in her garden.* Gardens and Vineyards are places for *fruit, for fruit* according to the *nature* of the plant or flowers. Suppose such a *slip* as I told you of before, should be in your garden, and there die: *Would you let it abide in your Garden?* No! away with it, away with it. The woman comes into her garden towards the Spring, where first she gives it a *slight* cast with her eye; then she sets to gathering out the *weeds,* and *nettles,* and *stones;* takes a *beesom* and *sweeps* the *walks:* this done, she falls to *prying* into her *herbs* and *slips,* to see if *they* live, to see if they are likely to grow: Now, *if she comes to one that is dead,* that she is confident will not grow, up she pulls that, and makes to the heap of rubbish with it, where she despisingly casts it down, and valueth it *no more* than a *nettle,* or a *weed,* or than the *dust* she hath swept out of her *walks.* Yea, if any that see her should say, Why do you so? The answer is ready, 'Tis dead, 'tis dead at root: If I had let it stand, 'twould but have cumbered the ground. *The strange slips* (and

---

10 *Objections? Why, 1688*] *Objections, Why?*

also the dead ones) *they must be an heap in the day of grief, and of desperate* Isa. 17. 10,
Sorrow. 11.

Cut it down.

There be *two* manner of cuttings down;
5 *First,* When a man is cast out of the Vineyard.
Secondly, When a man is cast out of the World.
First, When a man is cast out of the Vineyard. And that is done *two*
waies.
 1. *By an immediate hand of God.*
10 2. *By the Churches due execution of the Laws and Censures which Christ
for that purpose hath left with his Church.*
 First, God cuts down the Barren Fig-tree *by an immediate hand,* 1.
smiting his roots, blasting his branches, and so takes him away from
among his people. *Every branch,* saith Christ, *that beareth not fruit in me,* Joh. 15. 2.
15 *He,* my Father, *taketh away.* He taketh him out of the Church, He
taketh him away from the Godly. There are *two* things by which God
taketh the *barren* Professor from among the Children of God.
 First, *Strong Delusions.*
 Secondly, *Open Prophaneness.*
20 *First,* By strong Delusions, such as beguile the Soul with damnable Isa. 66. 3, 4.
Doctrines, that *swerve* from Faith and Godliness, *They have chose their* Isa. 6. 9, 10.
own ways, saith God, and their Soul delighteth in their abominations; I also 1 Kin. 22.
will chuse their delusions, and will bring their fears upon them. I will smite 20, 21, 22.
them with blindness, and hardness of heart, and failing of eyes, and
25 will also suffer the Tempter to tempt and effect his hellish designs
upon them; *God will send them strong delusions, that they may believe a* 2 Thes. 2.
Lie, that they all may be damned, who believe not the truth, but had pleasure 10, 11, 12.
in unrighteousness.
 Secondly, Sometimes God takes away a *barren* Professor by open
30 Profaneness. There is one hath taken up a profession of that *worthy
name, the Lord Jesus Christ*; but this Profession is but a cloak, he
secretly practiseth wickedness; He is a Glutton, a Drunkard, or
Covetous, or Unclean. Well, saith God, I will loose the reins of this
Professor, I will give him up *to his vile Affections*, I will loose the reins of
25 Tempter *1688*] Temper.

his lusts before him, he shall be entangled with his beastly lusts, he shall be overcome of ungodly company. Thus they that turn aside to their own crooked waies, *The Lord shall lead them forth with the workers of Iniquity.* This is God's hand immediately: God is now dealing with this man *himself.* *Barren Fig-tree,* hearken, Thou art crouded into a Profession, art got among the Godly, and there art a scandal to the holy and glorious Gospel, but withal so cunning, that like the Sons of *Zerviah,* thou art too hard for the Church. She knows not how to deal with thee; well, saith God, I will deal with that man my self: *I will answer that man by my self;* he that sets up his Idols in his heart, and puts the stumbling block of his iniquity before his Face, and yet comes and appears before me; *I will set my face against that man, and will make him a Sign and a Proverb, and I will cut him off from the midst of my People, and ye shall know that I am the Lord.*

But *Secondly,* God doth somtimes cut down the *barren Fig-tree* by the Church, by the Churches due execution of the Laws and Censures, which Christ for that purpose hath left with his Church. This is the meaning of that in *Matth.* 18. 1. *Cor.* 5. And that in *Timothy,* upon which now I shall not enlarge. But which way soever God dealeth with thee, *O thou barren Fig-tree,* whether by himself immediatly, or by his Church, it amounts to one and the same. For if timely Repentance prevent not, *The end of that Soul is damnation.* They are blasted, and withered, and gathered by men, Gods enemies, and at last being cast into the fire, *burning must be their end. That which beareth Briars and Thorns, is nigh unto cursing, whose end is to be burned.*

But again, sometimes by *cut it down,* God means, cast it out of the world: Thus he *cut* down *Nadab* and *Abihu,* when *he burned them up with fire from Heaven;* Thus He *cut down* Corah, Dathan, *and* Abiram, *when he made the earth to swallow them up.* Thus he *cut* down *Saul, when he gave him up to fall upon the edge of his own sword, and died.* Thus He *cut down* Ananias *with* Saphira *his wife, when he struck them down dead in the midst of the Congregation.* I might here also discourse of *Absalom, Ahithophel* and *Judas,* who were *all three hanged;* The *first* by Gods revenging hand, the *other* were given up of God to be their own Executioners. These were barren and unprofitable *Fig-trees,* such as God took no pleasure in, therefore he commanded, *To cut them down.*

16 marg. Mat. 18.] Mat. 8.

Psal. 125. 5.

Ezek. 14. 7, 8.

2.
Mat. 18. 17, 18.
1. Cor. 5. 4, 5.
1 Tim. 1. 20.

Joh. 15. 6.

Heb. 6. 8.

Lev. 10. 1, 2, 3.

Numb. 16. 31, 32, 33.
1 Sam. 31. 4.
Act. 5. 5, 10.
Mat. 27. 3, 4, 5.

The *Psalmist* saith, *He shall take them away as with a whirlwind, both* Psal. 58. 9.
living, and in his wrath.

   Barren Figtree, hearken; God calls for the Ax, his Sword, bring it
hither, here is a barren Professor, *Cut him down, why cumbereth he the* Ezek. 21. 9,
5 *ground.* 10.

Why cumbereth it the ground.

   By these words the Lord suggesteth *reasons* of his displeasure
against the Barren Fig-tree, *It cumbereth the ground.* The Holy Ghost
doth not only take an Argument from its *barrenness,* but because it is a
10 *cumber-ground, Therefore* cut it down; Wherefore it must needs be a
provocation.

   1. Because, as much as in him lieth, he disappointeth the design of
God in planting his Vineyard. *I looked that it should bring forth fruit.*

   2. It hath also abused his Patience, his **long,** *his three years*
15 *patience.*

   3. It hath also abused *his labour;* his pains, his care, and providence
of * protection and preservation: for he hedges his Vineyard, and walls *Isa. 51. 2,
it about. *Cumber-ground! all these things thou abusest.* He waters his 3.
Vineyard, and looks to it night and day, but all these things thou hast & 27. 1,
20 abused. 2, 3.

   Further, There are other reasons of Gods displeasure; as *first,* a
cumber-ground is a very mock and reproach to Religion, a mock and
reproach to the waies of God, to the People of God, to the Word of
God, and to the name of Religion. It is expected of all hands, that *all*
25 *the trees* in the Garden of God, should be fruitful. *God* expects fruit, the
Church expects fruit, the *world,* even the *world* conclude that Professors
should be fruitful in good works; I say, the very *world* expecteth that
Profesors should be better than themselves: But, *barren Fig-tree,* thou
disappointest all: Nay, hast thou not learned *the wicked ones* **thy**
30 waies? Hast thou not learnt them to be more wicked by thy example:
(but that's by the by.) *Barren Fig-tree,* Thou hast disappointed others,
and *must be disappointed thy self. Cut it down, why cumbereth it the ground.*

   Secondly, The Barren Fig-tree *takes up the room where a better tree*
might stand; I say, it takes up the room, it keeps, so long as it stands

16 providence *1688*] providente.

where it doth, a fruitful tree out of that place, and therefore it must *be cut down. Barren Figtree,* Dost thou hear? Because the *Jews* stood

Mat. 21. 33-43.

fruitless in the Vineyard, Therefore, said God, *The Kingdom of Heaven shall be taken from you, and shall be given to a Nation that shall render him their fruits in their season.* The *Jews* for their barrenness were *cut down,* 5 and more fruitful people put in their room. As *Samuel* also said to

I Sam. 15. 28. Mat. 25. 30.

barren *Saul, The Lord hath rent the Kingdom from thee, and hath given it to thy neighbour, that is better than thou;* the unprofitable Servant *must be cast out,* must be cut down.

Cumber-ground! How many hopeful, inclinable, forward people, hast 10 thou by thy fruitless and unprofitable life, kept out of the Vineyard of God; for thy sake have these people stumbled at Religion; By thy life have they been kept from the love of their own Salvation. Thou hast been also a means of hardening others, and of quenching, and killing weak beginnings. Well, *Barren Fig-tree! Look to thy self,* (thou wilt not go 15 to Heaven thy self, and them that would, thou hinderest). Thou must not alwaies cumber the ground, nor alwaies hinder the Salvation of others: Thou shalt be *Cut down, and another shall be planted in thy room.*

Thirdly, The *Cumber-ground* is a *Sucker,* he draws away the heart and nourishment *from the other trees.* Were the *cumber-ground cut down,* the 20 other would be more fruitful; he draws away that fatness of the ground

Eccl. 9. 18.

to himself, that would make the other more hearty and fruitful. *One Sinner destroyeth much good.*

The *Cumber-ground* is a very *Droan* in the *Hive,* that eats up the *Honey* that should feed the labouring Bee; he is a *thief* in the *Candle,* 25 that wasteth the *Tallow,* but giveth no *Light;* he is the *unsavory* Salt, that is fit for nought but the Dung-hil. Look to it *Barren Fig-tree.*

> *And he answering, said unto him, Lord,*
> *let it alone this year also, until I*
> *shall dig about it, and dung it; and* 30
> *if it bear fruit, well; and if not, then*
> *after that, thou shalt cut it down,* v. 8, 9.

These are the words of the Dresser of the Vineyard, who, I told you,

Isa. 53. 12.

is Jesus Christ (for he made intercession for the transgressors.) And they contain a Petition, presented to an offended Justice, praying that a 35

3 marg. 33-43] 33-41.   8 marg. 25. 30] 25. 27.

little more time, and patience might be exercised towards the barren, cumber-ground *Fig-tree.*

In this Petition there are *Six* things considerable;

First, That Justice might be *deferred.* O that Justice might be *deferred.*
5 Lord let it *alone,* &c. a while longer.

Secondly, Here is *time* prefixed, as a space to try if more means *will cure a barren Fig-tree. Lord let it alone this year also.*

Thirdly, The means to help it, are propounded, *until I shall dig about it, and dung it.*

10 *Fourthly,* Here is also an insinuation of a Supposition, that by thus doing, Gods expectation may be answered, *And if it bear Fruit, Well.*

Fifthly, Here is a Supposition that the *barren* Fig-tree may *yet* abide *barren,* when Christ hath done *what he will unto it, and* if *it bear fruit,* &c.

15 *Sixthly,* Here is at last a *Resolution,* that if thou continue barren, *hewing days will come upon thee.* And if it bear fruit, well, *And if not, then after that thou shalt cut it down.*

But to proceed according to my former Method, by way of Exposition.

20   *Lord, let it alone this year also.*

Here is astonishing Grace indeed, astonishing Grace! I say, that the Lord Jesus should concern himself with a *barren Fig-tree*; that He should step in to stop the blow from a *barren Fig-tree.* True, He stopt the blow but for a time; but *why did he stop it at all?* Why did not he
25 fetch out the Ax? Why did he not do Execution? Why did not he *cut it down? Barren Fig-tree!* 'tis well for thee that there is a Jesus at Gods right hand, a Jesus of that largeness of bowels, *As to have compassion for a barren Fig-tree,* else Justice had never let thee alone to cumber the ground as thou hast done. When *Israel* also had sinned against God,
30 down they had gone, *But that* Moses *stood in the breach. Let me alone,* said God to him, *That I may consume them in a moment, and I will make of thee a great Nation. Barren Fig-tree,* Dost thou hear? Thou knowest not how oft the hand of Divine Justice hath been up to strike, and how many years since thou hadst been *cut down,* had not Jesus caught hold

Psal. 106. 23.
Exo. 32. 10.
Num. 16.
21.

15 *Sixthly*] Sixthly.   30 marg. 16. 21] 16. 20.

of his Fathers Ax. Let me alone, let me fetch my blow, or *cut it down, why cumbereth it the ground?* Wilt thou not hear yet, *Barren Fig-tree?* Wilt thou provoke still! *Thou hast wearied men,* and provoked the Justice of God; *And wilt thou weary my Christ also!*

Isa. 7. 13.

Lord, let it alone this year.

5

Lord, a little longer, lets not lose a Soul for want of means; *I will try,* I will see if I can make it fruitful, *I will not beg a long life,* nor that it might still be *barren,* and so provoke thee. I beg for the sake of the Soul, the immortal Soul, Lord spare it *one year only, one year longer, this year also*; if I do any good to it, it will be *in little time.* Thou shalt not be over-wearied with waiting, *one year and then.*

10

Barren Fig-tree, Dost thou hear what striving there is between the *Vine-dresser* and the *Husband-man* for thy life. *Cut it down,* saies one; *Lord spare it,* saith the other; *'Tis a cumber-ground,* saith the Father, one year longer praies the Son, *Let it alone this year also.*

15

Until I shall dig about it, and
dung it.

The Lord *Jesus* by these words supposeth *two* things, as Causes of the want of fruit in a *barren Fig-tree,* and *two* things he supposeth as a Remedy.

20

The things that are a cause of want of fruit, are

1. *'Tis earth-bound,* Lord, the Fig-tree is *earth bound.*

2. *A want of warmer means, of fatter means.*

Wherefore accordingly he propoundeth;

First, *To loosen the earth, to dig about it.*

25

Secondly, *And then to supply it with dung; to dig about it, and dung it. Lord, let it alone this year also, until I shall dig about it.* I doubt it is too much ground-bound, *The Love of this world, and the deceitfulness of Riches,* lie too close to the roots of the heart of this Professor. The love of Riches, the love of Honours, the love of Pleasures, are the Thorns that choak the Word. *For all that is in the world, the lusts of the flesh, the lusts of the eyes, and the pride of life, are not of the Father, (but enmity to*

Luke 14.

30

1 Joh. 2. 15, 1.

5 *this year.*] *this year,*   12 striving] striving,

God); how then (where these things bind up the heart) can there be
fruit brought forth to God? *Barren Fig-tree*, See how the Lord *Jesus*, by
these very words, suggesteth the cause of thy fruitlesness of Soul. The
things of this world *lie too close to thy heart*; the earth with its things have
5 *bound up thy roots. Thou art an earth-bound Soul, thou art wrapt up in
thick clay. If any man love the world, the love of the father is not in him*: how
then can he be fruitful in the Vine-yard. This kept *Judas* from the fruit   Joh. 12. 6.
of caring for the poor. This kept *Demas* from the fruit of *Self-denial*.   2 Tim. 4.
And this kept *Ananias* and *Saphirah* his wife, from the goodly fruit of   Acts 5.
10 sincerity and truth. What shall I say, *These are foolish and hurtful Lusts,*   5–10.
which drown men in destruction and perdition; for the love of money, is the   1 Tim. 6. 9,
root *of* **all** *evil*. How then can good fruit grow from such a **root**, the
root of all evil, *Which while some covet after, they have erred from the
Faith, and pierced themselves through with many sorrows*. Mark, I say, it is
15 an *evil* **root**, Nay more, it is the **root** of all *evil*: how then can the
Professor that hath such a **root**, or a **root** wrapt up in such earthly
things, as the Lusts, and Pleasures, and Vanities of this world, bring
forth fruit to God!

Until I shall (dig) *about it.*

20   Lord, I will loose his roots, *I will dig up this earth*, I will lay his roots
bare, my hand shall be upon him by Sickness, by Disappointments, by
cross Providences; I will dig about him until he stands shaking and
tottering, until he be ready to fall; Then, if ever, he will seek to take
faster hold. Thus, I say, deals the Lord Jesus oft-times with the barren
25 Professor, *he diggeth about him*; He smiteth *one* blow at his heart,
another blow at his lusts, a *third* at his pleasures, a *fourth* at his
Comforts, *another* at his Self-conceitedness; Thus he diggeth about
him: This is the way to *take* bad earth from his roots, and to loosen his
roots from the earth. *Barren Fig-tree*, See here the *care*, the *love*, the
30 *labour* and *way*, which the Lord Jesus, the Dresser of the Vineyard, is
fain to take with thee, if happily thou maist be made fruitful.

1 *to God*); *1688*] *to God*)   19 *it. 1688*] *it.*

Until I shall dig about it, and (dung) *it.*

As the earth, by binding the *roots* too closely, may hinder the trees being fruitful: So the want of better means, may be also a cause thereof. And this is more than intimated by the Dresser of the Vineyard, *until I shall dig about it, and dung it,* I will supply it with a 5 more fruitful Ministry, with a warmer Word. I will give them Pastors *after mine own heart, I will dung them*; you know *dung* is a more warm, more fat, more hearty, and suckering matter, than is commonly the place in which trees are planted.

I will dig about it, and dung it, I will bring it under an *heart-awakening* 10 Ministry, the means of Grace *shall be fat,* and good. I will also visit it with Heart-awakening, heart-warming, heart-encouraging Considera-tions, I will apply warm dung to *his roots,* I will strive with him by my Spirit, and give him some tasts of the heavenly Gift, and the power of the world to come. I am loath to loose him for want of digging, *Lord,* 15 *Let it alone this year also, until I shall dig about it, and dung it.*

Gen. 6. 3.
Heb. 6. 2, 3.

And if it bear fruit, well:

And if the fruit of all my labour, doth make this *Fig-tree* fruitful, I shall count my *time,* my *labour,* and *means* well bestowed upon it; And thou also, O *my God,* shalt be therewith much delighted: *For thou art* 20 *gracious, and merciful, and repentest thee of the evil, which thou threatnest to bring upon a people.*

These words therefore inform us, that if a *Barren Fig-tree,* a barren Professor, shall now at last bring forth fruit to God, it shall go *well* with that Professor, it shall go *well* with *that poor Soul.* His *former* 25 barrenness, his *former* tempting of God, his *abuse* of Gods Patience, and long-Suffering; his *mispending* year after year, shall now be *all forgiven him.* Yea, God the Father, and our Lord Jesus Christ will now pass by, and forget *all,* and say, *Well done,* at the last. When I say to the wicked, *O wicked man, thou shalt surely die*; if he then do that which 30 is lawful and right, if he walk in the Statutes of life, without committing iniquity, he shall surely live, *he shall not die.*

Barren Fig-tree, *Dost thou hear!* the Ax is laid to thy roots, the Lord

Jonah 4. 2.

Ezek. 33.

32 marg. Ezek. 33 *1688*] Ezek. 3. 3.

Jesus prayes God to spare thee; Hath he been *digging* about thee? Hath he been *dunging* of thee? *O Barren Fig-tree, Now* thou art come to the point; if thou shalt *now* become good, if thou shalt after a gracious manner suck in the Gospel-dung, and if thou shalt bring forth fruit
5 unto God, **Well**; But if not, *the fire is the last*. Fruit or the Fire. Fruit or the Fire, *Barren Fig-tree. If it bear Fruit, well.*

> *And if not, then after that*
> *thou shalt cut it down.*

And if not, &c. The Lord Jesus by this, *if*, giveth us to understand,
10 that there is a generation of Professors in the world, that are incureable, that *will not*, that *cannot* repent, nor be profited by the means of Grace; A generation, I say, that will retain a Profession, *But will not bring forth fruit*; A generation that will *wear out* the patience of God, *Time* and *Tide*, Threatnings and Intercessions, Judgments and
15 Mercies, *And after all will be unfruitful.*

O the desperate Wickedness that is in thy heart; Barren Professor, Dost thou hear, the Lord Jesus stands *yet in doubt about thee!* There is an (**if**) stands *yet in thy way*. I say, the Lord Jesus stands *yet* in doubt about thee, whether or no, at last thou wilt be good. Whether he may
20 not labour in vaine, whether his digging and dunging will come to more then lost labour. *I gave her space to repent, and she repented not.* I ⟨Rev. 2. 21.⟩ digged about it, I dunged it, I gained time, and supplied it with means; but I laboured herein in vain, and spent my strength for nought and in vain. Dost thou hear, *Barren Figtree!* There is yet a question, *Whether*
25 *'twill be well with thy Soul at last.*

> *And if not, then after that*
> *thou shalt cut it down.*

There is nothing more exasperating to the mind of a man, than to find all his kindness and favour slighted: neither is the Lord Jesus so
30 provoked with any thing, as when Sinners abuse his means of Grace, if it be barren and fruitless under my Gospel, if it turn my Grace into

---

2 thee? *1688*] thee!

wantonness; if after digging, and dunging, and waiting, it yet remain unfruitful, I will let *thee cut it down.*

Gospel-means applied, is the *last remedy* for a barren Professor; if the Gospel, if the grace of the Gospel will not do, there can be nothing expected, but *cut it down. Then after that thou shalt cut it down.*   5

Mat. 23. 37, 38. *O* Jerusalem, Jerusalem, *Thou that killest the Prophets, and stonest them that are sent unto thee, how often would I have gathered thy Children together, as an Hen gathereth her Chickens under her wings, and ye would not? therefore your houses are left unto you desolate.* Yet it cannot be, but that this Lord Jesus, who at first did put stop to the execution of his   10 Fathers Justice, because He desired to try more means with the *Fig-tree*: I say, it cannot be, but that an heart so full of Compassion, *as his is,* should be touched, to behold this Professor must **now** be cut down; Luke 19. 41, 42. *And when he was come near, he beheld the City, and wept over it, saying, If thou hadst known, even thou, at least in this thy day the things that belong to*   15 *thy peace, but now they are hid from thine eyes.*

After that, thou shalt cut it down.

When Christ *giveth thee over,* there is *no* Intercessor, *no* Mediator, *no* Heb. 10. 26, 27, 28. more Sacrifice for Sin: all is gone but *Judgment,* but the *Ax,* but *a*   20 *certain fearful looking for of Judgment, and fiery indignation, which shall devour the adversaries.*

Barren Fig-tree, Take heed that thou comest not to these *last words,* for these words are a *give-up,* a cast-up, a cast-up of a cast-away: **after** *that thou shalt cut it down.* They are as much, as if Christ had   25 said, Father, I begg'd for *more time* for this barren Professor. I begged until I should *dig about it, and dung it;* But now, Father, the *time is out,* the year is ended, *the Summer is ended,* and no good done; I have also tried with my *means,* with the *Gospel,* I have digged about it; I have laid also the *fat* and *hearty* dung of the Gospel to it; *but all comes to nothing.*   30 Father, I deliver up this Professor to thee again, I have *done,* I have *done* all, I have *done praying,* and endeavouring, *I will hold the head of thine Ax*

3 Gospel-means *1688*] Gospel means
18 *After that, thou shalt cut it down* printed as a separate heading *1688*] Printed as part of the previous paragraph.

no *longer*: Take him into the hands of Justice, do Justice, do the Law, *I will never beg for him more. After that thou shalt cut it down. Wo unto them* Hos. 9. 12. *when I depart from them.* Now is this Professor left *naked* indeed, *naked* to God, *naked* to Satan, *naked* to Sin, *naked* to the Law, *naked* to Death, Mar. 9.
5 *naked* to Hell, *naked* to Judgement, and *naked* to the gripes of a *guilty* 43–48. Conscience, and to the torment of that *worm* that never dies, and to that *fire* that never shall be quenched. *See that ye refuse not him that* Heb. 12. 25. *speaketh; for if they escaped not, who refused him that spake on earth, much more shall not we escape, if we turn away from him that speaketh from*
10 *Heaven.* From this brief pass through this *Parable*, you have these *two* general Observations;

   First, That even then when the Justice of God cries out, *I cannot* Doct. 1. *endure to wait on this barren Professor any longer*: Then Jesus Christ intercedes for a *little more* Time, and a *little more* Patience, and a *little*
15 *more* striving with this Professor, if possible he may make him a fruitful Professor. *Lord, let it alone this year also, until I shall dig about it and dung it, and if it bear fruit, Well*, &c.

   Secondly, There are some Professors whose Day of Grace will end Doct. 2. with, *cut it down*, with Judgment; when Christ, by his means, hath been
20 used for their Salvation.

   The *First* of these *Observations* I shall pass, and not meddle at all therewith; But shall briefly speak to the *Second*, to wit, *That there are some Professors, whose day of Grace will end with, cut it down, with Judgment, when Christ by his means hath been used for their*
25 *Salvation.*

   This the Apostle sheweth in that *third* Chapter of his Epistle to the *Hebrews*; when he tells us, that the people of the *Jews*, after a *forty years* Heb. 3. 10, *patience*, and endeavour to do them good by the means appointed for 11. that purpose, their end was to be *cut down*, or excluded the Land of
30 Promise, for their final incredulity, *So we see they could not enter in, because of Unbelief.* Wherefore saith he, *I was grieved with that generation, and said, they do alwaies erre in their hearts, and they have not known my waies: So I sware in my wrath, they shall not enter into my rest.* As who should say, I would they should have entered in, and for that purpose I
35 brought them out of *Egypt*, led them through the Sea, and taught them in the Wilderness, but they did not answer my work, nor designs in that matter; wherefore, they shall not, I sware they shall not, *I swore in my*

wrath they should not enter into my Rest. Here is *cutting down with*

Heb. 4. 2, 3, 4.

judgment. So again *Chapter* the *fourth,* he saith, *As I have sworn in my wrath,* if *they shall enter into my rest, although the works were finished from the foundation of the world.* This word *if,* is the same with (they shall not) in the Chapter before. And where he saith, *Although the works were* 5 *finished from the foundation of the world.* He giveth us to understand, that what Preparations soever are made for the Salvation of Sinners, and of how long continuance soever they are, yet the God-tempting, God-provoking, & fruitless Professor is like to go without a share there in; *although the works were finisht from the foundation of the world.* 10

Jude 5, 6.

I will therefore put you in remembrance, though ye once knew this, how that the Lord having saved the people out of the land of Egypt, *afterwards destroyed them that believed not. And the Angels that kept not their first estate, but left their own habitation, he hath reserved in everlasting chains under darkness unto the Judgment of the great Day.* Here is an instance to 15 purpose, an instance of men and Angels. Men saved out of the Land of *Egypt,* and in their Journey towards *Canaan,* the type of Heaven (cut down), Angels created, and placed in the Heavens in great Estate and Principality, yet both these, because unfruitful to God in their places, were *cut down,* the men destroyed by God (for so saith the Text) and 20 the Angels reserved in everlasting chains under darkness, *to the Judgment of the great day.*

Now, in my handling of this point, I shall discourse of the *cutting down,* or the Judgement here denounced, as it respecteth the doing of it by Gods hand immediately, and that too, with respect to his *casting* 25 *them out of the world.* And *not* as it respecteth an *act* of the Church, *&c.* And as to this cutting down or Judgment, it must be concluded that it *cannot be before the day of grace be past with the fig-tree.* But according to the observation, *There be some Professors whose day of grace will end, with cut it down,* and according to *the* words of the text, *then* **after that,** 30 *thou shalt cut it down. After that,* that is, after all my attempts and ·endeavours to make it fruitful, after I have left it, given it over, done with it, and have resolved to bestow *no more* daies of Grace, opportunities of Grace, and means of Grace upon it; then *after* **that** thou shalt cut it down. 35

18 (cut down),] (cut down)   25 too, *1688*] to,
30 according *1688*] accarding

Besides, the *giving up* of the *Figtree*, is *before* the execution. *Execution is not alwaies presently* upon the *Sentence* given; for **after** *that* a convenient time is thought on, and *then* is *cutting down*: and so it is here in the Text. The Decree that he shall perish, is gathered from its
5 continuing fruitless quite through the *last year*, from its continuing fruitless *at the end of all endeavours*: But *cutting down* is not yet, for that comes with an **after** word. *Then after* **that** *thou shalt cut it down.*

So then, that I may orderly proceed with the Observation, I must lay down these two Propositions.

10 *First, that the day of grace ends with some men* before God takes them out of this world. And,

Secondly, the death, or *cutting down* of such men will be dreadful. For this *cut it down*, when it is understood in the largest sense (*as here indeed it ought*) it sheweth, not only the wrath of God against a mans life in
15 this world, but his wrath against him body & Soul. And is as much as to say; cut him off from all the priviledges, and benefitts that come by grace, both in this world, and that which is to come.

But to proceed, *The day of grace ends with some men, before God taketh them out of this world.* I shall give you some instances of this, and so go
20 on to the last Proposition.

First, I shall instance, *Cain*; *Cain* was a Professor, * a Sacrificer, a worshipper of God; Yea the first worshiper that we read of *after the fall*; But his grapes were wild ones *, *his works were evil*, he did not doe what he did, from true Gospel-motives. Therefore God disallowed his
25 worke, at this his countenance falls; Wherefore he envies his brother, disputes him, takes his opertunity, and kills him. Now in *that* day that he *did this* act, was the heavens closed up against him, and that himself did smartingly and fearfully feel, when God made inquisition for the blood of *Abel, And now cursed*, said God, *shalt thou be from the earth,*
30 *which hath opened her mouth to receive thy brothers blood from thy hand, and, &c.* And Cain *said, my punishment is greater than I can bear. Mine Iniquity is greater than that it may be forgiven. Behold, thou hast driven me out this day from the face of the earth, and from thy face shall I be hid.* Now thou art cursed, saith God. Thou hast driven me out *this* day, saith
35 *Cain*, and from thy face shall I be hid; I shall never more have Hope in

The first
Proposition.

*Gen. 4. 3.

*1 Joh. 3.
12.

Gen. 4.
5, 7, 8.

Gen. 4. 8,
11, 12, 13,
14.

27 him. Now *1688*] him now

thee, Smile from thee, nor expect mercy at thy hand. Thus therefore,
Cain's day of Grace ended, and the Heavens, with Gods own heart,
were shut up against him; *yet after this,* he lived long. *Cutting down,* was
not come yet: after *this* he lived to marry a wife, to beget a cursed
brood, to build a City, (and what els I know not) all which could not be   5
quickly done; Wherefore *Cain* might live after the day of Grace was
past with him, several *hundred* of years.

Secondly, I shall instance, *Ishmael* : *Ishmael* was a Professor, was
brought up in *Abraham's* family, and was circumcised at *thirteen years of
age,* but he was the son of the *bond-woman,* he brought not forth good   10
fruit; he was *A wild Professor.* For all his Religion, he would scoff at
those that were better then himself. Well, upon a day his brother *Isaac*
was weaned, at which time his father made a feast and rejoyced before
the Lord, for that he had given him the promised Son, *at this* Ishmael
mocked them, their Son, and Godly rejoyceing. Then came the Spirit of   15
God upon *Sarah* and she cried, *Cast him out, cast out this bond-woman,
and her Son; for the Son of* * *this bond-woman shall not be Heir with my
Son, with Isack.* Now *Paul* to the *Galatians* makes this casting out to be,
not only a casting out of *Abraham's* family, but a casting out also *from a
lot* * *with the Saints in heaven.* Also *Moses* giveth us a notable proof   20
thereof, in saying, that when he died, *he was gathered to his † People;* his
people by his Mothers side, for he was reckoned from her, the Son of
Hagar, the Son of the Bondwoman. Now she came of the * *Egyptians*;
So that he was gathered when he died, notwithstanding his Profession,
to the place that *Pharoah* and his hoast were gathered to, who were   25
drowned in the *Red Sea,* these were his People, and he was of them,
both by Nature and Disposition, by persecuting as they did. But now,
When did the day of Grace end with this man. Observe, and I will shew
you: *Ishmael* was *thirteen years old,* when he was Circumcised, and then
was *Abraham* * *ninety years* old and *nine.* The *next year Isaac* was born.   30
So that *Ishmael* was *now Fourteen* years of Age. Now *when* Isaac *was
weaned* (suppose he suckt four years) by that account *The day of Grace
must be ended with* Ishmael, *by that he was* Eighteen *years old.* For that
day he mocked, that day it was said, *Cast him out,* and of that casting
out, the Apostle makes what I have said. Beware ye young, barren   35
Professors. Now *Ishmael* lived an *hundred* and *nineteen* years after this,

Marginal notes:

Gen. 4. 16.

Gen. 17. 25,
26.
& 16. 12.

*Gen. 21. 9,
10, 11.

*Gal. 4. 29,
30, 31.
†Gen. 25.
17.
*Gen. 21. 9.

*Gen. 17.
24, 25, 26.

Gen. 25. 12,
13, 14, 15,
16, 17.

· 13 weaned, *1688*] weaned   30 was born.] was † born.

in great tranquillity and honour with men; after this he also begat *twelve* Princes, even after his day of Grace was past.

Thirdly, I shall instance *Esau*. *Esau* also was a Professor, he was born unto *Isaac*, and circumcised according to the Custom: but *Esau* was a 5 *gamesom Professor*, an hunts-man, *a man of the field*; also he was wedded to his Lusts, which he did also venture to keep, *rather than the Birthright*. Well, upon a day, when he came from hunting, and was faint, he sold his Birthright to *Jacob* his brother. Now the Birth-right, in those days, had the Promise and Blessing annexed to it. Yea, they were so 10 entailed *in this*, that the one could not go without the other, wherefore the Apostles Caution is here of weight; *Take heed*, saith he, *lest there be among you a Fornicator, or profane person as* Esau, *who for one Morsel of meat sold his Birthright; for ye know how that afterwards, when he would have inherited the Blessing, he was rejected; for he found no place of* 15 *Repentance, though he sought it carefully with tears*. Now the ending of *Esau*'s day of Grace is to be reckoned from his selling of his Birthright: For there the Apostle points it, lest there be among you any, that like *Esau*, sells his Birth-right: for then goes hence the Blessing also.

But *Esau* sold his Birth-right long before his death. *Twenty* years 20 after this, *Jacob* was with *Laban*, and when he returned home, his brother *Esau* met him. Further, after this when *Jacob* dwelt again some time with his Father, then *Jacob* and *Esau* buried him. I suppose he might live above *forty*, yea for ought I know, above *fourscore* years after he had sold his Birth-right. And so consequently had put himself out 25 of the Grace of God.

Three things I would further note upon these *three* Professors.

First, Cain an angry Professor, *Ishmael* a mocking one, *Esau* a lustful, gamesome one: *Three Symptomes* of a barren Professor. For he that can be angry, and that can mock, and that can indulge his Lusts, cannot 30 bring forth fruit to God.

Secondly, The Day of Grace ended with these Professors at that time when they committed some grievous Sin; *Cain's*, when he killed his Brother; *Ishmael's* when he mocked at *Isaac*, &c. and *Esau* when out of love to his Lusts, he despised, and sold his Birth-right. Beware barren 35 Professor. *Thou maist do that in half a quarter of an hour, from the evil of which thou maist not be delivered for ever and ever.*

35 Professor. *1688*] Professur.

Gen. 25. 27, 28, 29, 30–34.

Heb. 12. 16, 17.

Gen. 31. 34. & 32. 6.

& 35. 28, 29.

Thirdly, Yet these *three, after their day of Grace was over*, lived better

Gen. 4. 17.
& 17. 20.
c. 25. 16.
& 33. 8, 9.

lives, as to outward things, than ever they did before. Cain, *after this*, was Lord of a City, *Ishmael* was *after this*, father of *twelve* Princes, and *Esau after this*, told his Brother, *I have enough, my brother, keep that thou hast to thy self.* Ease, and Peace, and a prosperous life in outwards, is no 5 sign of the favour of God to a barren and fruitless Professor; But rather of his *wrath*, that thereby he may be capable to treasure up *more* wrath, against the *day of wrath and revelation of the righteous judgment of God.*

Let thus much serve for the proof of the *first* Proposition, namely, 10 *That the day of Grace ends with some men, before God takes them out of this world.*

Now then, to shew you, by some Signs, how you may know that the day of Grace is ended, or near to ending with the Barren Professor; *And after that thou shalt cut it down.* 15

First, He that hath stood it out against God, and that hath withstood all those means for fruit, that God hath used for the making of him (if it might have been) a fruitful tree in his garden, he is in this danger; and this indeed is the *sum* of the *Parable*; The Fig-tree here mentioned, was blessed with the application of means, had time 20 allowed it to receive the nourishment; But it out-stood, with-stood, over-stood **all**, **all** that the Husband-man did, **all** that the Vine-dresser did.

Signs of being past Grace.

But a little distinctly to particularize in *four* or *five* Particulars: 25

1. Sign

First, The day of Grace is like to be past, when a Professor hath withstood, abused, *and worn out Gods patience*, then he is in danger, this is a provocation, then God cries, *cut it down.* There are some men that *steal* into a Profession, *no body knows how*; even as this Fig-tree was brought into the Vine-yard, by other hands than Gods: and there they 30 abide liveless, graceless, careless, *and without any good Conscience to God*

Joh. 6. 26.

at all. Perhaps they came in for the loaves, for a trade, for credit, for a blind; or it may be stifle, & choak the checks, & grinding pangs of an awakened, and disquieted, Conscience. Now having obtain'd their purpose, *like the Sinners of Sion*, they are at ease, and secure; Saying 35

---

2 marg. & 17. 20. c. 25. 16] & 19. 20. c. 23. 26.
32 marg. Irrelevant reference, Gen. 21. 20, 22, 23, removed.

like *Agag, Surely the bitterness of Death is past*; I am well, shall be saved, and go to Heaven: Thus in these vain conceits *it spends a year, two, or three*; not remembring that at every Season of Grace, and at every opportunity of the Gospel, *the Lord comes seeking fruit. Well*, Sinner, *well*
5 *barren Fig-tree*, this is but a course *beginning*; God comes for fruit. What have I here, saith God, what a *Fig-tree* is this, that hath stood this year in my Vineyard, and brought me forth no fruit. I will cry unto him, Professor! *Barren Fig-tree*, be fruitful! I look for fruit, I expect fruit, I must have fruit, therefore bethink thy self. At these the Professor
10 pauses; but these are words, *not blows*, therefore off goes this consideration from the heart: When God comes the next year, he finds him still as he was, a *barren*, fruitless *cumber-ground*. And now again he complains, here are *two years gone*, and *no* fruit appears; Well, I will defer mine anger for my name sake. I will defer mine anger for my
15 praise, *I will refrain from thee, that I cut thee not off* (as yet.) I will wait, I will yet wait to be gracious. But this helps not, this hath not the least influence upon the barren Fig-tree, *Tush*, saith he, here is *no* Threatning: *God is merciful*, he will defer his anger, He waits to be gracious: *I am not yet afraid.* O how ungodly Men, that are at unawares
20 crept into the Vineyard, *how do they turn the Grace of our God into lasciviousness.* Well, he comes the third year for fruit, as he did before, but still he finds *but a barren Fig-tree; No* fruit: now he cries out again, *O thou dresser of my Vineyard*, come hither, here's a *Fig-tree* hath stood these *three years* in my Vineyard, and hath at every season disappointed
25 my expectation, for I have looked for fruit in vain. *Cut it down*, my patience is worn out, *I shall wait on this Fig-tree no longer.*

2. And now He begins to shake the *Fig-tree* with his threatnings; fetch out the Ax, now the *Ax* is death, Death therefore is called for, Death come, smite me *this* Fig-tree, and withal the Lord shakes this
30 Sinner, and *whirls* him upon a Sick-bed, saying, *Take him Death*, he hath abused my Patience and Forbearance, not remembring that it should have led him to Repentance, and to the fruits thereof. *Death, fetch away this Fig-tree to the fire*, fetch this barren Professor to Hell. At this, Death comes with *grim* looks into the Chamber, yea and * Hell
35 follows with him to the Bed-side, and both stare this Professor in the

Amos 6. 1.
1 Sam. 15. 32.

Isa. 48. 9.

Isa. 30. 18.

Rom. 2. 3, 4.

*Rev. 6. 8.

1 marg. Irrelevant reference, 1 Sam. 15. 30, removed.
19 marg. Isa. 48. 9, removed.

face, yea, begin to lay hands upon him; one smiting him with pains in his Body, with Head-ach, Heart-ach, Back-ach, Shortness of Breath, Fainting, Qualms, Trembling of Joints, Stopping at the Chest, and almost all the *Symptomes* of a man past all recovery. Now while *Death* is thus tormenting the Body, *Hell* is doing with the Mind and Conscience, striking them with its Pains, casting sparks of Fire in thither, wounding with sorrows and fears of everlasting damnation, the spirit of this poor creature: And now he begins to bethink himself, and to cry to God for mercy; *Lord, spare me, Lord, spare me.* Nay, saith God, you have been a Provocation to me, *these three years.* How many times have you disappointed me? How many seasons have you spent in vain? How many Sermons and other Mercies did I of my patience afford you? but *all* to no purpose at all. *Take him Death.* O good Lord, saith the Sinner, Spare me but *this once.* Raise me but *this once.* Indeed I have been a barren Professor, and have stood to no purpose at all in thy Vine-yard: But spare! O spare, *this one time*, I beseech thee, and I will be better. *Away, away*, you will not. I have tried you *these three years* already, you are nought; If I should recover you again, you would be as bad as you was before (and all this talk is while Death stands by.) The Sinner cries again, Good Lord, try me *this once*, let me get up again *this once*, and *see* if I do not mend. But will you promise me to mend? yes indeed, Lord, and vow it too; I will never be so bad again, *I will be better.* Well, saith God, *Death*, let this Professor alone *for this time.* I will try him a while longer, he hath promised, he hath *vowed* that he will amend his waies. It may be he will mind to keep his Promises. *Vows* are solemn things, it may be he may *fear to break his vows*: arise from off thy bed, and *now God laies down his Ax.* At this the poor Creature is very thankful, praises God, and fawns upon him, shews as if he did it heartily, and calls to others to thank him too. He therefore riseth as one would think, to be a new-creature indeed. But by that he hath put on his cloaths, is come down from his bed, and ventured into the Yard, or Shop, and there sees how all things are gone to *Sixes* and *Sevens*, he begins to have *Second* thoughts: and saies to his folks, What have you all been doing? How are all things out of order? I am I cannot tell what behind-hand; one may see if a man be but a little a to-side, that you have neither wisdome, nor prudence to order things: And now, instead of seeking to spend the rest of his time to God, *he doubleth his diligence after this world.* Alas, all must not be lost, *we must have a provident Care*: and thus quite forgetting the sorrows of Death, the pains of Hell, the Promises and Vows which he made to God to be better: *Because Judgment was not* (now) *speedily executed, therefore the heart of this poor* 5 *creature is fully set in him to do evil.*

These things proving ineffectual, *God takes hold of his* Ax *again*, sends Death to a Wife, to a Child, to his Cattle, (*your young men have I* * *slain, and taken away your horses*) I will blast him, cross him, disappoint him, and cast him down, and will set my self against him, *in* 10 *all that he putteth his hand unto.* At this the poor *Barren Professor* cries out again, Lord, I have sinned, spare me once more, I beseech thee. O take not away *the desire of mine eyes*, spare my Children, bless me in my labours, and I will mend, and be better. No, saith God, you lyed to me last time, I will trust you, *in this*, no longer, and with all he tumbleth the 15 Wife, the Child, the Estate, into a grave:

And then returns to his place, till this Professor more unfeignedly acknowledgeth * his offence.

At this the poor creature is afflicted and distressed, rents his cloaths, and begins to call the breaking of his Promise and Vows to mind, he 20 mourns and praies, and like *Ahab, a while walks softly*, at the remembrance of the justness of the hand of God upon him. And now he renews his Promises, Lord try me *this one time more*, take off thy hand and see. *They go far as never turn.* Well, God spareth him again, sets down his *Ax* again (*Many times He did deliver them, but they provoked* 25 *him with their Counsels, and were brought low for their Iniquities*). Now they seem to be thankful again, and are as if they were resolved to be Godly indeed. Now they Read, they Pray, they go to Meetings, and seem to be serious a pretty while, but at last they forget. Their Lusts prick them, suitable Temptations present themselves: wherefore they 30 turn to their own crooked waies again. *When he slew them, then they sought him, and returned early after God, nevertheless they did flatter him with their mouth, and lyed unto him with their tongue.*

4. Yet again, The Lord will not leave this Professor, but will take up his *ax* again, and will put him under a more heart-searching Ministry, a 35 Ministry that shall search him, and turn him over and over, a Ministry that shall meet with him, as *Elijah* met with *Ahab*, in all his acts of

11 I have *1688*] I, have

*Amos 4. 9, 10.

*Hos. 5. 14, 15.

1 Kin. 21, 27.

Psal. 106. 43.

Psal. 78, 34–36.

wickedness (and **now** *the* Ax *is laid to the roots of the trees*) Besides, this Ministry doth not only search the heart, but presenteth the Sinner with the *Golden* raies of the glorious Gospel; *Now is Christ Jesus set forth evidently*, now is Grace displaied sweetly; Now, now are the Promises broken like *Boxes* of *Ointment*, to the perfuming of the whole room. *But* 5 *alas, there is yet no fruit on this fig-tree.* While his heart is searching, he wrangles; while the glorious Grace of the Gospel is unvailing, this Professor wags and is wanton, gathers up some *scraps* thereof, *Tastes the good word of God, and the powers of the world to come.* Drinketh in this rain that comes oft upon him, *But bringeth not forth fruit meet for him,* 10 *whose Gospel it is; takes no heed to walk in the Law of the Lord God of Israel, with all his heart*; but counteth that the glory of the Gospel consisteth in talk and shew, and that our obedience thereto, is a matter of *Speculation*; that good *works* lie in good *words*, and if they can finely talk, they think they *bravely* please God. They think the Kingdom of 15 God consisteth only in word, not in power: and thus proveth ineffectual this *Fourth* means also.

5. Well, Now the *Ax* begins to be heaved higher, for now indeed God is ready to smite the Sinner, yet before he will strike the stroak, he will try one way more at the last, and if that misseth, *down goes the Fig-* 20 *tree.* Now this last way is *to tug, and strive with this Professor by his Spirit.* Wherefore the Spirit of the Lord is now come to him: But *not alwaies to strive with man*, yet a while he will strive with him, he will *awaken*, he will *convince*, he will call to remembrance former Sins, former Judgments, the breach of former Vows and Promises, the mispending 25 of former Days; he will also present perswasive Arguments, encouraging Promises, dreadful Judgments, the shortness of time to repent in; and that there is hope if he come. Further, he will shew him the certainty of Death, and of the Judgment to come; yea, He will pull and strive with this Sinner. But, behold, the mischief now lies here, here is tugging 30 and striving on both sides. The *Spirit* convinces, the *man* turns a deaf ear to God; The *Spirit* saith, Receive my instruction and live; but the *man* pulls away his Shoulder; the *Spirit* shews him whither he is going, but the *man* closeth his eyes against it; the *Spirit* offereth violence, the *man* strives and resists, *They have done despite unto the Spirit of Grace.* 35 The Spirit *parlieth* a *Second* time, and urgeth Reasons of a new nature;

Jude 4.
Heb. 6. 3–7, 8.

2 Kin. 10. 31.

1 Cor. 4. 19.

Gen. 6. 3.

Acts 7. 51.

Zac. 7. 11, 12, 13.

Heb. 10. 29.

22 marg. 3.] 8.   31 marg. 51.] 50.

But the Sinner answereth, No, *I have loved Strangers, and after them I will go.* At this Gods fury comes up into his face, now he comes out of his holy place, and is terrible: now He *sweareth in his wrath, they shall never enter into his rest.* I exercised towards you my Patience, yet you 5 have not turned unto me, saith the Lord. I smote you in your Person, in your Relations, in your Estate, yet you have not returned unto me, saith the Lord, *In thy filthiness is lewdness, because I have purged thee, and thou wast not purged; thou shalt not be purged from thy filthiness any more, till I cause my fury to rest upon thee. Cut it down, why doth it cumber the* 10 *ground.*

Amos 4. 6, 8, 9, 10, 11.

Ezek. 24. 13.

A Second *Sign.*

Another *Sign* that such a Professor is almost (if not quite) past Grace, is, *When God hath given him over, or lets him alone,* and suffers him to do any thing, and that without controul, helpeth him not either 15 in works of Holiness, or in streights & difficulties. *Ephraim is joyned to Idols, let him alone; Wo be to them when I depart from them. I will laugh at their Calamities, and will mock when their fear cometh.*

The 2 Sign of

Hos. 4. 17.

Pro. 1. 24, 25, 26, 27, 28.

Barren Fig-tree, thou hast heretofore been digged about, and dunged, God's mattock hath heretofore been at thy roots, Gospel- 20 dung hath heretofore been applyed to thee; thou hast heretofore been strove with, convinced, awakened, made to taste and see, and crie, *O the blessedness!* Thou hast heretofore been met with under the Word, thy heart hath melted, thy Spirit hath fallen, thy Soul hath trembled, and thou hast felt something of the Power of the Gospel. But thou hast 25 sinned, thou hast provoked the eyes of his Glory, thy iniquity is found to be hateful, and now perhaps God hath left thee, given thee up, *and lets thee alone.*

Heretofore thou wast tender, thy Conscience startled at the temptation to wickedness, for thou wert taken off from *the pollutions of* 30 *the world, through the knowledg of our Lord and Saviour Jesus Christ;* but that very *vomit* that once thou wert turned from, now thou lappest up, with the *dog* in the *Proverb* again, and that very *Mire,* that once thou seemest to lie washed from, *in that very mire thou now art tumbling*

2 Pet. 2. 20, 21, 22.

19–20 Gospel-dung *1688*] Gospel dung

afresh. But to particularize, there are *three* Signs of a mans being given over of God.

1. When he is let alone in Sinning, *when the reins of his lusts are loosed,* and he given up to them. *And even as they did not like to retain God in their knowledg, God gave them over to a reprobate mind, to do those things* 5 *which are not convenient; being filled with all unrighteousness.* Seest thou a man that heretofore had the knowledg of God, and that had some awe

of his Majesty upon him; I say, seest thou such an one *Sporting himself in his own deceivings,* turning the Grace of our God into Lasciviousness, and walking after his own ungodly Lusts; his Judgment now of a long 10

time lingereth not, *and his Damnation slumbereth not.* Dost thou hear, barren Professor? It is astonishing to see, how those that once seemed

Sons of the Morning, and were making Preparations for Eternal Life, now at last, for the rottenness of their hearts, by the just Judgment of God, to be permitted, being past feeling, to give themselves over unto 15

lasciviousness, *to work all uncleanness with greediness.* A great number of such were in the *first* Gospel-days; against whom *Peter,* and *Jude,* and

John pronounceth the heavy Judgment of God. *Peter* and *Jude couple them with the fallen Angels*; and *John* forbids that prayer be made for them, because that is happened unto them, that hath happened to the 20

Angels that fell. *Who for forsaking their* first *state, and for leaving their own habitation, are reserved in chains under everlasting darkness, unto the Judgment of the great Day. Barren Fig-tree,* Dost thou hear?

First, These are beyond all Mercy.

Secondly, These are beyond all Promises. 25

Thirdly, These are beyond all hopes of Repentance.

Fourthly, These have no Intercessor, nor any more share in a Sacrifice for Sin.

Fifthly, For these remains nothing, but a fearful looking for of Judgment. 30

Sixthly, Wherefore these are the true Fugatives and Vagabonds, that being left of God, of Christ, of Grace, of the Promise, and being beyond all hope, wander and straggle to and fro, even as the Devil, their associate, until their time shall come to die, or until they descend in Battle, and perish. 35

2. Wherefore they are let alone in hearing. If these at any time come

10 marg. 3] 13.   11 Professor? *1688*] Professor,

under the word, there is for them *no* God, *no* savour of the means of
Grace, *no* stirrings of heart, *no* pity for themselves, *no* love to their own
Salvation. Let them look on this hand or that, there they see such
effects of the Word in others, as produceth signs of Repentance, and
5 love to God and his Christ, *These men only have their backs bowed down* Rom. 11, 8,
alway. These men only, *have the spirit of slumber, eyes that they should not* 9, 10.
see, and ears that they should not hear to this very day. Wherefore as they
go to the place of the holy; *So they come from the place of the holy, and* Eccl. 8. 10.
soon are forgotten in the places where they so did. Only they reap this
10 damage, *They treasure up wrath against the day of wrath, and revelation of* Rom. 2. 3,
the righteous judgment of God. Look to it, *barren Professor.* 4, 5.

3. If he be visited after the common way of Mankind, either with He is left
Sickness, Distress, or any kind of Calamity, still no God appeareth, no in his
Affliction.
sanctifying hand of God, no special Mercy is mixed with the Affliction.
15 But he falls sick, and grows well, *like the beast*; or is under distress, as
Saul, who when he was engaged by the *Philistines*, was forsaken and 1 Sam. 28.
left of God. *And the* Philistins *gathered themselves together, and came and* 4, 5, 6.
pitched in Shunem; *and* Saul *gathered all* Israel *together, and they pitched*
in Gilboa: *And when* Saul *saw the Host of the* Philistins, *he was afraid, and*
20 *his heart greatly trembled. And when* Saul *enquired of the Lord, the Lord*
answered him no more, neither by Dreams, nor by Urim, *nor by Prophets.*
The Lord answered him *no* more, He had done with him, cast him off,
and rejected him, and left him to stand and fall with his sins by himself.
But of this more in the *Conclusion*, therefore I here forbear.
25 4. These men may go whither they will, do what they will, they may He is left to
range from Opinion to Opinion, from Notion to Notion, from *Sect* to do what he
will, or go
Sect, but are stedfast no where, they are left to their own uncertainties: where he
will.
they have not Grace to establish their hearts, and though some of them
have boasted themselves of this Liberty; yet *Jude* calls them *wandering* Jude 13.
30 *Stars, to whom is reserved the blackness of darkness for ever.* They are left,
as I told you before, to the Fugatives and Vagabonds in the Earth, to
wander every where, but to abide no where, until they shall descend *to* Acts. 1. 25.
their own place, with *Cain* and *Judas*, men of the same fate with
themselves.

32 marg. 25.] 5.

A Third *Sign.*

Thirdly, Another *Sign,* that such a Professor is quite past Grace, is, when his heart is grown so hard, so stony and inpenetrable, that nothing will pierce it. *Barren Fig-tree, Dost thou consider?* A hard and impenitent heart is the Curse of God. A heart that cannot repent, is 5 instead of all plagues at once; And hence it is that God said of *Pharaoh,* when he spake of delivering him up in the greatness of his Anger, *I will at this time,* saith he, *send all my Plagues upon thy heart.*

To some men that have grievously sinned under a Profession of the Gospel; God giveth this *Token* of his Displeasure, they are denied the 10 Power of Repentance, their heart is bound, they cannot repent: It is impossible that they should ever repent should they live a *thousand* years, *It is impossible for those* Fall-a-waies *to be renewed again unto Repentance, seeing they crucifie to themselves the Son of God afresh, and put him to open shame.* Now to have the heart so hardened, *so judicially* 15 *hardened,* this is as a bar put in by the Lord God, against the Salvation of *this* Sinner. This was the burden of *Spira's* complaint, *I cannot do it: O now I cannot do it.*

This man sees what he hath done, what should help him, and what will become of him, yet he cannot repent; he pulled away his shoulder 20 before, he stopped his ears before, he shut up his eyes before, *and in that very posture God left him,* and so he stands to this very day. I have had a fancy, that *Lot's* wife, when she was turned into a Pillar of Salt, stood yet looking over her shoulder, or else with her face towards *Sodom*; as the judgment caught her, so it bound her, and left her a 25 Monument of Gods anger to after-Generations.

We read of some that are *seared with an hot iron,* and that are *past feeling,* for so seared persons, in seared parts are. Their Conscience is seared. The Conscience is the thing that must be touched with feeling fear and *remorse,* if ever any good be done with the Sinner. How then 30 can any good be done to those whose Conscience is *worse than that, that is fast asleep in sin.* For that Conscience that is fast asleep, may yet be effectually awakened and savèd; but that Conscience *that is seared,* dried, as it were into a *Cinder,* can never have sense, feeling, or the least regret in this world. *Barren Fig-tree, hearken, judicial hardening* 35

Rom. 2. 5.

Exo. 9. 14.

Heb. 6. 4, 5, 6.

Zec. 7. 12, 13, 14.

1 Tim. 4. 2.

Eph. 4. 19.

28 marg. 2. *1688*] 3.

is dreadful. There is a difference betwixt that hardness of heart, that is incident to all men, and that which comes upon some as a signal or special Judgment of God: and although all kind of hardness of Heart, in some sense, may be called a Judgment, yet to be hardened with this
5 *Second* kind, is a Judgment peculiar only to them that perish; An hardness that is sent as a punishment, *for the abuse of light received, for a reward of Apostacy.*

This *Judicial* hardness is discovered from that which is incident to all men in these particulars.

10 1. It is an hardness that comes after some great Light received, *Because of some great Sin committed against that Light, and the Grace that gave it.* Such hardness as *Pharaoh* had, after the Lord had wrought wonderously before him: Such *hardness* as the *Gentiles* had, a *hardness* which darkened the heart, a *hardness* which made their minds *reprobate.*

15 *This hardness* is also the same with that the *Hebrews* are cautioned to beware of; an *hardness* that is caused by Unbelief, and a departing from the Living God; an *hardness* compleated through the deceitfulness of Sin: Such as that in the Provocation, of whom God sware, that they should not enter into his *Rest.* 'Twas this kind of *hardness* also that both
20 *Cain,* and *Ishmael,* and *Esau* were hardened with, after they had committed *their great Transgressions.*

2. It is the *greatest* kind of *Hardness,* and hence they are said to be *Harder than a Rock,* or than an *Adamant,* that is, *harder than Flint.* So hard that nothing can enter.

25 3. It is an *Hardness* given in much anger, and that to bind the Soul up in an impossibility of Repentance.

4. It is an *Hardness* therefore which is incurable, of which a man must die and be damned. *Barren Professor, hearken to this.*

A Fourth *Sign.*

30 *Fourthly,* Another *Sign* that such a Professor is quite past Grace, is when he fortifies his hard heart against the *tenour* of God's Word. This is called *hardening themselves against God, and turning of the Spirit against him.* As thus, When after a Profession of Faith in the Lord Jesus, and of the Doctrine that is according to Godliness, they shall embolden

23 marg. 12| 13.

Margin notes:
1 Sam. 6. 6.
Rom. 1. 20, 21.
Heb. 3. 7, 8, 9, 10, 11, 12, 13.
Jer. 5. 3.
Zac. 7. 12.
Rom. 2. 5.
Heb. 6. 6.
Job 9. 4.
& 5. 12, 13.

themselves in courses of Sin, *by promising themselves that they shall have Life and Salvation notwithstanding. Barren Professor*, hearken to this.

Deut. 29.
18.
& 19. This man is called, *A root that beareth Gall and Wormwood, or a poisonful herb*, such an one as is abominated of God; yea the abhorred of his Soul. For this man saith, *I shall have peace, though I walk in the* 5 *imagination, or stubborness of my heart, to adde drunkenness to thirst*; an opinion flat against the whole Word of God, yea against the very nature

Deut. 29.
20. of God himself. Wherefore he adds that, *Then the anger of the Lord, and his jealousie shall smoak against that man, and all the Curses that are written in God's Book shall lie upon him, and God shall blot out his name* 10 *from under Heaven.*

Yea, that man shall not fail to be effectually destroyed, saith the

Deut. 29.
21. Text, *The Lord shall separate that man unto evil, out of all the Tribes of Israel, according to all the Curses of the Covenant.*

He shall separate him unto evil, He shall give him up, he shall leave 15 him to his heart, he shall separate him to *that*, or *those* that will assuredly be too hard for him.

Now this judgment is much effected, when God hath given a man up unto *Satan*, and hath given *Satan* leave, *without fail*, to compleat his destruction. I say, *When God hath given Satan leave effectually to compleat* 20 *his destruction*: For all that are delivered up unto Satan, have not, nor do not come to this end. But *that* is the man, whom God shall *separate* to evil, and shall *leave* in the hands of *Satan*, to *compleat*, without fail, his destruction.

I Kin. 21.
25. Thus he served *Ahab*, a man, *That sold himself to work wickedness in* 25 *the sight of the Lord. And the Lord said, Who shall perswade* Ahab, *that he may go up, and fall at* Ramoth-Gilead? *And one said on this manner, and another said on that manner: And there came forth a Spirit, and stood before*

I Kin. 22.
20, 21, 22. *the Lord, and said, I will perswade him. And the Lord said unto him, wherewith? And he said, I will go forth, and be a lying Spirit in the mouth of* 30 *all his Prophets. And he said, Thou shalt perswade him, and prevail also, go forth and do so.* Thou shalt perswade him *and prevail*, do thy will, I leave him in thy hand, *Go forth, and do so.*

Wherefore in these Judgments, the Lord doth much concern himself for the management thereof, because of the Provocation, 35

---

3 marg. & 19.] 19, v, *1688, 1673.*   8 marg. 29.] 19.
13 marg. Deut. 29. 21.] 21. *vers.*   27 Ramoth-Gilead? *1688*] Ramoth-Gilead:

wherewith they have provoked him. This is the man, *whose ruine God
contriveth, and bringeth to pass by his own contrivance. I will chuse their* Isa. 66. 4.
delusions for them, I will bring their fears upon them, I will chuse their
Devices, or the Wickednesses that their hearts are contriving of. I, even
5 I, will cause them to be accepted of, and delightful to them. But who v. 3.
are they that must thus be feared? Why, those among Professors, that
have chosen *their own waies, those whose Soul delighteth in their
Abominations.*

Because they received not the love of the Truth, that they might be saved;
10 *for this cause God shall send them strong Delusions, that they should believe a
Lye, that they all might be damned, who believed not the Truth, but had
pleasure in Unrighteousness.*

God shall send them, It is a great word; Yea, *God shall send them strong
Delusions;* Delusions that shall do, that shall make them believe a Lye.
15 Why so? *That they all might be damned, every one of them, who believe not* 2 Thes. 2.
the Truth, but had pleasure in Unrighteousness. 10, 11, 12.

There is nothing more provoking to the Lord, than for a man to
promise, when God threatneth; for a man to be light of conceit, that he
shall be safe; and yet to be more wicked than in former daies: This
20 mans Soul abhorreth the Truth of God, no marvel therefore if God's
Soul abhorreth him: he hath invented a way contrary to God, to bring
about his own Salvation, no marvel therefore, if God invent a way to Jer. 44. 26,
bring about this mans Damnation: And seeing that these rebels are at 27, 28.
this point, We shall have peace; God will see whose word shall stand,
25 His or theirs.

A Fifth *Sign.*

Fifthly, Another *Sign* of a man being past Grace, is, When he shall at
this, scoff, and inwardly *grin,* and fret against the Lord, secretly
purposing to continue his course, and put all to the venture, despising
30 the Messengers of the Lord. *He that despised* Moses*'s Law, died without* Heb. 10. 28.
*Mercy, of how much sorer punishment suppose ye, shall he be thought worthy,
who hath troden under foot the Son of God,* &c.

Wherefore, against these Despisers *God hath set himself,* and
foretold, that they *shall* not believe but perish. *Behold ye Despisers, and* Acts 13. 41.
3 *them, 1688*] *them*   15 marg. 2.] 5.

wonder, and perish, for I work a work in your days, which ye shall in no wise
believe, though a man declare it unto you.

After that thou shalt cut
it down.

Thus far we have treated of the *Barren Fig-tree*, or fruitless 5
Professor, with some Signs to know him by; whereto is added also
some *Signs* of one who neither will or can, by any means, be fruitful,
but they must miserably perish. Now being come to the time of
Execution, I shall speak a word to that also, *After that thou shalt cut it*
down. Christ at last turns the *Barren Fig-tree* over to the Justice of God, 10
shakes his hands of him, *And gives him up to the fire for his*
unprofitableness.

Thou shalt cut it down.

Two things are here to be
considered. 15

1. The Executioner, *thou*, the great, the dreadful, the eternal God.
These words therefore, as I have already said, signifie that Christ the
Mediator, through whom alone Salvation comes, and by whom alone
Execution hath been deferred, *Now giveth up the Soul*, forbears to speak
one *Syllable* more for him, or to do the least Act of Grace further, to try 20
for his recovery; but delivereth him up to that fearful Dispensation, *To*
fall into the hand of the living God.

Heb. 10. 31.

2. The *Second* to be considered, is, *The instrument by which this*
Execution is done, and that is *Death*, compared here to an *Ax*; and
forasmuch as the Tree is not fellen at one Blow, therefore the strokes 25
are here continued, till all the blows be struck at it, that are requisite
for its *felling*; For now *cutting* time, and *cutting* work is come, *cutting*
must be his portion, till he be cut down. *After that thou shalt cut it down.*
Death, I say, is the *Ax*, which God often useth, therewith to take the
Barren Fig-tree out of the Vineyard, out of a Profession, *and also out of* 30

16 dreadful, *1688*] dreadful   28–29 *down. 1688*] down,

the world at once. But this *Ax* is now new-ground, it cometh well-edged to the roots of this *Barren Fig-tree.* It hath been whetted by Sin, by the Law, and by a *formal* Profession, and therefore must, and will make deep gashes, not only in the natural life, but in the Heart, and Conscience also of this Professor. *The wages of Sin is Death, the sting of Death is Sin.* Wherefore Death comes not to this man as he doth to Saints, *muzzled,* or without his Sting, but with open mouth, in all his strength; yea, he sends *his First-born,* which is guilt, to devour his strength, *and to bring him to the King of Terrors.* Rom. 5.

1 Cor. 15.

Job 18. 13, 14.

But to give you, in a few *Particulars,* the manner of this mans dying.

1. Now he hath his fruitless *Fruits* beleague him round his Bed, together with all the *bands* and *legions* of his other wickedness. *His own Iniquities shall take the wicked himself, and he shall be holden in the cords of his sins,* Prov. 5. 22.

2. Now some terrible discovery of God is made out unto him, to the perplexing and terrifying of his guilty Conscience, *God shall cast upon him, and not spare, and he shall be afraid of that which is high.* Job. 27, 22.

3. The dark Entry he is to go through, will be a sore amazement to him; *For fear shall be in the way,* yea terrors will take hold on him, when he shall see the *yawning* Jaws of Death to gape upon him, and the Doors of the Shadow of Death open, to give him passage out of the World. Now who will meet me in this dark entry, how shall I pass through this dark Entry into another world. Eccl. 12. 5.

Job. 38. 17.

4. For by reason of guilt, and a shaking Conscience, *His life will hang in continual doubt before him, and he shall be afraid day and night,* and shall have no assurance of his life. Deut. 28. 66, 67.

5. Now also *Want* will come up against him, he will come up *like an armed man.* This is a terrible Army to him that is graceless in heart, and fruitless in life. This *Want* will continually cry in thine ears, here is a New birth *wanting,* a *new* Heart, and a *new* Spirit *wanting,* here is Faith *wanting,* here is Love and Repentance *wanting;* here is the Fear of God *wanting;* and a good Conversation *wanting; Thou art weighed in the ballance, and art found wanting.* Prov. 24. 34.

Dan. 5. 27.

6. Together with these, standeth by *the companions of Death;* Death and Hell, Death and Devils, Death and endless Torment in the

27 marg. 34.] *ult. 1673.*

everlasting flames of devouring Fire. *When God shall come up unto the people, he will invade them with his troops.*

But how will this man die? Can *now* his heart endure, or *can his hands be strong?*

1. God, and Christ, and Pity *have left him*: Sin against Light, against 5
Mercy, and the Long-suffering of God, *Is come up against him*; his
Hope and Confidence *now lie a dying by him*, and his Conscience *totters
and shakes* continually within him.

2. Death is at his work, *Cutting of him down*, hewing both bark and
heart, both Body and Soul asunder; The man groans, but Death hears 10
him not: He looks gastly, carefully, dejectedly; he sighs, he sweats, he
trembles, but Death matters nothing.

3. Fearful *Cogitations* haunt him, misgivings, direful apprehensions
of God terrifie him. Now he hath time to think what the loss of Heaven
will be, and what the torments of Hell will be; now he looks no way, but 15
he is frighted.

4. Now would he live, but may not; he would live, though it were but
the life of a Bed-rid man, but must not. He that cuts him down, swaies
him, as the Feller of wood, *swaies the tottering tree*; now this way, then
that, at last a root breaks: an heart-string, an eye-string snaps asunder. 20

5. And now, could the Soul be *anihilated*, or brought to nothing, for
how happy would it count it self; but it sees that may not be. Wherefore
it is put to a wonderful strait: stay in the Body it may not, go out of the
Body it dares not. *Life* is going, the *Blood* settles in the *Flesh*, and the
Lungs being now no more able to draw breath through the Nostrils, at 25
last out goes the weary trembling Soul, who is immediatly seized by
Devils, who lay lurking in every hole in the Chamber, for that very
purpose: His Friends take care of the Body, wrap it up in the *Sheet* or
Coffin, the Soul is out of their thought and reach, going down to the
Chamber of Death. 30

I had thought to have enlarged, but I forbear: God, who teaches man
to profit, bless this brief and plain Discourse to thy Soul, who yet
standest a Professor in the Land of the Living, among the Trees of his
Garden. *Amen.*

FINIS.

---

4 *strong?*] *strong.*

THE STRAIT GATE

THE
STRAIT GATE,

OR,

Great Difficulty of Going
to HEAVEN;

PLAINLY

Proving by the Scriptures, that
not only the rude and profane ; but
many great professors will come
short of that Kingdom.

By *John Bunyan.*

*Enter ye in at the strait gate, for wide is the
gate, and broad is the way that leadeth to destruction, and many there be that go in thereat. Because strait is the gate, and narrow is
the way that leadeth unto life, and few there
be that find it.* Matt. 7. 13, 14.

LONDON.

Printed for *Francis Smith* at the Elephant
and Castle near the Royall Exchange
in *Cornhill.* 1676.

THE STRAIT GATE

Note on the Text

ONLY one edition, the first of 1676, was published in Bunyan's lifetime. Only two copies are extant, one in the Bodleian Library, and the other in the Cambridge University Library.

THE FIRST EDITION, 1676

Title-page: [within rules] THE | STRAIT GATE, | OR, | Great Difficulty of Going | to HEAVEN; | PLAINLY | Proving by the Scriptures, that | not only the rude and profane; but | many great professors will come | short of that Kingdom. | [rule] By *John Bunyan*. | [rule] *Enter ye in at the strait gate, for wide is the* | *gate, and broad is the way that leadeth to de-* | *struction, and many there be that go in there-* | *at. Because strait is the gate, and narrow is* | *the way that leadeth unto life, and few there* | *be that find it*. Matt. 7. 13, 14. | [rule] *LONDON*. | Printed for *Francis Smith* at the Elephant | and Castle near the Royall Exchange | in *Cornhill*. 1676. |

Collation: 12°; A–F¹², $5, G⁶, $4. Pages [i–iv] + 152 = 156. Page 83 has '3' from the wrong fount.

Contents: A1ʳ title-page, A1ᵛ blank, A2ʳ To the READER | — A2ᵛ *So prays thy friend*, | J.B. | [rule] catch-word 'Luke'. A3ʳ [double row of ornaments] *Luke* 13. 24. | *Strive to enter in at the strait gate, for* | *many, I say unto you, seek to enter* | *in, and shall not be able*. | text — G6ᵛ [rule] *FINIS*.

Running titles: *The Strait Gate*. Pages 7, 55, 105 have 'Starait' for 'Strait'; pages 14, 21, 37, 41, 51, 65, 71, 77, 97, 101, 115, 117, 131 have 'G' from a different fount; pages 21 and 97 have roman 'T' instead of italic; pages 134 and 150 have roman 'S' instead of italic; pages 14, 44, 142 lack the final full-stop; pages 22 and 86 have a comma instead of the final full-stop.

Catchwords: (incorrect) A2ᵛ Luke, [*Luke*] A4ʳ word [word,] D5ᵛ birth [birth,] E6ʳ God [God,] F8ʳ victions [ctions] F9ʳ beware [Beware] G3ᵛ kills [kils].

The spelling of the first edition has been retained, with a few exceptions. Obvious typographical errors have been silently corrected. The original punctuation has for the most part been retained. It has been silently corrected where full-stops or question marks have obviously been wrongly used or omitted. Where more radical repunctuation has taken place, this has been noted.

Mistakes in the scriptural references have been corrected, and the false references appear in the footnotes. The punctuation around them, which is quite haphazard in the text, has been regularized throughout, references at the end of sentences being preceded by a full-stop, references in the midst of a sentence being preceded by a comma. Sentences after these references have been given an initial capital letter in all cases. These alterations of reference punctuation have not been separately noted.

TO THE READER.

COURTEOUS Reader,
  God (I hope) hath put it into my heart to write unto thee
  another time, and that about matters of greatest moment (for
  now we discourse not about things controverted among the godly,
but directly about the saving or damning of the soul, *yea, moreover this*
discourse is about the fewness *of them that shall* be saved, *and it proves,*
that many an high professor will come short of eternal life;) *wherefore*
the matter must needs be sharp *and so disliked by some, but let it not be*
rejected by thee. The text calls for sharpness, so do the times, yea, the faithful
discharge of my duty towards thee, hath put me upon it.
  I do not now pipe *but* mourn, *and 'twill be well for thee, if thou canst*
gratiously lament. Matt. 11. 17. *Some (say they) make the* gate *of heaven*
too wide, *and some make it too narrow: for my part I have here presented*
thee with as true a measure of it as by the word of God I can: reade me
therefore, yea, reade me and compare me with the bible; *and if thou findest*
my *doctrine, and* that *book of God concur; embrace it, as thou wilt answer the*
contrary in the day of Judgment: This awaking work (if God will make it so)
was prepared for thee: If there be need and it wounds, *get healing* by blood;
if it disquiets get peace by blood: *if it takes away all thou hast because 'twas*
naught, (for this book is not prepared to take away true grace from any) then
buy of Christ gold tried in the fire, that thou maist be rich, and white
rayment that thou maist be cloathed, and that the shame of thy
nakedness doth not appear, and anoint thine eyes with eye-salve that
thou maiest see. Revel. 3. 18. *Self-flatteries, self-deceivings, are easie and*
pleasant, but damnable! the Lord give thee an heart to Judge right of thy self,
right of this book, and so to prepare for eternity, that thou maist not only
expect entrance, but be received into the kingdome of Christ and of God,
Amen.

                    So prays thy friend,

                         J.B.

Luke. 13. 24.

Strive to enter in at the strait gate, for
many, I say unto you, seek to enter in, and
shall not be able.

THESE are the words of our Lord Jesus Christ, and are
therefore in an especial manner to be heeded; besides, the
subject matter of the words, is the most weighty, to wit,
how we should attain salvation, and therefore also to be
heeded.

The occasion of the words, was *a question* which one that was at this
time in the company of the disciples, put to Jesus Christ; the *question*
was this, *Lord, are there few that be saved?* ver. 23. *A serious question*, not
such as tended to the subvertion of the hearers, as too many now
adaies do, but such as in its own nature tended to the awakening of the
company to good, and, that called for such an answer that might profit
the people also: This question also, well pleased Jesus Christ, and
therefore he prepareth, and giveth such an answer, as was without the
least retort, or shew of distaste, such an answer I say, as carried in it
the most full resolve to the question it self, and help to the persons
questioning; *And he said unto them, strive to enter in*, &c. The words are
an answer, and an instruction also.

1. An answer, and that in the affirmative, *the gate is strait many that*
seek will not be able, therefore but few shall be saved.

2. The answer, is an instruction also, *strive to enter in*, &c. good
counsel, and instruction; pray God help me, and my Reader, and all
that love their own salvation to take it.

My manner of handling the words will be, first by way of *Explication*,
and then by way of *Observation*.

By way of *Explication*.

1. The words are to be considered, with reference to their *general*
scope.

2. And then with reference to their several phrases.

1. The general *scope* of the text is to be considered, and that is that
great thing *Salvation*; for these words do immediatly look at, point to,

and give directions about *salvation. Are there few that be saved? strive to enter in at the strait gate.*

The words, I say, are to direct us, not only to talk of, or to wish for, but to understand how we shall, & to seek that we may be effectualy saved; and therefore of the greatest importance. To be saved! what is 5 like being saved? to be saved from sin, from hell, from the wrath of God, from eternal damnation, what is like it? To be made an heir of God! of his grace! of his kingdome and eternal glory! what is like it? and yet all this is included in this word, *saved,* and in the answer to that question, *are there few that be saved?* indeed this word, *saved,* is but of 10 little use in the world, *save* to them that are heartily afraid of *damning.* This word lies in the Bible, as excellent salves lie in some mens houses, thrust into a hole, and not thought on for many moneths, because the houshold people have no wounds nor sores: In time of sickness, what so set by, as the Doctors glasses, and gally-pots full of 15 his excellent things; but when the person is grown well, the rest is thrown to the dunghil. Oh when men are sick of sin, and afraid of damning, what a text is that, where this word *saved* is found? yea, what a word of worth and goodness and blessedness is it to him that lies continually upon the wrath of a guilty conscience? *but the whole need not* 20 *the phisitian:* He therefore, and he only, knows what *saved* means, that knows, what *hell* and *death* and *damnation* means: *what shall I do to be saved?* is the language of the trembling sinner; *Lord save me,* is the language of the sinking sinner, and none admire the glory that is in that word *saved,* but such as see without being saved, all things in heaven 25 and earth are emptyness to them, they also that believe themselves priviledged in all the blessedness that are wrapped up in that word, blesse and admire God that hath saved them: wherefore, since the thing intended both in the question and the answer is no less then the salvation of the soul, I beseech you to give the more earnest heed. *Heb.* 30 21.

But to come to the particular phrases in the words, and to handle them orderly, in the words I finde four things.

1. An intimation of the kingdom of heaven.

2. A description of the entrance into it.   35

3. An Exhortation to enter into it; and,

33 orderly,] orderly

4. A motive to inforce that exhortation.

First, An Intimation of the kingdom of heaven, for when he saith, *strive to enter in*; and in such phrases there is supposed a place or state or both to be enjoyed; enter *in*, enter into what, or whether but into a state or place or both; and therefore when you read this word, *enter in*, you must say there is certainly included in the text that good thing that yet is not expressed; *enter in, into heaven*, that's the meaning: where the saved are, and shall be, *into heaven*, that place, that glorious place, where God, and Christ, and Angels are: and the souls or spirits of just men made perfect: *enter in*; that thing included, though not expressed in the words, is called in another place, the *Mount Sion*, the heavenly *Jerusalem*, the *general assemblie and Church of the first born* which are written in heaven. *Heb.* 12. And therefore the words signifie unto us, *that there is a state most glorious, and that when this world is ended; and that this place and state is likewise to be enjoyed, and inherited by a generation of men for ever.* Besides, this word, *enter in*, signifieth that salvation to the full is to be enjoyed *only there*, and that there *only* is eternal safety; all other *places*, and *conditions*, are hazzardous, dangerous, full of snares, imperfections, temptations and afflictions, but *there all is well*; there is no devil to tempt, no desperately-wicked heart to deliver us up, no deceitful lusts to intangle, nor any inchanting world to bewitch us: *there all shall be well to all eternity.* Further all the parts of, and circumstances that attend salvation, are *only* there to be enjoyed: there *only* is immortalitie and eternal life; there is the glory, the fulness of joy, and the everlasting pleasures; there is God and Christ to be enjoyed by open vision, and more; there are the Angels, and the Saints; further, there is no death, nor sickness, no sorrow, nor sighing, for ever: there is no pain, nor persecutor, nor darkness to eclipse our glory. O this *Mount Sion*! O this *heavenly Jerusalem*! 2 *Cor.* 5. 1, 2, 3, 4. *Psal.* 16. 11. *Luk.* 20. 35, 36. *Heb.* 12. 22, 23, 24.

Behold therefore what a great thing the Lord Jesus hath included by this little word, *in*, in this word is wrapt up an whole heaven, and eternal life: even as there is also by other little words in the holy Scriptures of truth; as where he saith, *knock, and it shall be opened unto you*, and the elect have obtained *it*.

This should teach us, not only to reade but to attend in reading, not

30 *Heb.* 12. 22, 23, 24.] *Heb.* 12. 12, 13, 14.

only to read, but to lift up our hearts to God in reading, for if we be not heedful, if he give us not light and understanding; we may easily pass over without any great regard, such a word as may have a glorious kingdom and eternal salvation in the bowels of it: yea somtimes, as here, a whole heaven is intimated, where it is not at all expressed. The Apostles of old, did use to fetch great things out of the Scriptures, even out of the very order and timeing of the several things contained therein, see *Rom.* 4. 9, 10, 11. *Gala.* 3. 16, 17. *Heb.* 8. 13. but,

Secondly, As we have here an intimation of the kingdom of heaven, so we have a description of the entrance into it, and that by a double similitude.

1. It is called a *gate.*

2. *A strait gate: strive to enter in at the strait gate.*

1. It is set forth by the similitude of a *gate.* A *gate*, you know, is of a double use, it is to *open* and *shut*, and so consequently, to let in, or to keep out; and to do both these *at the season*; as he said, *let not the gates of* Jerusalem *be opened till the sun be hot*; and again, *I commanded that the gates should be shut, and charged that they should not be opened till after the Sabbath.* (*Neh.* 7. 3. *chap.* 13. 19, 20.) And so you finde of this gate of heaven, when the five wise virgins came, the gates were open, but *afterward came the other virgins, and the door was shut. Matt.* 11.

So then, the entrance into heaven, is called *a gate*, to shew, there is a time when there *may be* entrance, and there will come a time *when there shall be none*; and indeed this is a chief truth contained in the text: *strive to enter in at the strait gate, for many I say unto you will seek to enter in and shall not be able.*

I reade in the Scriptures of two gates or doors, through which they that go to heaven must enter.

1. *There is the door of faith*, the door which the grace of God hath opened to the gentiles, this door is Jesus Christ, as also himself doth testifie, saying, *I am the door*, &c. (*Acts.* 14. 27. *Joh.* 10. 9.) By this door men enter into Gods favour, and mercy, and finde forgiveness through faith in his blood, and live in hope of eternal life; and therefore himself also hath said, *I am the door, by me if any man enter in, he shall be saved*, that is, received to mercy and inherit eternal life: but

2. There is another door, or gate; (for that which is called in the text, *a gate*, is twice in the next verse, called, *a door*): there is, I say another

gate, and that is the passage into the very heaven it self; the entrance into the celestial mansion-house, and that is the *gate* mentioned in the text, and the door mentioned twice in the verse that follows. And thus *Jacob* called it, when he said *Bethel was the house of God, and this is the* 5 *gate of heaven*, that is, the entrance, for he saw the entrance into heaven, *one end of Jacobs ladder stands in Bethel, Gods house, and the other end reacheth up to the gate of heaven. Gen.* 28. 10, 11, 12, 13, 14, 15, 16, 17. *Jacobs* ladder was the figure of Christ, which ladder was not the gate of heaven, but the way from the Church to that gate which he saw above 10 at the top of the ladder. *Gen.* 28. 12. and *Joh.* 1. 51.

But again that the gate in the text, is the gate, or entrance into heaven, consider,

1. It is that gate that letteth men into, or shuteth men out of that place or kingdom where *Abraham*, and *Isaac*, and *Jacob* is, which place 15 is that paradice where Christ promised the thief, that he should be that day, that he asked to be with him in his kingdom: it is that place into which *Paul* said, he was caught, when he heard words unlawful or impossible for a man to utter. *Luk.* 13. 20. *chap.* 23. 24. 2 *Cor.* 12. 1, 2, 3, 4, 5.

20 *Quest.* But is not Christ the gate or entrance into this heavenly place?

Answ. He is he without whom no man can get thither, because by *his merits* men obtain that world, and also because he (as the father) is the doner and disposer of that kingdom to whom he will: further, this place is called his house, and himself the master of it (*when once the master of* 25 *the house is risen up, and hath shut to the door (ver. 25.)* But we use to say, that the master of the house, is not the door: men enter into heaven then, by him, not as he is the gate or door, or entrance into the celestial mansion-house, but as he is the giver and disposer of that kingdom to them who he shall count worthy, because he hath obtained it for them.

30 2. That this gate is the very passage into heaven, consider the text hath special reference to the day of judgment, when Christ will have laid aside the mediatory office, which before he exercised for the bringing to the faith his own elect; and will then act, not as one that justifies the ungodly, but as one that judgeth sinners; he will now be 35 risen up from the throne of grace, and shut up the door against all the impenitent, and will be set upon the throne of judgment, from thence to proceed with ungodly sinners.

Object. But Christ bids *strive, strive now to enter in at the strait gate,* but if that *gate* be as you say, the *gate.* or entrance into heaven, then it should seem, that we should not strive till the day of judgment, for we shall not come at that gate till then.

Answ. Christ, by this exhortation, *strive,* &c. doth not at all admit of,   5
or countenance delayes, or that a man should neglect his own salvation, but putteth poor creatures upon preparing for the judgment, and counselleth them *now* to get those things that will then give them entrance into glory. This exhortation, is much like these, *be ye therefore ready also, for at such an hour as you think not, the son of man cometh: and*   10
they that were ready went in with him to the marriage, and the door was shut.
Matt. 24. 44. *Chap.* 25. 10.

So that when he saith, *strive to enter in,* it is as if he should say, blessed are they that shall be admitted another day to enter into the kingdom of heaven, but they that shall be counted worthy of so   15
unspeakable a favour, must be well prepared, and fitted for it before-hand: now the time to be fitted, is not the day of judgment, but the day of grace; not *then,* but *now*: therefore *strive now* for those things, that will *then* give you entrance into the heavenly kingdom: but,

Secondly, As it is called *a gate,* so it is called a *strait gate; strive to enter*   20
in at the strait gate.

The straightness of this gate, is not to be understood carnally, but mistically: you are not to understand it, as if the entrance into heaven was some little pinching wicket, no, the straightness of this gate is quite another thing. This gate is wide enough for all them that are the truly   25
gracious, and sincere lovers of Jesus Christ, but *so strait,* as that not one of the other can by any means enter in: *open to me the gates of righteousness, I will go into them, and I will praise the Lord, this gate of the Lord into which the righteous shall enter. Psal.* 118. 19, 20. By this word therefore Christ Jesus hath shewed unto us that without due   30
qualifications there is no possibility of entring into heaven; the straight gate will keep all others out: when Christ spake this parable he had doubtless his eye upon some passage or passages of the old testament, with which the Jews were well acquainted. I will mention two and so go on.   35

1. *The place by which God turned* Adam *and his wife out of paradise*; possibly our Lord might have his eye upon that, for though that was

wide enough for them to come *out* at, yet it was too strait for them to go *in* at, but what should be the reason of that? why they had sinned and therefore God set at the east of that garden, *cherubins and a flaming sword, turning every way, to keep the way of the tree of life. Gen.* 3. 24.

5 These Cherubins and this flaming sword, they made the entrance too strait for them to enter in: souls, there are Cherubins and a flaming sword at the gates of heaven to keep the way of the tree of life, therefore none but them that are duely fitted for heaven can enter in at this strait gate, the flaming sword will keep all others out. *Know you not*

10 *that the unrighteous shall not inherit the kingdom of God, be not deceived, neither fornicatours, nor Idolaters, nor adulterers, nor effeminate, nor abusers of themselves with mankind, nor thievs, nor covetous, nor drunkards, nor revilers, nor extortioners, shall inherit the kingdom of God.* 1. *Cor.* 6. 9.

2. Perhaps our Lord might have his eye upon the gates of the

15 temple, when he spoke this word unto the people, for though the gates of the temple were six cubits wide, yet they were so strait, that none that were unclean in any thing might enter in thereat, *Ezek.* 40. 48. because there were placed at them gates, porters whose office was to look that none but those that had right to enter, might go in thither:

20 and so it is written, *Jehojadah set porters at the gates of the house of the Lord, that none that were unclean in any thing might enter in.* 2 *Chro.* 23. 19. Souls, God hath porters at the gates of his temple, at the gate of heaven, porters, I say, placed there by God, to look that none that are unclean in any thing may come in thither. In at the gate *of the Church,*

25 none may enter *now,* that are open profane and scandalous to religion; no, though they pleade they are beloved of God; *What hath my beloved to do in mine house* (saith the Lord,) *seeing she hath wrought leudness with many. Jer.* 11. 15.

I say, I am very apt to believe, that our Lord Jesus Christ had his

30 thoughts upon these two texts, when he said, *the gate is strait,* and that which confirms me the more in the thing, is this, a little below the text he saith, *there shall be weeping, and gnashing of teeth, when you shall see* Abraham, *and* Isaac, *and* Jacob, *and all the prophets in the kingdom of heaven, and you your selves thrust out, ver.* 28. *thrust out,* which signifieth

35 a violent act, resisting with striving, those that would (though unqualified) enter: the porters of the temple were, for this very thing,

---

1 too strait] to strait.   35 striving,] striving;

to wear arms if need were, and to be men of courage and strength, lest the unsanctified or unprepared should by some means enter in.

We reade in the book of the *Revelations*, of the *holy citie*, and that it had twelve gates, and at the gates twelve Angels, but what did they do there? why amongst the rest of their service, this was one thing, *that there might in no wise enter in, any thing that defileth, or worketh abomination, or that maketh a lie. Revel.* 21. 12, 27.

But more particularly to shew what it is, that maketh this gate so strait: there are three things that make it strait.

1. There is sin.

2. There is the word of the law.

3. There are the Angels of God.

First, there is sin, the sin of the profane, and the sin of the professor.

1. The sin of the profane, but this needs not be inlarged upon, because it is concluded upon, at all hands, where there is the common belief of the being of God, and the judgment to come, that the *wicked shall be turned into hell, and all the nations that forget God. Psal.* 9. 17.

2. But there is the sin of professors, or take it rather thus, there is a profession that will stand with an unsanctified heart and life, the sin of such will overpoise the salvation of their souls, the sin-end being the heaviest end of the scale: I say, that being the heaviest end which hath sin in it; they tilt over; and so are, notwithstanding their glorious profession, drowned in perdition and destruction: *for none such hath any inheritance in the kingdome of Christ and of God, therefore let no man deceive you with vain words, for because of these things, comes the wrath of God upon the children of disobedience*; neither will a profession be able to excuse them. *Ephes.* 5. 3, 4, 5, 6. The gate will be too strait for such as these to enter in thereat. A man may partake of salvation in part, but not of salvation in whole: God saved the children of *Israel* out of *Egypt*, but overthrew them in the wilderness: *I will therefore put you in remembrance, though ye once knew this, how that the Lord, having saved the people out of the land of* Egypt, *afterwards destroyed them that believed not: so we see,* (that notwithstanding their beginning) *they could not enter in, because of unbelief. Jude.* 5. *Heb.* 3. 19.

Secondly, *There is the word of the Law, and that will make the gate strait* also: none must go in thereat but those that can go in by the leave of

7 *Revel.* 21. 12, 27.] *Revel.* 21. 12, 21.

the law, for though no man be or can be, justifyed by the works of the
law, yet unlesse the righteousness and holyness by which they attempt
to enter into this kingdom, be justified by the law, 'tis in vain once to
think of entring in at this *strait gate*: now the law justifieth not, but upon
5 the account of Christs righteousness; if therefore thou be not indeed
found in that righteousnes, thou wilt finde the law lie just in the
passage into heaven to keep thee out; every mans work must be tried by
fire, that it may be manifest of what sort it is. There are two errors in
the world about the law, one is, when men think to enter in *at the strait*
10 *gate by the righteousness of the law*, the other is, when men think, *they may*
enter into heaven without the leave of the law; both these, I say, are errors:
for, as by the works of the law, *no flesh shall be justified*, so without the
consent of the law, *no flesh shall be saved, heaven and earth shall passe*
away, before one jot, or title of the law shall fail, till all be fulfilled: he
15 therefore must be *damned*, that *cannot* be saved by the consent of the
law, and indeed this law is the flaming sword that turneth every way,
yea, that lieth to this day, in the way to heaven, for a barr to all
unbelievers and unsanctified professors, for it is taken out of the way
for the truly gracious *only*: it will be found as a roaring lion to devour all
20 others: because of the law therefore the gate will be found too strait for
the unsanctified to enter in; when the Apostle had told the *Corinthians*,
that *the unrighteous should not inherit the kingdom of God*, and, that *such*
were some of them, he adds, *but ye are washed, but ye are sanctified, but ye*
are justified, in the name of the Lord Jesus, & by the spirit of our God,
25 1. *Cor.* 6. 9, 10, 11. closely concluding, that had they not been washed,
and sanctified, and justified in the name of the Lord Jesus, the law, for
their transgressions, would have kept them out, it would have made the
gate too strait for them to enter in.

Thirdly, There are also the Angels of God, *and by reason of them the*
30 *gate is strait*. The Lord Jesus, calleth the end of the world, his *harvest*;
and saith moreover, that the Angels are his *reapers*; these Angels are
therefore to gather his wheat into his barn, but to gather the ungodly
into bundels to burn them, *Matt.* 13. 39, 41, 49. unless therefore, the
man that is unsanctified, can master the law, and conquer Angels:
35 unless *he* can, as I may say, pull them out of the gateway of heaven,
himself is not to come thither for ever: no man goeth to heaven but by

6 the law] the law,   17 way] way,

the help of the Angels, I mean at the day of Judgment, *For the son of man, shall send forth his angels with a great sound of a trumpet, and they shall gather together his elect from the four winds, from one end of heaven to the other. Mat.* 24. 31. If those that shall enter in at the strait gate shall enter in thither by the conduct of the holy Angels; pray when do you think those men will enter in thither, concerning whom the Angels are commanded, to gather them, to binde them in bundles, to burn them? This therefore is a third Difficulty: the Angels will make this enterance strait, yea, too strait for the unjustified and unsanctified to enter in thither.

I come now to the Exhortation, which is *to strive to enter in; strive to enter in at the strait gate.*

These words are fitly added, for since the gate is strait, it follows, *that they that will enter in must strive.*

Strive, this word *strive*, supposeth that great idleness is natural to professors, they think to get to heaven by lying as it were on their elbows. 2. It also suggesteth, that many will be the difficulties that professors will meet with before they get to heaven. 3. It also concludeth, that only the labouring Christian, man or woman will get in thither.

Strive, &c.

Three questions I will propound upon the word, an answer to which may give us light into the meaning of it.

1. *Quest.* What doth this word, *strive*, import?

2. *Quest.* How should we strive?

3. *Quest.* Why should we strive?

First, what doth this word *strive*, import?

Answ. When he saith, *strive*, It is as much as to say, bend your selves to the work with all your might: *Whatsoever thy hand findeth to do; do it with all thy might, for there is no work nor device, nor knowledge, nor wisdom in the grave, whither thou goest. Eccles.* 9. 10. Thus *Sampson* did, when he set himself to destroy the Philistins, *he bowed himself with all his might. Judg.* 16. 30. Thus *David* did also when he made provision for the building and beautifying of the temple of God. 1. *Chro.* 29. 2. and thus must thou do if ever thou entrest into heaven.

2*ly*, When he saith *strive*, he calleth for the *minde* and the *will*, that

7 burn them?] burn them;

they should be on his side, and on the side of the things of his kingdome; *for none strive indeed*, but such as have given the son of God their heart, of which the minde and will are a principal part, for saving conversion lieth more in the turning of the minde and will to Christ, and to the Love of his heavenly things, then in all knowledge and Judgment: and this the Apostle confirmeth when he saith, *stand fast in one spirit, with one minde, striving* &c. *Philip.* 1. 27.

3*ly*, And more particularly, this word *strive*, is expressed by several other terms, as,

1. It is expressed by that word, *so run that you may obtain.* 1 *Cor.* 9. 24. 25.

2. It is expressed by that word, *fight the good fight of faith, lay hold of eternal life.* 1 Tim. 6. 12.

3. It is expressed by that word, *labour not for the meat that perisheth, but for that meat that endureth to everlasting life. Joh.* 6. 27.

4. It is expressed by that word, *we wrestle with principalities and powers, and the rulers of the darkness of this world. Ephes.* 6. 12. Therefore when he saith, *strive*, it is as much as to say, *run* for heaven, *fight* for heaven, *labour* for heaven, *wrestle* for heaven, or you are like to go without it.

Secondly, the second question, is *how should we strive?*

Answ. 1. The answer in general is, thou must strive lawfully; *and if a man also strive for the mastery, yet is he not crowned, except he strive lawfully.* 2 *Tim.* 25.

But you will say, *what is it to strive lawfully?*

Answer 1. to strive against the things which are abhored by the Lord Jesus, yea, to resist to the spilling of your blood, *striving against sin, Heb.* 12. 4. to have all those things that are condemned by the word, yea, though they be thine own right hand, right eye, or right foot, in abomination; and to seek by all godly means the utter suppressing of them. *Mar.* 9. 43, 45, 47.

2*ly*, To strive lawfully is to strive for those things that are commended in the word; *But thou O man of God fly*, the world, *and follow after*, that is strive for *righteousness, godlyness, faith, love, patience, meekness, fight the good fight of faith, lay hold on eternal life*, &c. 1 *Tim.* 6. 11, 12.

34 that is strive for] *that is strive for.*

3*ly*, He that striveth lawfully must be therefore very temperate in all the good and lawful things of this life. *And every one that striveth for the mastery, is temperate in all things: now they do it to obtain a corruptible crown, but we an incorruptible.* 1 *Cor.* 9. 25. Most professors give leave to the world, and vanity of their hearts, to close with them and to hang about their necks, and make their striving to stand rather in an out-cry of words, then a hearty labour against the lusts, and love of the world, and their own corruptions, but this kind of striving is but a beating of the air, and will come to just nothing at last. 1 *Cor.* 9. 26.

4*ly*, He that striveth lawfully, must take God and Christ along with him to the work, otherwise he will certainly be undone: *whereunto,* said *Paul, I also labour, striving according to his working, which worketh in me mightily, Colo.* 1. 29. and for the right performing of this, he must observe these following particulars.

1. He must take heed, that he doth not strive about things, or words to no profit, for God will not *then* be with him: *of these things,* saith the Apostle, *put them in remembrance; charging them before the Lord, that they strive not about words to no profit, but to the subverting of the hearers.* 1. *Tim.* 2. 14. But alas! how many professors in our days are guilty of this transgression, whose religion stands chiefly, if not only, in a few unprofitable questions, and vain ranglings, about words and things to no profit, but to the destruction of the hearers. *Tit.* 3. 9.

2. He must take heed, that whilst he strives against one sin, he does not harbour and shelter another, or that whilst he cries out against other mens sins, he does not countenance his own.

3. In the striving, strive to believe, strive *for* the faith of the Gospel, for the more we believe the Gospel, and the realitie of the things of the world to come, with the more stomack and courage shall we labour to possess the blessedness. *Philip.* 1. 27. *Heb.* 4. *Let us labour therefore to enter into that rest, lest any man fall after the same example of unbelief.*

4. As we should strive for, and by faith, so we should strive by prayer, *Rom.* 15. 30. by fervent and effectual praiers; O the swarms of our praierless professors! what do they think of themselves! surely the gate of heaven was heretofore as wide as in these our dayes, but what striving by praier was there then among Christians for the thing that gives admittance into this kingdom, over there is in these latter days?

5. We should also strive by mortifying our members that are upon

the earth: *I therefore so run, said* Paul, *so fight I, not as one that beats the air, but I keep under my body, and bring it into subjection, lest that by any means when I have preached the Gospel to others I my self should be a castaway.* 1 *Cor.* 9. 27. But all this is spoken principally to professors, so
5 I would be understood.

I come now to the third question, namely *but why should we strive?* Answer 1. Because the thing for which you are here exhorted to strive, it is worth the striving for: it is for no less then for a whole heaven, and an eternity of felicity there; how will men that have before
10 them, a little honour, a little profit, a little pleasure, *strive?* I say again, how will they *strive* for *this? now they do it for a corruptible crown, but we an incorruptible.* Methinks this word *heaven,* and this eternal life, what is there again either in heaven or earth like them to provoke a man to strive?

15 2. *Strive,* because otherwise the devil, and hell, will assuredly have thee. *He goes about like a roaring Lion, seeking who he may devour.* 1 *Pet.* 5. 8. These fallen Angels, they are always watchful, diligent, unwearied, they are also mighty, subtle, and malicious, seeking nothing more then the damnation of thy soul; O thou that art like the heartless
20 dove, *strive.*

3. *Strive* because every lust strives and wars against thy soul; *the flesh lusteth against the spirit; dearly beloved, I beseech you,* said *Peter, as strangers and pilgrims, abstain from fleshly lusts, which war against the soul. Gal.* 5. 17. 'Tis a rare thing to see, or finde out a Christian, that indeed
25 can bridle his lusts, but no strange thing to see such professors that are not only bridled, but sadled too, yea, and ridden from lust to sin, from one vanitie to another, by the very devil himself, and the corruptions of their hearts.

4. *Strive,* because thou hast a whole world against thee, the world
30 hateth thee, if thou beest a christian: the men of the world hate thee, the things of the world are snares for thee, even thy bed and table, thy wife and husband, yea, thy most lawful enjoyments have that in them that will certainly sink thy soul to hell, if thou doest not *strive* against the snares that are in them. *Rom.* 11. 9.
35 The world will seek to keep thee out of heaven, with mocks, flouts, taunts, threatnings, goals, gibbits, halters, burnings, and a thousand

deaths, *therefore strive*. Again, if it cannot overcome thee with these, it will flatter, promise, allure, intice, intreat, and use a thousand tricks on this hand to destroy thee; and observe, many that have been stout against the threats of the world, have yet been overcome with the bewitching flatteries of the same: there ever was enmity betwixt the devil and the Church, and betwixt his seed and her seed too; *Michael and his Angels, and the dragon and his angels:* these make war continually. *Gen.* 3. *Revel.* 12. There hath been great desires and endeavors among men to reconcile these two in one, to wit, the seed of the serpent, and the seed of the woman, but it could never be yet accomplished: the world says, they will never come over to us, and we again say, by Gods grace, we will never come over to them, but the business has not ended in words, both they and we have also added our endeavours to make each other submit, but endeavours have proved ineffectual too: They for their part have devised all manner of cruel torments to make us submit, as flaying with the sword, stoning, sawing asunder, flames, wilde beasts, banishments, hunger, and a thousand miseryes; we again on the other side have laboured by praiers, and tears, by patience, and long-suffering, by gentleness, and love, by sound doctrine, and faithful witness-bearing against their enormities, to bring them over to us, but yet the enmitie remains; so that they must conquer us, or we must conquer them, one side must be overcome, *but the weapons of our warfare are not carnal but mighty through God.*

5. *Strive*, because there is nothing of Christianity got by idleness, idleness cloaths a man with rags, and the vineyard of the slothful is grown over with nettles. *Pro.* 23. 21. *chap.* 24. 30, 31, 32. Profession that is not attended with spiritual labour cannot bring the soul to heaven, the fathers before us were not slothful in business, but fervent in spirit, serving the Lord. *Therefore be not slothful, but followers of them who through faith and patience inherit the promises. Rom.* 21. 11. *Heb.* 6. 12.
Strive to enter in.

Methinks the words at the first reading, do intimate to us, that the Christian in all that ever he does in this world, should carefully heed and regard his soul, I say, in all that ever he does; many are for their souls by fits and starts, but a Christian indeed in all his doings, and

1 strive.] *strive*

designes which he contriveth and manageth in this world, should have
a special eye to his own future and everlasting good, in all his labours
he should strive to enter in. *Wisdom* (Christ) *is the principal thing:
therefore get wisdom, and in all thy gettings get understanding.* Pro. 4. 7.
5 Get nothing, if thou canst not get Christ and grace, and further hopes
of heaven, in that getting; get nothing with a bad conscience, with the
hazzard of thy peace with God, and that in getting it, thou weakenest
thy graces which God hath given thee, for this is *not to strive to enter in:*
adde grace to grace, both by religious and worldly duties, for *so an*
10 *entrance shall be ministred unto you abundantly into the everlasting kingdom
of our Lord and Saviour Jesus Christ.* 2 Pet. 1. 7, 8, 9, 10, 11. Religious
duties are not only the striving times, he that thinks so, *is out*: thou
maist help thy faith, and thy hope in the godly managment of thy
calling, and maist get further footing in eternal life, by studying the
15 glory of God, in all thy worldly imployment. I am speaking now to
Christians that are justified freely by grace, and am incouraging, or
rather counselling of them, to *strive to enter in*, for there is an entring in
by faith and good conscience *now*, as well as an entring in, in body and
soul *hereafter;* and I must add, that the more common it is to thy soul to
20 enter in now by faith, the more stedfast hope shalt thou have of entring
in hereafter in body and soul.
   Strive to enter in.
   By these words also the Lord Jesus giveth sharp rebuke to those
professors that have not eternal glory, but other temporal things in
25 their eye, by all the bustle that they make in the world about religion:
some there be, what a stir they make, what a noise and clamour, with
their notions and forms, and yet perhaps all is but for the loaves;
because they have eaten of the loaves and are filled, *Joh.* 6. 26. these
strive indeed to enter, but it is not into heaven; they finde, religion hath
30 a good trade at the end of it, or they finde, that it is the way to credit,
repute, preferment, and the like, and therefore they strive to enter into
these; but these have not the strait gate in their eye, nor yet in
themselves have they love to their poor, and perishing souls: wherefore
this exhortation nippeth such, by predicting of their damnation.
35 *Strive to enter in.*
   These words also sharply rebuke them who content themselves as
11 2 *Pet.* 1. 7, 8, 9, 10, 11.] 2 *Pet.* 1. 1, 8, 9, 10, 11.

the Angel of the *Church of Sardis* did, to wit, *to have a name to live, and be dead, Revel.* 3. 1. or as they of the *Laodiceans*, who took their religion upon trust, and was content, *with a poor, wretched, lukewarm profession*: For such as these do altogether unlike to the Exhortatian in the text; that says, *strive*; and they sit and sleep, that says *strive to enter in*, and they content themselves with a profession that is never like to bring them thither.

Strive to enter in.

Further, these words put us upon proving the truth of our graces, *now*: I say, they put us upon the proof of the truth of them *now*: for if the *strait gate* be the gate of heaven, and yet we are to strive to enter into it *now*, even while we live, and before we come thither, then, doubtless Christ means by this exhortation, that we should use all lawful means to prove our graces in this world whether they will stand in the judgment or no: *strive to enter in*, get those graces now that will prove true graces then, and therefore try them you have, and if upon tryall they prove not right, cast them away, and cry for better, lest they cast thee away, when better are not to be had: *Buy of me gold tried in the fire*, mark that. *Revel.* 13. 20. Buy of me faith and grace that will stand in the judgment, strive for that faith, buy of me that grace, *and also white raiment that thou mayest be cloathed, that the shame of thy wickedness doth not appear, and annoint thine eyes with eye-salve that thou maiest see*: minde you this advice, this is right striving to enter in.

But you will say, how should we try our graces? would you have us run into temptation to try if they be sound or rotten?

Answ. You need not run into tryals, God hath ordained that enow of them shall overtake thee to prove thy graces either rotten or sound before the day of thy death: *sufficient to the day is the evil thereof*, if thou hast but a sufficiency of grace to withstand. I say, thou shalt have tryals, enow, overtake thee, to prove thy graces sound or rotten: thou maiest therefore, if God shall help thee, see how it is like to go with thee before thou goest out of this world, to wit, whether thy graces be such as will carry thee in at the gates of heaven or no.

But how should we try our graces now?

Ans. How doest thou finde them in outward trials? See *Heb.* 11. 15, 16. how doest thou finde thy self in the inward workings of sin? (*Rom.* 7. 24.)

36 sin?] sin *1676*.

how doest thou find thy self under the most high enjoyment of grace in this world? *Phil.* 3. 14.

But what do you mean by these three questions?

Answ. I mean graces shew themselves at these their seasons whether
5 they be rotten or sound.

How do they shew themselves to be true under the first of these?

Ans. By mistrusting our own sufficiency, by crying to God for help, by desiring rather to die then to bring any dishonour to the name of God, and by counting, that if God be honoured in the trial, thou hast
10 gained more then all the world could give thee. 2 *Chro.* 20. 12. *chap.* 14. 11. *Acts.* 4. *Acts.* 20. 24. 2 *Cor.* 4. 17, 18. *Heb.* 11. 24, 25.

How do they shew themselves to be true under the second?

Answ. By mourning and confessing, and striving, and praying against them: by not being content, shouldest thou have heaven if *they* live, and
15 defile thee, and by counting of holyness the greatest beauty in the world, and by flying to Jesus Christ for life. *Zech.* 12. 10. *Joh.* 19. *Heb.* 12. 4. *Psal.* 19. 12.

How do they shew themselves to be true under the third?

By prizing the true graces above all the world, by praying heartily
20 that God will give thee more, by not being content with all the grace thou canst be capable of enjoying on this side heaven and glory. *Psal.* 84, 10. *Luk.* 17. 5. *Philip.* 3. *chapter.*

Strive to enter in.

The reason why Christ addeth these words, *to enter in*, is obvious; to
25 wit, because there is no true & lasting happiness on this side heaven; I say none that is both true and lasting, I mean, as to our sense and feeling, as there there shall, *for here have we no continuing city but we seek one to come. Heb.* 13. 14. The heaven is within, *strive therefore to enter in*; the glory is within, *strive therefore to enter in*; the *Mount Sion* is within,
30 *strive therefore to enter in*; the *heavenly Jerusalem* is within, *strive therefore to enter in*; Angels, and Saints are within, *strive therefore to enter in*; and to make up all, the God and father of our Lord Jesus Christ, and that glorious redeemer is within, *strive therefore to enter in.*

Strive to enter in.

35   *For without are dogs, sorcerers, and whoremongers, and murderers, and Idolaters, and whosoever loveth and maketh a lie*: without are also the devils, and hell, and death, and all damned souls; without is houling,

weeping, wailing, and gnashing of teeth; yea without are all the miseries, sorrows, and plagues that an infinite God can in justice and power inflict upon an evil and wicked generation: *strive therefore to enter in at the strait gate. Revel.* 22. 15. *Matt.* 25. 41. *Revel.* 12.9. *Isai.* 65. 13, 14. *Matt.* 22. 13. *Deut.* 29. 18, 19, 20.

Strive to enter in at the strait gate, [*for many*] *I say unto you, will seek to enter in, and shall not be able.*

We are now come to the motive which our Lord urges to inforce his exhortation: he told us *before*, that the gate was strait, he also *exhorted* us to *strive* to enter *in* thereat, or to get those things *now* that will further our entrance *then*, and to set our selves against those things that will hinder our entring in.

In this motive there are five things to be minded.

1. That there will be a disappointment to some at the day of judgment, *they will seek to enter in, and shall not be able.*

2. That not a few, *but many*, will meet with this disappointment, *for* [*many*] *will seek to enter in, and shall not be able.*

3. This doctrine of the miscariadge of *many*, then, it standeth upon the validity of the word of Christ; *for many* [*I say*] *will seek to enter in, and shall not be able.*

4. Professors shall make a great heap, among the many that shall fall short of heaven, *for many I say* [*unto you*] *will seek to enter in, and shall not be able.*

5. Where grace and striving are wanting *now, seeking*, and contending to enter in, will be unprofitable *then, for many, I say unto you will seek to enter in, and shall not be able.*

But I will proceed in my former method, to wit, to open the words unto you.

For many, &c,

If he had said, *for* [*some*] *will fall short*, it had been a sentence to be minded: If he had said, *for some that seek, will fall short*, it had been very awakening, but when he saith, *many, many will fall short*, yea many among professors will fall short, this is not only awakning, but dreadful.

For many, &c.

I finde this word *many*, variously applyed in the Scripture.

1. Sometimes it intendeth the open profane, the wicked, and

ungodly world, as where Christ saith, *wide is the gate, and broad is the way that leadeth to destruction, and many there be that go in thereat. Matt.* 7. 13. I say by the many *here*, he intends those chiefly, that go on in the broad way of sin, and prophanness, bearing the tokens of their

5 damnation in their foreheads, those whose dayly practise proclaims, that their *feet go down to death, and their steps take hold of hell. Job.* 21. 29, 30. *Isa.* 3. 9. *Pro.* 55.

2. Sometimes this word, *many*, intendeth those that cleave to the people of God deceitfully, and in hypocrisy; or as *Daniel* hath it, *many*

10 *shall cleave unto the Church with flatteries. Dan.* 11. 34. The word *many*, in this text, includeth all those who feign themselves better then they are in religion; it includeth I say those that have religion, *only*, for an holy-day saint to set them out at certain times and when they come among sutable company.

15 3. Sometimes this word *many*, intendeth them that apostatise from Christ, such as for a while believe and in time of temptation fall away, as *John* saith of some of Christs disciples, *from that time* many *of his disciples went back, and walked no more with him. Joh.* 6. 66.

4. Sometimes this word *many*, intendeth them that make a great

20 noyse, and do many great things in the Church, and yet want saving grace, *many*, saith Christ, *will say unto me in that day, Lord, Lord, have we not prophesied in thy name, and in thy name cast out devils, and in thy name done many wonderful works*: mark, there will be *many* of these.

5. Sometimes this word *many* intendeth those poor ignorant deluded

25 souls that are ledd away with every winde of doctrine: those who are caught with the cunning and crafty deceiver, who lieth in wait to beguile unstable souls. *And many shall follow their pernicious ways, by reason of whom the way of truth shall be evil spoken of.* 2. *Pet.* 2. 2.

6. Sometimes this word *many* includeth all the world, good and bad.

30 *And many of them that sleep in the dust of the earth shall awake, some to everlasting life, and some to everlasting shame and contempt. Dan.* 12. 2. compared with *Joh.* 5. 28, 29.

7. Lastly, Sometimes this word *many* intendeth the *good* only, even them that shall be saved. *Luk.* 1. 10. *chap.* 2. 34.

35 Since then that the word is so variously applied, let us enquire how it must be taken in the text, and,

1. It must not be applied to the *sincerely godly*, for they shall never perish. *Joh.* 10. 27. 28.

2. It cannot be applied to *all the world*, for then no flesh should be saved.

3. Neither is it to be applied to the open profane only, for then the hypocrite is by it excluded.

4. But by the *many* in the text our Lord intendeth in special the professor, the professor I say, how high soever he seems to be now, that shall be found without saving grace in the day of Judgment.

Now that the professor, *is in special intended in this text*, consider; so soon as the Lord had said, *many will seek to enter in, and shall not be able*, he pointeth, as with his finger, at the *many* that then he in special intendeth, to wit, them among whom he had taught; them *that had eat and drunken in his presence; them that had prophesied, and cast out devils in his name, and in his name done many wonderful works. Luk.* 13. 26. *Matt.* 7. 22. These are the *many* intended by the Lord in this text, though others are also included under the sentence of damnation by his word in other places.

For many, &c.

Matthew saith concerning this strait gate, *That there are but few that finde it*: but it seems the cast-aways in my text, did finde it, for you reade that they knocked at it, and cried, *Lord open unto us*: so then, the meaning may seem to be this, *many of the few that finde it, will seeke to enter in, and shall not be able*.

I finde at the day of Judgment, some will be crying to the rocks to cover them, and some at the gates of heaven for entrance: suppose that those that cry to the rocks to cover them, are they whose conscience will not suffer them, once to look God in the face because they are fallen under present guilt, and the dreadful fears of the wrath of the lamb. *Revel.* 6. 16. And that those that stand crying at the gate of heaven, are those whose confidence holds out to the last, even those whose boldness will enable them to contend even with Jesus Christ for entrance. Them, I say, that will have, profession, casting out of devils, and many wonderful works to pleade: of this sort are the *many* in my text; *for many, I say unto you, will seek to enter in, and shall not be able.*

For many, &c.

Could we compare the professors of the times with the everlasting word of God, this doctrine would more easily appear to the children of men. How few among the many, yea among the many swarms of professors have heart to make conscience of walking before God, in
5 this world, and to study his glory among the children of men: How few, I say, have his name lie nearer their hearts, then their own carnal concerns, nay, do not many make his word, and his name, and his ways a stalking-horse, to their own worldly advantages. God calls for faith, good conscience, moderation, self-denial, humility, heavenly-minded-
10 ness, love to Saints, to enemies: and for conformity in heart, in word, and life to his will, but where is it? *Mar.* 11. 22.1 *Pet.* 3. 16. *Heb.* 13.5. *Philip.* 4. 5. *Matt.* 10. 37, 38, 39. *Colo.* 3. 1, 2, 3, 4. *Mich.* 6. 8. *Revel.* 2. 10. *Joh.* 15. 17. 1 *Joh.* 4. 21. *Matt.* 5. 44. *Pro.* 23. 26. *Colo.* 4. 6.

For many [I say unto you].

15 These latter words carry in them a double argument to prove the truth asserted before. First, in that he directly pointeth at his followers. *I say unto [you]:* many I say unto *you,* even to *you* that are my disciples, to *you* that have eat and drunk in my presence. I know that sometimes Christ hath directed his speech to his disciples, not so much upon their
20 accounts, as upon the accounts of others: but here it is not so: the *I say unto you,* in this place, it immediatly concerned some of themselves. *I say unto you, ye shall begin to stand without, and to knock saying, Lord, Lord open to us, and he shall answer, and say unto* you, *I know* you *not, whence* you *are; then shall ye begin to say, we have eat, and drunk in thy presence,*
25 *and thou hast taught in our streets: But he shall say, I tell* you, *I know* you *not whence* you *are, depart from me, all ye workers of iniquity,* 'tis you, you, you, that I mean.

I say unto you.

It is common with a professing people, when they hear a smart and
30 thundring Sermon, to say, now has the preacher paid off the drunkard, the swearer, the lier, the covetous, and adulterer; forgetting that these sins may be committed in a spiritual and mistical way. There is spiritual drunkenness, spiritual adultery, and a man may be a lier *that calls God his father when he is not, or that calls himself a christian and is not.*
35 Wherefore perhaps all these thunders and lightnings in this terrible Sermon, may more concern thee then thou art aware of, *I say unto you:*

19–20 their] there

unto you professors may be the application of all this thunder. *Rev.* 2.
9. *chap.* 3. 9.

I say unto you.

Had not the Lord Jesus designed by these words, to shew what an
overthrow will one day be made among professors, he needed not to 5
have *you'ed* it at this rate, as in the text, and afterwards he has done, the
sentence had run intelligible enough without it; I say, without his
saying [*I say unto you*;] but the truth is, the professor is in danger, the
preacher, and hearer, the workers of miracles, and workers of wonders
may all be in danger of damning, notwithstanding all their attainments. 10
And to awaken us all about this truth therefore, the text must run *thus,
for many, I say unto you, will seek to enter in and shall not be able.*

See you not yet, that the professor is in danger, and that these
words, *I say unto you*, are a Prophesie of the everlasting perdition of
some that are famous in the congregation of Saints: I say, if you do not 15
see it, pray God your eyes may be opened, and beware that thy portion
be not as the portion of one of those that are wrapped up in the twenty
eight verse of the chapter. *There shall be weeping and gnashing of teeth,
when ye shall see* Abraham *and* Isaac *and* Jacob, *and all the prophets in the
kingdom of heaven, and you your selves thrust out.* 20

For many [*I say*] *unto you.*

These words, I told you, carry in them a double argument for
confirmation of the truth asserted before: first, the professors are here
particularly pointed at; and secondly it is the saying of the truth
himself; for these words *I say*, are words full of authority. I say it, I say 25
unto you, sais Christ, as he saith in another place, *It is I that speak,
behold it is I.* The person whose words we have now under
consideration, was no blundering raw-headed preacher, but the very
wisdom of God, his son, and him that hath lain in his bosom, from
everlasting, and consequently, had the most perfect knowledg of his 30
fathers will, and how it would fare with professors at the end of this
world. And now hearken what himself doth say of the words which he
hath spoken; *heaven and earth shall pass away, but* my *word shall not pass
away. Matt.* 24. 35.

[I say] *unto you.* 35

The Prophets used not to speak after this manner, nor yet the holy
Apostles; for thus to speak is to press things to be received upon their

own authority. They used to say, *thus saith the Lord, or* Paul, *or* Peter *an Apostle, or a servant of God.* But now we are dealing with the words of the son of God, it is *he* that hath said it, wherefore we finde the truth of the perishing of many professors, asserted, and confirmed by Christs
5 own mouth. This consideration carrieth great awakning in it, but into such a fast sleep are many now adays fallen, that nothing will awaken them but that shril and terrible cry, *behold the bridegroom comes, go ye out to meet him.*

I say unto you.
10 There are two things upon which this assertion may be grounded.
  1. *There is in the world a thing like grace that is not.*
  2. *There is a sin called, the sin against the holy Ghost, from which there is no redemption,* and both these things befall professors.
  First, *There is in the world a thing like grace that is not.*
15 1. This is evident, because we reade that there are some that not only *make a fair shew in the flesh, that glory in appearance, that appear beautiful outward, that do as Gods people, but have not the grace of Gods people. Gal.* 6. 12. 2 *Cor.* 5. 12. *Matt.* 23. 27. *Isa.* 57. 2.
  2. 'Tis evident also from those frequent cautions that are every
20 where in the Scriptures given us about this thing: *Be not deceived, let a man examine himself; examine your selves whether you be in the faith*: all these expressions intimate to us, that there may be a shew of, or a thing like grace where there is no grace indeed. *Galat.* 6. 7. 1 *Cor.* 11. 28. 2. *Cor.* 13. 5.
25 3. This is evident from the conclusion made by the holy Ghost upon this very thing, *for if a man thinketh himself to be something when he is nothing, he deceiveth himself. Gal.* 6. 3. The holy Ghost here concludeth, that a man may think himself to be something, may think he hath grace, when he hath none, may think himself something for heaven
30 and another world, when indeed he is just nothing at all with reference thereto: the holy Ghost also determines upon this point, to wit, that they do so *deceive themselves; for if a man thinketh himself to be something when he is nothing, he deceiveth himself,* he deceiveth his own soul, he deceiveth himself of heaven and salvation: so again, *let no man beguile*
35 *you of your reward. Col.* 2. 18.
  4. It is also manifest from the text, *for many I say unto you will seek to enter in, and shall not be able*: alas! great light, great parts, great works,

and great confidence of heaven may be where there is no faith of Gods elect, no love of the spirit, no repentance unto salvation, no sanctification of the spirit, and so consequently no saving grace, but

Secondly, as there is a *thing* like grace which is not, so there is a *sin* called the *sin against the holy Ghost*, from which there is no redemption, 5 and this sin doth more ordinarily befal professors.

1. There is a sin called the *sin against the holy Ghost*, from which there is no redemption; this is evident both from *Matthew* and *Mark: But whosoever speaketh against the holy Ghost, it shall not be forgiven him neither in this world, neither in the world to come. But he that shall* 10 *blaspheme against the holy Ghost, hath never forgiveness, but is in danger of eternal damnation, Matt.* 12. 32. *Mar.* 3. 29. wherefore when we know that a man hath sinned this sin, we are not to pray for him, or to have compassion on him. 1 *Joh.* 15. 16. *Judg.* 22.

2. This sin doth most ordinarily befal professors, for there are few, if 15 any, that are not professors, that are at present capable of sinning this sin. *They which were once enlightned, and have tasted the heavenly gift, that were made partakers of the holy Ghost, and have tasted the good word of God, and the powers of the world to come, Heb.* 6, 4, 5. of this sort are they that commit this sin; *Peter* also describes them *to be such*, that sin the 20 unpardonable sin. *For if after they have escaped the pollution of the world through the knowledg of our Lord and saviour Jesus Christ, they are again intangled therein and overcome, the latter end is worse with them then the beginning.* 2 *Pet.* 2. 2. That other passage in the tenth of the *hebrews* holdeth forth the same thing; *for if we sin wilfully after we have received* 25 *the knowledge of the truth, there remaineth no more sacrifice for sin, but a certain, fearful looking for of Judgment, and fiery indignation that shall devour the adversaryes. Heb.* 10. 26, 27.

These therefore are the persons that are the prey for this sin: this sin *feedeth upon professors*, and they that are such do very often fall into the 30 mouth of this eater. Some fall into the mouth of this sin, by delusions, and doctrins of devils, and some fall into the mouth of it, by returning *with the dog to his own vomit again, and with the sow that was washed, to her wallowing in the mire.* 1. *Pet.* 2. 22. I shall not here give you a particular description of this sin, that I have done elsewhere; *but such a* 35 *sin there is*, and they that commit it shall never have forgiveness; and I say again, there be professors that commit this unpardonable sin, yea

more then the most are aware of: let all therefore look about them; the
Lord awaken them that they may so do: for what with a profession
without grace, and by the venom of the sin against the holy Ghost,
many will seek to enter in, and shall not be able.

5   *Will seek to enter in.*

This kingdom, at the gate of which the reprobate will be stopt, will
be at the last Judgment, the desire of all the world, and *they*, especially
they in my text will *seek to enter in.* For then they will see that the
blessednesse is to those that shall get into this kingdom, according to
10 that which is written, *Blessed are they that do his Commandments, that they*
may have right to the tree of life, and may enter in through the gates into the
city. Revel. 22. 14.

To prove that they will seek, although I have done it already, yet
reade these texts at your leisure, *Matt.* 25. 11. *chap. 7. 22. Luk.* 13. 28.
15 And in a word to give you the reason why they will *seek to enter in.*

1. Now they will see what a kingdom it is, what glory there is in it,
and now they shall also see the blessednesse which they shall have that
shall then be counted worthy to enter in: the reason why this kingdom
is so little regarded, it is because it is not seen, the glory of it is hid
20 from the eyes of the world: *their eye hath not seen, nor their ear heard,* &c.
I, but then they shall hear and see too, and when this comes to passe,
then even then he that now most seldom thinks thereof, *will seek to*
enter in.

2. They will now see what hell is, and what damnation in hell is,
25 more clear then ever; They will also see how the breath of the Lord
like a stream of brimstone doth kindle it: O the sight of the burning
fiery furnace which is prepared for the devil and his Angels! this, this
will make work in the souls of castaways at that day of God almighty,
and then they will *seek to enter in.*

30   3. Now they will see what the meaning of such words as these are,
hell-fire, everlasting fire, devouring fire, fire that never shall be
quenched: now they will see what for ever, means: what eternity
means: now they will see what this word means, *the bottomless pit*: now
they will hear roaring of sinners in this place, howling in that, some
35 crying to the mountains to fall upon them, and others to the rocks to
cover them; now they will see blessedness is no where but within.

4. Now they will see what glory the godly are possessed with, how

they rest in *Abrahams* bosom, how they enjoy eternal glory, how they walk in their white robes, and are equal to the Angels. O the favour, and blessedness, and unspeakable happyness that now Gods people shall have, and this shall be seen by them that are shut out, by them that God hath rejected for ever, and this will make them seek to enter 5 in. *Luk.* 16. 22, 23. 13. 28.

Will seek to enter in.

Q. But some may say, *how will they seek to enter in?*

Answ. They will put on all the confidence they can, they will trick, and trim up their profession, and adorn it with what bravery they can. 10 *Thus the foolish virgins sought to enter in,* they did *trim up their lamps,* made themselves as fine as they could, they made shift to make their lamps to shine a while, but the son of God, discovering himself, their confidence failed, their lamps went out, the door was shut upon them, and they were kept out. *Matt.* 25. 1. 2, 3, 4, 5, 6, 7, 8, 9, 15 10, 11, 12.

2. They will seek to enter in, by crouding themselves in among the godly. *Thus the man without the wedding garment, sought to enter in,* he *goes* to the wedding, gets into the wedding-chamber, sits close among the guests, and then, without doubt, concluded, he should escape 20 damnation: *but you know, one black sheep is soon seen, though it be among an hundred white ones,* why even thus it faired with this poor man; *And when the king came in to see the guests, he saw* there *a man that had not on a wedding-garment.* He spied him presently, and before one word was spoken to any of the other, he had this dreadful salutation, *friend how* 25 *camest thou in hither, not having on a wedding-garment?* and he was speechless, though he could swagger it out amongst the guests, yet the Master of the Feast, at first coming in, strikes him dumb, and having nothing to say for himself, the King had something to say against him: *Then said the king to the servants* (the Angels) *bind him hand and foot, and* 30 *take him away, and cast him into outer darkness, there shall be weeping and gnashing of teeth. Matt.* 22. 11, 12, 13.

3. They will seek to enter in by pleading their profession and admittance to the Lords Ordinances, when they were in the world, *Lord we have eat and drunk in thy presence and thou hast taught in our* 35 *streets,* we sat at thy table and used to frequent sermons and Christian assemblies; we were well thought of by thy saints, and were admitted

into thy Churches, we professed the same faith as they did, *Lord, Lord, open unto us.*

4. They will seek to enter in, *by pleading their virtues*; how they subjected to his ministry, how they wrought for him, what good they did in the world, and the like, *Matt.* 7. 22. but neither will this help them; the same answer that the two former had, the same have these; *depart from me ye workers of iniquity.*

5. *They will seek to enter in* by pleading excuses, where they cannot evade conviction. The slothful servant went this way to work, when he was called to account for not improving his Lords mony. *Lord,* says he, *I knew thou wast an hard man, reaping where thou hast not sowed, and gathering where thou hast not strewed, and I was afraid,* &c. (either that I should not please in laying out thy mony, or that I should put it into hands, out of which I should not get it again at thy need) *and I went and hid thy talent in the earth, lo, there thou hast that is thine*; as if he had said, true Lord, I have not improved, I have not got, but consider also, I have not imbezled, I have not spent, nor lost thy mony, *lo there thou hast that is thine. Matt.* 25. 24, 25, 26, 27. There are but few will be able to say these *last words* at the day of judgment; the most of professors are for imbezzeling, mispending and slothing away their time, their talents, their opportunities to do good in; but, I say, if he that can make so good an excuse as to say, *lo, there thou hast what is thine*: I say if such an one shall be called *a wicked and slothful servant*, if such an one shall be put to shame at the day of judgment, yea if such an one shall, notwithstanding this care to save his Lords mony, *be cast as unprofitable into utter darkness, where shall be weeping and gnashing of teeth*, what will they do that have neither took care to lay out, nor care to keep what was committed to their trust?

6. They will seek to enter in by pleading, that ignorance was the ground of their miscarrying in the things wherein they offended; wherefore when Christ charges them with want of love to him, and with want of those fruits that should prove their love to be true, as, *that they did not feed him, did not give him drink, did not take him in, did not cloth him, visit him, come unto him, and the like*: they readyly reply, *Lord, when saw we thee an hungred, or athirst, or a stranger, or naked, or sick, or in prison, and did not minister unto thee. Matt.* 25. 41, 42, 43, 44. As who

35 *thee*] the

should say, Lord, we are not conscious to our selves, that this charge is worthyly laid at our door. God forbid that we should have been such sinners, but Lord, give an instance; when was it, or where? true, there were a company of poor sorry people in the world very inconsiderable, set by with no body, but for thy self we professed thee, we loved thee, and hadst thou been with us in the world, wouldest thou have worn gold, wouldest thou have eaten the sweetest of the world, we would have provided it for thee; and therefore, *Lord, Lord open to us*. But will this plea do? no, then shall he answer them, *inasmuch as you did it not to one of the least of these my brethren, ye did it not to me*. This plea then though grounded upon ignorance, which is one of the strongest pleas for neglect of duty, would not give them admittance into the kingdom. *These shall go away into everlasting punishment, but the righteous into life eternal*.

I might add other things by which t'will appear how they *will seek to enter* in; as,

1. They will make a stop at this gate, this beautiful gate of heaven, they will *begin to stand without at the gate*, as being loath to go any further: never did malefactor so unwillingly turn off the ladder, when the rope was about his neck, as these will turn away, in that day, from the gates of heaven to hell.

2. They will not only make a stop at the gate; but there *they will knock and call*, this also argueth them willing to enter: they *will begin to stand without and to knock at the gate saying, Lord, Lord, open to us*. This word, *Lord*, being doubled, shews the vehemency of their desires: Lord, Lord, *open unto us*. The devils are coming; Lord, Lord, the pit opens her mouth upon us: Lord, Lord there is nothing but hell and damnation left us, if Lord, Lord thou hast not mercy upon *us*; *Lord, Lord open to us*.

3. Their last argument for entrance is their tears, when groundless confidence, pleading of vertues, excuses and ignorance, will not do; when standing at the gate, knowing and calling *Lord Lord, open to us*, will not do, then they betake themselves to their tears: tears are sometimes the most powerful arguments, but they are nothing worth here: *Esau* also *sought it carefully, with tears*, but it helped him nothing at all. *Heb*. 12. 15. 16. *There shall be weeping, and gnashing of teeth*, for the

11 strongest] strangest

gate is shut for ever, mercy is gone for ever, Christ hath rejected them for ever: all their pleas, excuses, and tears, will not make them able to enter into this kingdom.

For many, I say unto you, will seek to enter in and shall not be able.

5 I come now to the latter part of the words which closely shews us the reason of the rejection of these many that must be damned, *they will seek to enter in, and shall not be able.*

An hypocrite, a false professor may go a great way, they may pass thorow the first and second watch, to wit, may be approved of 10 Christians and Churches, *but what will they do when they come at this iron gate that leadeth into the city?* there the workers of iniquity will fall, be cast down, and shall not be able to rise.

And shall not be able.

The time, as I have already hinted, which my Text respecteth, it is 15 the day of judgement, a day when all masks and vizzards shall be taken off from all faces: It is a day wherein *God will bring to light the hidden things of darknesse, and will make manifest the counsels of the heart.* 1 Cor. 4. 5. It is also the day of his wrath, the day in which he will pay vengeance, even a recompence to his adversaries.

20 At this day those things that now these *many* count sound and good, will then shake like a quagmire, even all their naked knowledge, their feigned faith, pretended love, glorious shews of gravity in the face, their holy-day words and specious carriages will stand them in little stead: I call them holy day ones, for I perceive that some professors do 25 with religion, just as people do with their best apparrel, hang it against the wall all the week, and put them on on Sundays: for as some scarce ever put on a Sute, but when they go to a Fair or a Market, so little house-religion will do with some; they save religion till they go to a Meeting, or till they meet with a godly chapman: O poor religion! O 30 poor professor, what wilt thou do at this day, at the day of thy trial & judgement? cover thy self thou canst not, go for a Christian thou canst not, stand against the Judge thou canst not; what wilt thou do? *The ungodly shall not stand in judgement, nor sinners in the congregation of the righteous.*

35 *And shall not be able.*

The ability here intended, is not that which standeth in carnal power or fleshly subtilty, but in the truth and simplicity of those things, for the sake of which, God giveth the kingdom of heaven to his people.

There are five things, *for the want of which*, this people will not be able to enter.   5

First, this kingdom belongs to the *elect*, to those for whom it was prepared from the foundation of the world, *Matt.* 25. hence Christ saith, when he comes, *he will send forth his angels with a great sound of a trumpet, and they shall gather together his elect from the four winds, from one end of heaven to another, Matt.* 24. and hence he saith again, *I will bring* 10 *forth a seed out of* Jacob, *and out of* Judah, *an inheritor of my mountains, and mine elect shall inherit it, and my servants shall dwell there; they shall deceive, if it were possible, the very elect, but the elect hath obtained it, and the rest were blinded.* Rom. 11. 7.

Secondly, They will not be able to enter, because they will want the 15 *birth right*; the kingdom of heaven is for the *heirs*, and if children then *heirs*, if born again then *heirs*: wherefore it is said expresly, *except a man be born again he cannot see the kingdom of God*; by this one word, down goes all carnal priviledge of being born of flesh, and bloud, and of the will of man, canst thou produce the *birth-right*, but art thou sure thou 20 canst? for it will little profit thee to think of the blessed kingdom of heaven, if thou wantest a *birthright* to give thee inheritance there. *Esau*, did dispise his birth-right, saying, *what good will this birth-right do me?* and there are many in the world of his mind to this day: tush (say they,) they talk of being born again, what good shall a man get by that? they 25 say, no going to heaven without being born again, but God is merciful, Christ died for sinners, and we will turn when we can tend it, and doubt not but all will be well at last. But I will answer thee, thou childe of *Esau*, that the birth-right and blessing go together, miss of one, and thou shalt never have the other; *Esau* found this true, for having first 30 despised the birth-right, when he would afterwards have inherited the blessing he was rejected, for he found no place of repentance though he sought it carefully with tears. *Gen.* 25. *Heb.* 12. 14, 15, 16.

Thirdly, they shall not be able to enter in who have not believed with the faith of Gods operation, the faith that is most holy, even the faith of 35 Gods elect: *He that believeth on the son of God hath everlasting life, he that*

17 again then *heirs*:] again then heirs:

believeth not the son, shall not see life, but the wrath of God abideth on him.
Joh. 3. But now, this faith is the effect of electing love, and of a new
birth, *Joh.* 1. 11, 12. therefore all the professors that have not that faith
which floweth from being born of God, will seek to enter in and shall
5 not be able.

Fourthly, they shall not be able to enter in, that have not Gospel-
holyness; holyness that is the effect of faith is that which admits into
the presence of God, and into his kingdom too. *Blessed and holy are they*
that have part in the first resurrection, on such the second death (which is
10 hell and eternal damnation *Revel.* 20. 14.) *hath no power.* Revel. 20. 6.
Blessed and holy, with the holiness that flows from faith which is in
Christ, for to these the inheritance belongs. *That they may receive*
forgiveness of sins and inheritance among them that are sanctified by faith
(said Christ) *which is in me. Acts.* 26. 18. This holyness which is the
15 natural effect of faith in the son of God, Christ Jesus the Lord, will at
this day of judgment, distinguish from all other shews of holiness, and
sanctitie be they what they will, and will admit the soul that hath this
holiness into his kingdom, when the rest will seek to enter in, and shall
not be able.

20 Fifthly, *They shall not be able to enter in,* that do not persevere in this
blessed faith and holiness, not that they that have them indeed, can
finally fall away, and everlastingly perish, but it hath pleased Jesus
Christ to bid them that have the right, to hold fast that they have, to
endure to the end, and then tells them they shall be saved: though 'tis
25 as true, that none is of power to keep himself, but God worketh
together with his children, and *they are kept by the power of God through*
faith unto salvation, which is also laid up in heaven for them. 1 Pet. 1. 3, 4, 5.
The foolish shall not stand in thy sight, thou hatest the workers of iniquity.
The foolish are the unholy ones, that neither have faith nor holiness,
30 nor perseverance in godliness, and yet lay claim to the kingdom of
heaven: but *better is a little with righteousness, then great revenues without*
right. Psal. 55. *Pro.* 16. 8. What is it for me to claim a house, or a farm
without right; or to say, all this is mine, but have nothing to shew for it:
this is but like the revenues of the foolish: his estate lieth in his conceit;
35 *he hath nothing by birth-right, and law,* and therefore shall not be able to
inherit the possession: *for many I say unto you will seek to enter in, and*
shall not be able.

Thus you see, that the *non* elect, shall not be able to enter, that he that is not born again, shall not be able to enter, that he that hath not saving faith, with holiness and perseverance flowing therefrom, shall not be able to enter: wherefore consider of what I have said.

I come now to give you some Observations from the words, and they may be three. 5

First, *When men have put in all the claim they can for heaven, but few will have it for their inheritance; for many I say unto you, will seek to enter in, and shall not be able.*

Secondly, *Great therefore will be the disappointment that many will meet* 10 *with at the day of judgement; for many will seek to enter in, and shall not be able.*

Thirdly, *Going to heaven therefore will be no trivial businesse, salvation is not got by a dream, they that would then have that kingdom must now strive lawfully to enter: for many I say unto you will seek to enter in, and shall not* 15 *be able.*

I shall speak chiefly, and yet but briefly to the first of these Observations, to wit,

That when men have put in all the claim they can to the kingdom of heaven, but few will have it for their inheritance: The Observation 20 standeth of two parts.

First, that the time is coming when every man will put in whatever claim they can to the kingdom of Heaven.

Secondly, there will be but few of them that put in claim thereto that shall enjoy it for their inheritance. 25

I shall speak but a word or two to the first part of the Observation, because I have prevented my enlargement thereon by my explication upon the words; but you finde in the 25. of *Matthew*, that all they on the left hand of the Judge, did put in all the claim they could for this blessed kingdome of heaven: If you shall take them on the left hand, as 30 most do, for all the sinners that shall be damned, then that compleatly proveth the first part of the Observation, for it is expressly said, *then shall they*, (all of them jointly, and every one apart) also answer him saying, *Lord, when saw we thee thus and thus, and did not minister unto thee. Matt.* 25. 44. I could here bring you in the plea of the slothful 35 servant, the cry of the foolish virgins; I could also here inlarge upon that passage *Lord, Lord, have we not eat and drunk in thy presence, and*

thou hast taught in our streets; but these things are handled already, in
the handling of which, this first part of the Observation is proved;
wherefore without more words, I will, God assisting by his grace,
descend to the second part therof, to wit,

5 *There will be but few of them that put in claim thereto, that will enjoy it for
their inheritance.*

I shall speak distinctly to this part of the Observation, and shall first
confirm it by a Scripture or two.

*Straight is the gate and narrow is the way that leadeth unto life, and few
10 there be that finde it. Matt.* 7. 13, 14.

*Fear not little flock, it is your fathers good pleasure to give you the
kingdome. Luk.* 12. 32. By these two Texts, and by many more that will
be urged anon you may see the truth of what I have said. To enlarge
therefore upon the truth; and,

15 First, more generally,
Secondly, more particularly.

First, more generally I shall prove that in all ages, but few have been
saved.

Secondly, more particularly, I shall prove but few of them that
20 professe have been saved.

First, in the old world, when it was most populous, even in the days
of *Noah*, we reade but of eight persons that were saved out of it; well
therefore might *Peter* call them *but few*, but how few? why but *eight
souls; wherein few, that is, eight souls were saved by water.* 1 *Pet.* 3. 20. He
25 touches a second time upon this truth, saying, *he spared not the old
world, but saved* Noah *the eight person, a preacher of righteousness, bringing
in the floud upon the world of the ungodly*: mark all the rest are called the
ungodly, and there were also a *world* of *them.* 2 *Pet.* 2. 5. These are also
taken notice of in *Job*, and go there also, by the name of wicked men,
30 *Hast thou marked the old way, which wicked men have trodden, which were
cut down out of time, whose foundation was overflown with a floud, which
said unto God, depart from us, and what can the almighty do for them? Job.*
22. 15, 16, 17, 18.

There were therefore but eight persons that escaped the wrath of

---

3 I will, God assisting by his grace,] I will God assisting by his grace,
4 wit,] wit.   14 the truth; and,] the truth. and.
31 *time*] nine

God, in the day that the floud came upon the earth, the rest were ungodly; there was also a world of them, and they are to this day in the prison of hell. *Heb.* 11. 7. 1 *Pet.* 3. 19, 20.

Nay I must correct my pen, there were but seven of the eight that were good, for *Ham* though he scaped the Judgment of the water, yet the curse of God overtook him to his damnation.

Secondly, when the world began again to be replenished, and people began to multiply therein: how few even in all ages do we reade of, that were saved from the damnation of the world.

1. One *Abraham* and his wife, God called out of the land of the *Caldeans, I called* (said God) *Abraham alone. Isa.* 51. 1, 2.

2. One *Lot* out of *Sodom* and *Gomorah*, out of *Adma* and *Zeboim*, one *Lot* out of four cities; indeed, his wife and two daughters, went out of *Sodom* with him, but they all three proved naught, as you may see in the nineteenth of *Genesis*: wherefore *Peter* observes, that *Lot* only was saved: *He turned the citys of* Sodom *and* Gomorah *into ashes, condemning them with an overthrow, making them an example unto those that often should live ungodly, and delivered just* Lot; *that righteous man*, reade 2 *Pet.* 2. 6, 7, 8.

Jude says, that in this condemnation, God over-threw, not only *Sodom* and *Gomorah*, but the cities about them also: and yet you finde none but *Lot*, could be found that was righteous either in *Sodom* or *Gomorah*, or the cities about them, wherefore they, *all of them*, suffer the vengance of eternal fire. *vers.* 7.

Thirdly, come we now to the time of the *Judges*, how few then were the godly, even then when the inhabitants of the villages ceased, they ceased in *Israel*, the high-ways (of God) were then unoccupied. *Judg.* 5, 6, 7.

Fourthly, there were but few in the days of David; *help Lord* says he, *for the godly man ceaseth, for the faithful fail from among the children of men. Psal.* 12. 1.

Fifthly, In *Isaia's* time the saved were come to such a few, that he positively says, but that there were a very small number left, God had made them like *Sodom*, and they had been like unto *Gomorah. Isa.* 1. 8, 9.

Sixthly, It was cryed unto them in the time of *Ieremiah*, that they

3 *Heb.* 11. 7.] *Heb.* 6. 11. 6.   11 *I called*] (I *called*

should run to and fro through the streets of Jerusalem, *and see, and know, and seek in the broad places thereof, if ye can finde a man, if there be any that executeth judgment, that seeketh the truth, and I will pardon it. Ier.* 5. 1.

Seventhly, God shewed his servant *Ezekiel* how few there would be
5 saved in his day, by the vision of a *few hairs*, saved out of the midest of a *few hairs*; for the saved were a few saved out of a few. *Ezek.* 5. 3, 4, 5.

Eighthly, you finde in the time of the Prophet *Micha* how the godly complain, that as to *number* they then were, *so few*, that he compares them to those that are left behinde when they had gathered the
10 summer-fruit. *Mic.* 7. 1.

Ninthly, when Christ was come, how did he confirm this truth, *that but few of them that put in claim for heaven will have it for their inheritance.* But the common people could not hear it, and therefore upon a time when he did but a little hint at this truth, the people, even all in the
15 Synagogue where he preached it, *were filled with wrath, rose up, thrust him out of the City, and led him unto the brow of the hill (whereon their city was built) that they might cast him down headlong. Luke* 4. 24, 25, 26, 27, 28, 29.

Tenthly, *John*, who was after Christ, saith, that the whole world lies
20 in wickedness, that all the world wondred after the beast, and that power was given to the beast, over all kindreds, tongues and nations; power to do what? why to cause all, both great and small, rich and poor, bond and free, to receive his mark, and to be branded for him. 1. *Joh.* 5. 19. *Revel.* 13. 3, 8, 16.

25 Eleventhly, should we come to observation and experience, the shew of the countenance, of the bulk of men, doth witness against them, *they declare their sin like* Sodom, *they hide it not. Isa.* 3. 9. Where is the man that maketh the almighty God his delight, and that designeth his glory in the world; do not even almost all, pursue this world, their lusts and
30 pleasures? and so, consequently, *say unto God, depart from us, for we desire not the knowledg of thy ways,* or what's the Almighty that we should serve him? it's in vain to serve God, *&c.*

So that without doubt, it will appear a truth in the day of God, *that but few of them, that shall put in their claim to heaven, will have it for their*
35 *inheritance.*

23–24 1. *Joh.* 5. 19.] Joh 5. 19.

Before I pass this head, I will shew you to what the saved are compared in the Scriptures.

First, they are compared to an handful, *there shall be an handful of corn in the earth upon the top of the mountains*, &c. *Psal.* 27. 16. This corn is nothing else but them that shall be saved. *Matt.* 3. 12. *chap.* 13. 30. 5

But mark, there shall be an handful; what's an handful when compared with the whole heap, or what's an handful out of the rest of the world?

Secondly, As they are compared to an handful, so they are compared to *a lillie among the thorns*, *Song.* 2. 2. which is rare, and not so 10 commonly seen. *As the lillie among thorns*, saith Christ, *so is my beloved among the daughters*. By *thorns* we understand the worst and best of men, even all that are destitute of the grace of God, *for the best of them is as a bryer, and the most upright of them as a thorn-hedge. Mich.* 7. 4. 2 *Sam.* 23. 6. 2. I know that she may be called a *lillie amongst thorns* also, 15 because she meets with the pricks of persecution. *Ezek.* 2. 6. *chap.* 29. 24. 3. she may also be thus termed, to shew the disparitie that is betwixt hypocrites and the Church. *Luk.* 8. 14. *Heb.* 8. But this is not all, the saved are compared to a *lillie among thorns*, to shew you, that they are but few in the world; to shew you, that they are few and rare; 20 for as Christ compares her to a *lillie among thorns*, so she compares him to an *apple-tree among the trees of the wood*, which is rare, and scarce, not common.

Thirdly, they that are saved, are called but *one* of many, for though there be *threescore queens, and fourscore concubines, and virgins without* 25 *number, yet my love*, saith Christ, *is but* one, *my undefiled is but* one, *Song.* 6. 8, 9. according to that of *Jeremiah, I will take you, one of a city. Jer.* 3. That saying of *Paul* is much like this, *know you not, that they which run in a race run all, but* one *receiveth the prize*, 1 *Cor.* 9. 24. but *one*, that is, few of many, few of them that run, for he is not here comparing them 30 that run, with them that sit still, but with them that run, some run and lose, some run and win; they that run and win, are few in comparison of them that run and lose: *They that run in a race run all, but* one *receives the prise*: let there then be threescore queens, and fourscore concubines, and virgins without number, *yet the saved are but few.* 35

Fourthly, they that are the saved, are compared to the *gleaning after the vintage is in: wo is me*, said the Church, *for I am as when they have*

gathered the summer fruit, as the grape gleanings after the vintage is in.
Mich. 7. 1. The gleanings! what's the gleanings to the whole crop? and
yet you here see, *to the gleanings* are the saved compared; 'tis the devil
and sin that carry away the cart-loads, while Christ and his ministers
5 come after a gleaning: *But the gleaning of the grapes of* Ephraim *are better*
then the vintage of Abiezer. *Jud.* 8. Them that Christ and his ministers
glean up and binde up in the bundle of life, are better then the loads
that go the other way: you know it is often the cry of the poor in
harvest, *poor gleaning, poor gleaning*: And the ministers of the Gospel,
10 they also cry, *Lord who hath believed our report? and to whom is the arm of*
the Lord revealed? Isa. 53. 1.

   When the prophet speaks of the saved under this metaphor of
gleaning, how doth he amplify the matter? *Gleaning grapes shall be left,*
says he, *two or three berries in the top of the uppermost bough, four or five, in*
15 *the outmost fruitful branches thereof, saith the Lord. Isa.* 17. 6. Thus you
see what gleaning is left in the vineyard, after the vintage is in, two or
three here, four or five there. Alas! they that shall be saved, when the
devil and hell have had their due, they will be but as the gleaning, they
will be but few, they that go to hell, go thither in clusters, but the saved
20 go not so to heaven, *Matt.* 13. 30. *Mich.* 7. wherefore when the
prophet speaketh of the saved, he saith, *there is no cluster,* but when he
speaketh of the damned, he saith, they are *gathered by clusters. Revel.* 14.
18, 19. O sinners, but few will be saved. O professor, but few will be
saved!

25   Fifthly, they that shall be saved, are compared *to jewels*; *And they shall*
be mine, saith the Lord, in the day that I make up my jewels. Malachi. 3. 13.
Jewels, you know, are rare things, things that are not found in every
house: Jewels will lie in little room, being few and small; though
lumber takes up much. In almost every house, you may find brass, and
30 iron, and lead; and in every place you may finde hypocritical professors,
but the saved are not these common things: they are Gods peculiar
treasure, *Psal.* 35. 4. wherefore *Paul* distinguisheth betwixt the lumber,
and the treasure in the house; there *is*, saith he, *in a great house, not only*
vessels of gold and of silver, but also of wood, and of earth, and some to
35 *honour, and some to dishonour.* 2. *Tim.* 2. 20. Here is a word for wooden
and earthy professors, the jewels and treasure are vessels to honor,

they of *wood* & *earth* are vessels of dishonour, that is, vessels for
destruction. *Rom.* 9. 21.

Sixthly, they that shall be saved are compared to a *remnant; except the
Lord had left in us a very small remnant, we should have been as* Sodom,
and should have been like unto Gomorrah. *Isa.* 1. 9. A remnant, a small 5
remnant, a very small remnant: O how doth the holy Ghost word it,
and all to shew you, how few shall be saved: every one knows, what a
remnant is, but this is a *small* remnant, a *very* small remnant. So again,
sing with gladness for Jacob, *and shout among the chief of the nations,
publish ye, praise ye, and say, O Lord, save thy people, the remnant of* Israel. 10
Jer. 31. 7. What shall I say, the saved are often in Scripture called, *a
remnant. Ezr.* 9. 8, 14. *Isa.* 10. 20, 21, 22, *chap.* 11. 11. 16. *Ier.* 23.3. *Ioel*
2. 32. But what's a remnant, to the whole piece: what's a remnant of
people to the whole kingdom, or what's a remnant of wheat to the
whole harvest.   15

Eightly, the saved are compared to the tithe, or tenth part, wherefore
when God sendeth the prophet to make the hearts of the people fat,
their ears dull, and to shut their eyes: The prophet asketh, *how long*! to
which God answereth, *until the cities be wasted without inhabitant, and
the houses without man, and the land be utterly desolate, and the Lord have* 20
*removed man far away, and there be a great forsaking in the middest of the
land: but yet,* (as God saith in another place, *I will not make a full end,) in
it shall be a tenth, so the holy seed shall be the substance thereof. Isa.* 6. 10,
11, 12, 13. But what's a tenth: what's one in ten? and yet so speaks the
holy Ghost when he speaks of the *holy seed*, of those that was to be 25
reserved from the Judgment; and observe it, the fatning, and blinding
of the rest, it was to their everlasting destruction, and so both Christ
and *Paul* expounds it often in the new Testament. *Matt.* 13. 14, 15.
Mar. 4. 12. *Luk.* 8. 10. *Joh.* 12. 40. *Acts.* 28. 26. *Rom.* 11. 8. So that
those that are reserved from them that perish, will be very few, one in 30
ten. *A tenth shall return, so the holy seed shall be the substance thereof.*

I shall not add more generals at this time, I pray God that the world
be not offended at these: but without doubt, *but few of them that shall
put in their claim for heaven will have it for their inheritance;* which will yet
further appear in the reading of that which follows.   35

24 what's a tenth: what's] whats a tenth: whats

Secondly, therefore I come more particularly to shew you, that *but few will be saved*, I say, but *few of professors themselves will be saved*, for that is the truth that the text doth more directly look at and defend. Give me therefore thy hand (good reader) and let us soberly walk
5 through the rest of what shall be said, and let us compare as we go each particular with the holy Scripture.

First, 'tis said, *The daughter of Zion is left as a cottage in a vinyard, as a lodge in a garden of cucumbers, as a besieged citie. Isa.* 18. The vineyard was the Church of *Israel, Isa.* 5. 1. the cottage in that vinyard, was
10 the daughter of *Zion*, or the truly gracious amongst or in that Church: a cottage: God had but a cottage there, but a little habitation in the Church, a very few that were truly gracious amongst that great multitude that professed; and had it not been for these, for this cottage, the rest had been ruined as *Sodom: Except the Lord of hosts had left in us,*
15 *in the Church, a very few, they had been as* Sodom, *v.* 9. wherefore among the multitude of them that shall be damned, professors will make a considerable party.

Secondly, *for though* thy *people* Israel, *be as the sand of the sea, a remnant shall return, a remnant shall be saved, Isa.* 10. 22. *Ro.* 9. 27. for
20 though *thy* people *Israel*, whom thou brought'st out of *Egypt*, to whom thou hast given Church-constitution, holy laws, holy ordinances, holy prophets, and holy covenants: *thy* people, by seperation from all people, and *thy* people by profession: though this *thy people* be as the sand of the sea, a remnant shall be saved: wherefore among the
25 multitude of them that shall be damned, professors will make a considerable party.

Thirdly, *Reprobate silver shall men call them because the Lord hath rejected them. Jer.* 6. 30. The people here under consideration, are called in *verse* 27. *Gods people*, his people by profession. *I have set thee for*
30 *a tower and a fortress among my people, that thou maiest know and try their way*, what follows? *They are all grievous revolters, walking with slanders, reprobate silver, the Lord hath rejected them.* In *chapter* 7. *ver.* 29. they are called also the generation of his wrath: *for the Lord hath rejected, and forsaken the generation of his wrath.* This therefore I gather out of these
35 holy Scriptures; that with reference to profession, and Church-constitution, a people may be called the people of God, but with

31 slanders] standers

reference to the event and final conclusion that God will make with
some of them, they may be truly the generation of his wrath.

Fourthly, In the 5. of *Isa.* you read again of the *vinyard of God,* and
that it was planted on a very fruitful hill, planted with the choicest
vines, had a wall, a tower, a wine-press belonging to it, and all things   5
that could put it into right order and good government, as a Church,
but this vinyard of the Lord of hosts brought forth wild grapes, fruits
unbecoming her constitution and government, wherefore the Lord
takes from her his hedge and wall, and lets her be troden down: reade
Christs exposition upon it in *Matt.* 2. *and* 33. &c. look to it professors,   10
these are the words of the text, *for many, I say unto you, will seek to enter
in, and shall not be able.*

Fifthly, *Son of man,* said God to the Prophet, *the house of* Israel *is to
me become dross, all they are brass and tin, and iron and lead, in the midest of
the furnace, they are the dross of silver.* Ezek. 22. 18. God had silver there,   15
some silver, but it was but little, the bulk of that people was but the
dross of the Church, though they were the members of it, but what
doth he mean by the dross? why he looked upon them as no better
notwithstanding their Church-membership, then the rabble of the
world, that is, with respect to their latter end, for to be called dross, it is   20
to be put among the rest of the sinners of the world in the judgment of
God, though at present they abide in his house: *Thou puttest away all
the wicked of the earth like dross, therefore I love thy testimonies.* Psal. 119.
119.

God saith of his saved ones, *he hath chosen them in the furnace of*   25
affliction. The refiner, when he putteth his silver into his furnace, he
puts lead in also among it; now this lead being ordered as he knows
how, works up the dross from the silver, which dross still as it riseth, he
putteth by, or taketh away with an instrument; and thus deals God with
his Church, there is silver in his Church, I, and there is also dross; now   30
the dross are the hypocrites, and graceless ones that are got into the
Church, and these will God discover and afterwards put away as dross.
So that it will without doubt prove a truth of God, that many of their
professors that shall put in claim for heaven, will not have it for their
inheritance.
                                                                            35
Sixthly, It is said of Christ, *his fan is in his hand, and he will throughly*

13 said God to the Prophet,] *said God to the Prophet,*

purge his floor, and will gather his wheat into his garner, but will burn up the chaff with unquenchable fire. Mat. 3. 12.

1. The floor, is the Church of God. (*O my threshing and the corn of my floor,*) said God by the prophet, *Isa.* 21. 10. to his people.

5 2. The wheat are those good ones in his Church that shall be undoubtedly saved, therefore he saith, *gather my wheat into my garner.*

3. The chaff groweth upon the same stalk, and ear, and so is in the same visible body with the wheat, but there is not substance in it, wherefore in time, they must be severed one from the other, the wheat
10 must be gathered into the garner, which is heaven: and the chaff, or professors, that want true grace, must be gathered into hell, that they may be *burned up with unquenchable fire*: therefore let professors look to it.

Seventhly, Christ Jesus casts away two of the three grounds that are
15 said to receive the word. *Luk.* 8. *The stony ground, received it with joy, and the thorny ground brought forth fruit almost to perfection*: indeed the high-way ground was to shew us that the *carnal*, while such, receive not the word at all, but here is the pinch, *two* of the *three* that received it, fell short of the kingdom of heaven; for but *one* of the three received it,
20 so as to bring forth fruit to perfection; look to it professors.

Eighthly, The parable of *the unprofitable servant*, the parable of the *man without a wedding garment*, and the parable of *the unsavory salt*, do each of them justifie this for truth. *Matt.* 25. 24, 25. *chap.* 22. 11, 12, 13. *chap.* 5. 13. That of *the unprofitable servant*, is to shew us, the sloth
25 and idleness of some professors; that of *the man without a wedding-garment*, is to shew us, how some professors have the shame of their wickedness seen by God, even when they are among the children of the bridegroome; and that parable of *the unsavory salt*, is to shew, that as the salt that hath lost its savor is fit for nothing, no, not for the
30 dunghill, but to be troden under the foot of men; So some professors (yea and great ones too, for this parable reached *one* of the Apostles:) will in Gods day be counted fit for nothing but to be troden down as the mire in the streets: oh the slothful, the naked and unsavory professors, how will they be rejected of God and his Christ, in the
35 judgment; look to it professors.

Ninthly, The parable of the *tares* also giveth countenance to this truth: for though it be said, *the field is the world*, yet it is said, the tares were sown even in the Church; *And while men slept, the enemy came and sowed tares among the wheat, and went his way. Matt.* 13. 24, 25.

Obj. But some may object, the tares might be sowed in the world among the wheat, though not in the Churches.

Answer, But Christ by expounding this parable tells us, the tares 5 were sown in his kingdom (the tares, that is, the children of the devil, *ver.* 30. 39.) *As therefore the tares are gathered and burned in the fire, so shall it be in the end of this world. The son of man shall send forth his angels, and they shall gather out of his kingdom, all things that offend, and them that do iniquitie, and shall cast them into a furnace of fire, there shall be wailing* 10 *and gnashing of teeth, ver.* 40, 41, 42, 43. Look to it professors.

Tenthly, the parable of the ten virgins also, suiteth our purpose; them ten are called *the kingdom of heaven, Matt.* 25. 1. that is, the Church of Christ, the visible rightly-constituted Church of Christ, for they went all out of the world, had all lamps and all went forth to meet 15 the bridegroom, yet behold what an overthrow the one half of them met with at the gate of heaven, they were shut out, bid to depart, and Christ told them he did not know them. *ver.* 10. 11. Tremble professors, pray professors.

Eleventhly, the parable of the *net that was cast into the sea, Matt.* 13. 20 41, 42. that also countenanceth this truth: the substance of that parable is to shew, that souls may be gathered by the Gospel, there compared to a net, may be kept in that net, drawn to shore, to the worlds end by that net; and yet may then prove bad fishes, and be cast away: the parable runs thus, *The kingdome of heaven* (the Gospel) *is like unto a net,* 25 *which was cast into the sea* (the world) *and gathered of every kind* (good and bad) *which when it was full, they drew it to shore* (to the end of the world) *and sat down* (in judgment) *and gathered the good into vessels, and cast the bad away*: some bad fishes, nay I doubt a great many will be found in the net of the Gospel, at the day of Judgment; watch and be 30 sober, professors.

Twelfthly, *and many shall come from the east, and from the west, and shall sit down with* Abraham, *and* Isaac, *and* Jacob, *in the kingdome of heaven, and the children of the kingdom shall be cast out. Matt.* 8. 12. The children of the kingdom whose priviledges were said to be these, *to* 35 *whom pertained the Adoption, and the glory, and the covenants, and the*

23 drawn] drown

giving of the law, and the service of God, and the promise. Rom. 9. 4. I take liberty to harp the more upon the first Church, because that that happened to them, hapned as tipes and examples, intimating there is ground to think, that things of as dreadful a nature are to happen
5 among the Church of the gentiles, 1. *Cor.* 10. 11, 12. neither indeed have the gentile-Churches security from God, that there shall not as dreadful things happen to them. And concerning this very thing sufficient caution is given to us also. 1. *Cor.* 6. 9, 10. *Gal.* 5. 19, 20, 21. *Ephes.* 5. 3, 4, 5, 6. *Phil.* 3. 10. 19. 2. *Thes.* 2. 11, 12. 2 *Tim.* 2. 20, 21.
10 *Heb.* 6. 4, 5, 6, 7, 8, *chap.* 10. 26, 27, 28. 2 *Pet.* 2. *chap.* 3. 1 *Joh.* 5. 10. *Revel.* 2. 20, 21, 22.

Thirteenthly, the parable of the *true vine and its branches*, confirm what I have said. *Joh.* 15. 1, 2, 3, 4, 5. By the vine there, I understand Christ, Christ as head; by the branches I understand his Church, some
15 of these branches proved fruitless cast-aways, were in time cast out of the Church, were gathered by men and burned.

Fourteenthly, and Lastly, I will come to particular instances.

1. The twelve had a devil among them. *Joh.* 6. 70.

2. *Ananias* and *Saphira* were in the Church of *Jerusalem. Acts.* 5.

20 3. *Simon Magus* was among them at *Samaria. Acts.* 8.

4. Among the Church of *Corinth* were them that had not the knowledg of God. 1. *Cor.* 15.

5. *Paul* tells the *Galatians*, false brethren crept in unawares, and so does the Apostle *Jude*, and yet they were as quick-sighted to see as any
25 now adays. *Gala.* 2. *Jude.* 3. 4.

6. The Church in *Sardis* had but a few names in her to whom the kingdom of heaven belonged, *Thou hast a few names even in* Sardis *which have not defiled their garments, and they shall walk with me in white, for they are worthy.*

30 7. As for the Church of the *Laodiceans*, it is called a wretched, and miserable, and poor, and blind, and naked. *Rev.* 3. So that put all things together, and I may boldly say as I also have said already, *That among the multitude of them that shall be damned, professors will make a considerable party*; or to speak in the words of the observation, *when men*
35 *have put in all the claim they can for heaven, but few will have it for their inheritance.*

10 *Heb.*] 2 *Heb.*

I will now shew you some reasons of the point, besides those five that I shewed you before.

But first, I will shew you why the poor carnall ignorant world miss of heaven, and then why the knowing professors miss of it also.

First, the poor carnal ignorant world miss of heaven, even because they love their sins, and cannot part with them; *men love darkness rather then light because their deeds be evil, Joh.* 3. the poor ignorant world miss of heaven, because they are enemies in their minds to God, his word and holyness: *They all must be damned who take pleasure in unrighteousness.* 2. *Thes.* 2. 10, 11, 12. The poor ignorant world miss of heaven because they stop their ears against convictions, and refuse to come when God calls, *because I have called and ye refused, I have stretched out my hand, and no man regarded, but have set at nought all my counsels, and would none of my reproofs; I also will laugh at your calamities, and mock when your fear cometh as desolation, and your destruction like a whirlwinde, when distress and anguish cometh upon you; then shall you call upon me, but I will not answer, they shall seek me early but shall not finde me. Pro.* 1. 24, 25, 26, 27, 28.

Secondly, the poor ignorant world miss of heaven because the God of this world hath blinded their eyes, that they can neither see the evil, and damnable state they are in at present, nor the way to get out of it, neither do they see the beauty of Jesus Christ, nor how willing he is to save poor sinners. 2. *Cor.* 4. 2, 3.

Thirdly, the poor ignorant world miss of heaven, because they putt off and defer coming to Christ, until the time of Gods patience and grace is over: some indeed are resolved never to come, but some again say, we will come hereafter, and so it comes to pass, that *because God called and they did not hear, so they shall cry and I will not hear, saith the Lord. Zech.* 7. 11, 12, 13.

Fourthly, the poor ignorant world miss of heaven, because they have false apprehensions of Gods mercy, *they say in their hearts, we shall have peace, though we walk in the imagination of our heart, to add drunkenness to thirst:* but what saith the word, *the Lord will not spare him, but then the anger of the Lord and his jealousie shall smoak against that man, and all the curses that are written in this book shall be upon him, and God shall blot out his name from under heaven. Deut.* 29. 19, 20, 21.

33 but what] *but what*

Fifthly, the poor ignorant world miss of heaven, because they make light of the Gospel that offereth mercy to them freely, and because they lean upon their own good meanings and thinkings and doings. *Matt.* 22. 1, 2, 3, 4, 5. *Rom.* 9. 30, 31.

5 Sixthly, The poor carnal world miss of heaven, because by unbelief, which reigns in them, they are kept for ever from being cloathed with Christs righteousness, and from washing in his blood, without which there is neither remission of sin, nor justification.

But to pass these till anon.

10 I come in the next place to shew you some reasons why the professor falls short of heaven.

First, In the general, they rest in things below special grace, as in awakenings that are not special, in repentance that is not special, in faith that is not special, *&c.* and a little to run the parallel betwixt the 15 one and the other, that if God will, you may see and escape.

1. Have they that shall be saved awakenings about their state by nature, so have they that shall be damned: they that never go to heaven may see much of sin and of the wrath of God due thereto: this had *Cain,* and *Judas,* and yet they came short of the kingdom. *Gen.* 4. *Matt.* 20 27. 4. The saved have convictions in order to their eternal life, but the others convictions are not so: the convictions of the one doth drive them sincerely to Christ, the convictions of the other doth drive them to the law, and the law to desperation at last.

2. There are also convictions that shew a man his necessity of 25 Christ, but wanting grace to lay hold effectually on Christ, they joyn the law also with the Savior, and so perish, or through despair of obtaining the power of grace, they rest in the notions and profession of grace, and so perish.

3. There is a repentance that will not save, a repentance to be 30 repented of, and a repentance to salvation, not to be repented of, 2. *Cor.* 7. 10. yet so great a similitude, and likeness there is betwixt the one and the other, that most times the wrong is taken for the right, and through this mistake professors perish.

As 1. In saving repentance there will be an acknowledgement of sin; 35 and one that hath the other repentance may acknowledg his sins also. *Matt.* 27. 4.

2. In saving repentance there is a crying out under sin, but one that hath the other repentance may cry out under sin also. *Gen.* 4. 13.

3. In saving repentance there will be humiliation for sin, and one that hath the other repentance may humble himself also. 1. *King.* 21. 29.

4. Saving repentance is attended with self-loathing, but he that hath the other repentance may have loathing of sin too. 2. *Pet.* 2. 22. A loathing of sin, *because* it is sin, that he cannot have, but a loathing of sin because it is offensive to him, that he may have: the dog doth not loath that which troubleth his stomach because it is there, but because it troubleth him; when it has done troubling of him, he can turn to it again, and lick it up as before it troubled him.

5. Saving repentance is atended with prayers and tears, but he that hath none but the other repentance, may have prayers and tears also. *Gen.* 27. 34, 35. *Heb.* 12. 14, 15, 16.

6 In saving repentance there is fear and reverence of the word, and Ministers, that bring it; but this may be also where there is none but the repentance that is not saving: *for* Herod *feared* John, *knowing that he was a just man, and holy, and observed him; when he heard him, he did many things, and heard him gladly. Mark.* 6. 20.

7. Saving repentance makes a mans heart very tender of doing any thing against the word of God: But *Balaam* could say, *If* Balak *would give me his house full of silver and gold, I cannot go beyond the word of the Lord. Numb.* 24. 13. Behold, then how far a man may go in repentance, and yet be short of that which is called *repentance unto salvation not to be repented of.*

1. He may be awakened. 2. he may acknowledge his sin. 3. he may cry out under the burden of sin. 4. he may have humility for it. 5. he may loath it. 6. may have prayers and tears against it. 7. may delight to do many things of God. 8. may be afraid of sinning against him, and after all this may perish for want of saving repentance.

Secondly, Have they that *shall* be saved, *faith*; why they that *shall not* be saved, *may have faith also.* Yea a faith in many things, *so like* the faith that *saveth*, that they can *hardly* be distinguished (though they differ, both in root and branch:) to come to particulars.

1. Saving faith hath Christ for its object, and so may the faith have that is not saving; those very *Jews*, of whom it is said, they believed on

Christ; Christ tells them, and that after their believing: *you are of your father the devil, and the lusts of your father ye will do. Jo.* 8. from *v.* 30. to *v.* 44.

2. Saving faith is wrought by the word of God, and so may the faith
5 be, that is not saving. *Luk.* 3. 13.

3. Saving faith looks for justification without works, and so may a faith do that is not saving. *Jam.* 2. 18.

4. Saving faith will sanctifie and purify the heart and the faith that is not saving may work a man off from the pollutions of the world, as it
10 did *Judas* and *Demas*, and others, see 2. *Pet.* 2.

5. Saving faith will give a man tasts of the world to come, and also joy by them tasts, and so will the faith do that is not saving. *Heb.* 6. 4, 5. *Luk.* 8. 13.

6. Saving faith will help a man, if called thereto, to give his body to
15 be burned for his religion, and so will the faith do too that is not saving. 1 *Cor.* 13. 1, 2, 3, 4.

7. Saving faith will help a man to look for an inheritance in the world to come, and that may the faith do that is not saving: *all those virgins took their lamps, and went forth to meet the bridegroom. Matt.* 25. 1.

20 8. Saving faith will not only make a man look for, but prepare to meet the bridegroom, and so may the faith do that is not saving; *then all these virgins arose and trimmed their lamps. Matt.* 25. 7.

9. Saving faith will make a man look for an interest in the kingdom of heaven with confidence, and the faith that is not saving will even
25 demand entrance of the Lord: *Lord, Lord, open unto us. Matt.* 25. 11.

10. Saving faith will have *good* works follow it *into heaven*, and the faith that is not saving, may have *great* works follow it, *as far as to heaven gates. Lord, have we not prophesied in thy name, and in thy name cast out devils, and in thy name done many wondrous works. Matt.* 7. 22.

30 Now then, if the faith that is not saving, may have Christ for its object, be wrought by the word, look for justification without works, work men off from the pollutions of the world, and give men tasts of, and joy in the things of another world; I say, again, if it will help a man to burn for his Judgment, and to look for an inheritance in another
35 world, yet if it will help a man to prepare for it, claim interest in it, and if it can carry *great* works, *many* great and glorious works as far as

15 too] to

heaven gates, then no marvel if abundance of people take this faith for the saving faith, and so fall short of heaven thereby. Alas friends! there are but few that can produce such for repentance, and such faith, as yet you see, I have proved even reprobates have had in several ages of the Church. But,   5

Thirdly, they that go to heaven are a praying people, but a man may pray that shall not be saved; pray! he may pray, pray dayly, yea, he may ask of God the ordinances of Justice, and may take delight in approaching to God, nay further, such souls may as it were cover the altar of the Lord with tears, with weeping, and crying out. *Isa.* 28. 2.   10 *Mala.* 12. 13.

Fourthly, do Gods people keep holy-fasts, they that are not his people may keep fasts also, may keep fasts often, even twice a week, *The pharisee stood, and prayed thus with himself, God I thank thee, that I am not as other men are, extortioners, unjust, adulterers, or even as this* 15 *publican: I fast twice a week, I give tithes of all that I possess. Luk. 16. 11, 12.* I might enlarge upon things, but I intend but a little book: I do not question but many *Balaamites* will appear before the Judgment-seat to condemnation: men that have had visions of God, and that knew the knowledge of the most high, men that have had the spirit of God come 20 upon them, and that have by that been made other men, yet these shall go to the generations of their fathers, they shall never see light. *Numb.* 24. 2, 4, 16. 1 *Sam.* 10. 6, 10. *Psal.* 49. 19.

I reade of some men, whose *excellency* in religion *mounts up to the heavens, and their head reaches unto the clouds, who yet shall perish for ever* 25 *like their own dung, and he,. that in this world hath seen them, shall say, at the Judgment, where are they? Job.* 20. 5, 6, 7. There will many an one that were gallant professors in this world, be wanting among the saved in the day of Christs coming: yea many whose damnation was never dream't of: which of the twelve ever thought that *Judas* would have 30 proved a devil? nay, when Christ suggested that one among them were naught, they each were more afraid of themselves then of him. *Matt.* 26. 21, 22, 23. Who questioned the salvation of the foolish virgins? The wise ones did not, they gave them the priviledge of communion with themselves. *Matt.* 25. The discerning of the heart, and the 35 infallible proof of the truth of saving-grace, is reserved to the

33-34 virgins? The] virgins, the   35 heart,] heart;

Judgment of Jesus Christ at his coming; the Church and best of saints, sometimes hit, and sometimes miss in their judgments about this matter; and the cause of our missing in our judgment, is; 1. partly because we cannot infallibly, at all times, distinguish grace that saveth,
5 from that which doth but appear to do so. 2. partly also because some men have the art to give right names to wrong things. 3. and partly because we being commanded to receive *him that is weak*, are afraid to exclude the least Christian; by a hid means, hypocrites creep into the Churches, but what saith the Scripture? *I the Lord search the heart, I try*
10 *the reins*: And again, *all the Churches shall know that I am he that searches the reins and hearts, and I will give to every one of you, according to your works. Jer.* 11. 20. *chap.* 17. 10. *Revel.* 2. 23. To this searcher of hearts, is the time of infallible discerning reserved, and then you shall see how far grace that is not saving, hath gone; and also how few will be saved
15 indeed. The Lord awaken poor sinners by my little book.

I come now to make some brief Use and Application of the whole: and my first word shall be to the open profane: poor sinner, thou readest here, that but a few will be saved, that many that expect heaven, will go without heaven; what saist thou to this, poor sinner?
20 Let me say it over again: There are but few to be saved, but very few, let me add, but few professors; but few eminent professors; what saist thou now sinner? *If Judgment begins at the house of God, what will the end of them be that obey not the Gospel of God?* This is *Peters* question, canst thou answer it, sinner? yea, I say again, if judgement must begin at
25 them, will it not make thee think, what shall become of me? and I add, when thou shalt see the stars of heaven to tumble down to hell, canst thou think that such a muck-heap of sin as thou art, shalt be lifted up to heaven? *Peter* asks thee another question, to witt, *If the righteous scarcely be saved, where shall the ungodly, and sinners appear?* 1. *Pet.* 14.
30 18, 19. Canst thou answer this question sinner? stand among the righteous thou maiest not; (*the ungodly shall not stand in the judgment, nor sinners in the congregation of the righteous. Psal.* 1. 5.) stand among the wicked thou then wilt not dare to do; where wilt thou appear sinner? to stand among the hypocrits will avail thee nothing: *the hipocrite shall not*
35 *come before him*, that is, with acceptance, but shall perish. *Job.* 13. 16. Because it concerns thee much, let me over with it again: when thou

8 Christian; by a hid means,] Christian, by a hid means;

shalt see lesse sinners then thou art bound up by angels in bundles to burn them, where wilt thou appear sinner? Thou maist wish thy self another man, but that will not help thee sinner; thou maist wish, *would I had been converted in time,* but that will not help thee neither; and if like the wife of *Jeroboam, thou shouldest fain thy self to be another woman,* 5 the prophet, the Lord Jesus would soon finde thee out; what wilt thou do poor sinner: heavy tidings, heavy tidings will attend thee, except thou repent, poor sinner! 1. *King.* 14. 2, 5, 6, *Luk.* 13. 3, 5. O the dreadful state of a poor sinner, of an open profane sinner: every body that hath but common sense knows that this man is in the broad way to 10 death, yet he laughs at his own damnation.

Shall I come to particulars with thee?

1. *Poor unclean sinner,* the harlots house is *the way to hell, going down to the chambers of death. Pro.* 2. 18. *chap.* 5. 5. *chap.* 7.27.

2. *Poor swearing, and theivish sinner,* God hath prepared the curse, 15 *that every one that stealeth shall be cut off, as on this side, according to it, and every one that sweareth, shall be cut off on that side, according to it. Zech.* 5. 3.

3. *Poor drunken sinner,* what shall I say to thee? *Wo to the drunkards of* Ephreim; *wo to them that are mighty to drink wine, and men of strong drink; they shall not* inherit the kingdom of heaven. *Isa.* 28. *chap.* 5. 11, 20 12. 1. *Cor.* 6. 9, 10.

4. *Poor covetous worldly man,* Gods word saies, that *the covetous the Lord abhorreth; that the covetous man is an idolater, and that the covetous shall not inherit the kingdom of God. Psal.* 10. 3. *Ephes.* 5. 5. *Joh.* 2. 15. 1. *Cor.* 6. 9, 10. 25

5. And thou lyar, what wilt thou do? *All lyars shall have their part in the lake that burneth with fire and brimstone. Revel.* 21. 8, 27.

I shall not inlarge, poor sinner, let no man deceive thee, *for because of these things cometh the wrath of God upon the children of disobedience. Ephes.* 5. 6. I will therefore give thee a short call and so leave thee. 30

Sinner awake, yea, I say unto thee awake: sin lieth at thy door, and Gods axe lieth at thy root, and hellfire is right underneath thee: I say again, awake. *Every tree therefore that bringeth not forth good fruit, is hewn down, and cast into the fire. Gen.* 4. 7. *Matt.* 3. 10.

Poor sinner awake, *eternity* is coming, & his son,. they are both 35 coming to judge the world, awake; art yet asleep? poor sinner! let me

18 thee?]thee   19 wo to them] wo them

set the trumpet to thine ear once again. The heavens will be shortly on a burning flame, the earth and the works thereof shall be burned up, and then wicked men shall go into perdition, dost thou hear this sinner? 2. *Pet.* 3.

5   Hark again, the sweet morsels of sins will then be fled, and gone, and the bitter burning fruits of them only left, what saist thou now sinner? canst thou drink hell fire? will the wrath of God be a pleasant dish to thy tast? this must be thine every days meat and drink in hell, sinner.

10   I will yet propound to thee Gods ponderous question, and then for this time leave thee. *Can thine heart endure, or can thy hands be strong in the day that I shall deal with thee saith the Lord? Ezek.* 22. 14. What saist thou? wilt thou answer this question now? or wilt thou take time to do it? or wilt thou be desperate and venture all? And let me put this text in
15 thine ear to keep it open, and so the Lord have mercy upon thee; *upon the wicked shall the Lord rain snares, fire, and brimstone, and an horrible tempest, this shall be the portion of their cup. Psal.* 11. 6. Repent sinners.

Secondly, my second word is to them that are upon the potters wheel, concerning whom, we know not, as yet, whether their
20 convictions, and awaknings will end in conversion or no; several things I should say to you, both to further your convictions, and to caution you from staying any where below, or short of saving grace.

1. Remember that but few shall be saved, and if God should count thee worthy to be one of that few, what a mercy would that be. *Ephes.* 2.
25 45.

2. Be thankful therefore for convictions, conversion begins at conviction, though all conviction doth not end in conversion. It is a great mercy to be convinced that we are sinners, and that we need a Saviour, count it therefore a mercy, and that thy convictions may end
30 in conversion; do thou.

1. Take heed of stiffling of them: it is the way of poor sinners, to look upon convictions, as things that are hurtful, and therefore they use to shun the awakening ministry, and to check a convincing conscience: such poor sinners, are much like to the wanton boy that
35 stands at the maids elbow to blow out her candle as fast as she lights it at the fire: convinced sinner, God lighteth thy candle, and thou putst it out; God lights it again, and thou puttest it out; (*yea how oft is the candle*

of the wicked put out? Job. 21. 17.) At last God resolveth he will light thy candle no more, and then like the *Egyptians*, you dwell all your days in darkness, and never see light more, but by the light of hell-fire; wherefore *give glory to God*, and if he awakens thy conscience, quench not thy convictions, do it, saith the prophet, *before he cause darkness, and* 5 *before your feet stumble upon the dark mountains*; and he turn your convictions into the shadow of death, and make them gross darkness. *Ier.* 13. 16.

2. Be willing to see the worst of thy condition, 'tis better to see it here, then in hell: for thou maiest see thy misery here or there. 10

3. Beware of little sins, they will make way for great ones, and they again will make way for bigger, upon which Gods wrath will follow, and then may thy latter end be worse then thy beginning. 2. *Pet.* 2.

4. Take heed of bad company, and evil communications, for that will corrupt good manners: God saith, *evil company will turn thee away from* 15 *following him, and will tempt thee to serve other Gods*, devils: so the anger of the Lord, will be kindled against thee, and destroy thee suddenly. *Deut.* 7. 23.

5. Beware of such a thought as bids thee delay repentance, for that is damnable. *Pro.* 1. 24. *Zec.* 7. 12, 13. 20

6. Beware of taking example by some poor carnal professor, whose religion lies in the tip of his tongue. Beware I say of the man whose head swims with notions, but his life is among the unclean. *Job.* 36. 14. *He that walketh with wise men shall be wise, but a companion of fools shall be destroyed. Pro.* 13. 20. 25

7. Give thy self much to the word, and prayer, and good conference.

8. Labour to see the sin that cleaveth to the best of thy performances and know that all is nothing if thou beest not found in Jesus Christ.

9. Keep in remembrance that Gods eye is upon thy heart, and upon all thy wayes: *can any hide himself in secret places that I should not see him* 30 *saith the Lord? do not I fill heaven and earth, saith the Lord? Jer.* 23. 24.

10. Be often meditating upon death, and judgment. *Eccle.* 11. 9. *chap.* 12. 14.

11. Be often thinking what a dreadful end, sinners, that have

6 stumble] tumble

9 The sections 2 to 12 have been renumbered. The 1676 text numbers section 2 as 1, with subsequent misnumbering.

13 2 *Pet.* 2.] 2 *Pet.* 20   23 *Deut.* 7. 23.] *Deut.* 7. 3.

neglected Christ, will make at that day of death, and judgment. *Heb.*
10. 31.

12. Put thy self often, in thy thoughts, before Christs judgment-seat,
in thy sins, and consider with thy self, were I now before my judge,
how should I look, how should I shake and tremble.

13. Be often thinking of them that are now in hell past all mercy, I
say, be often thinking of them, thus,

1. They were *once* in the world, as I now am.

2. They once took delight in sin, as I have done.

3. They once neglected repentance as Satan would have me do.

4. But now they are gone, now they are in hell, now the pit hath shut
her mouth upon them.

Thou mayest also doubt thy thoughts of the damned, thus,

1. If these poor creatures were in the world again, would they sin as
they did before? would they neglect salvation as they did before?

2. If they had sermons, *as I have*; if they had the bible, *as I have*; if
they had good company, *as I have*; yea if they had a day of grace, *as I
have*; would they neglect it as they did before? sinner, couldest thou
soberly think of these things they might help (God blessing them) to
awaken thee, and to keep thee awake to repentance, to the repentance
that is to salvation never to be repented of.

Object. But you have said, few shall be saved, and some that go a
great way, yet are not saved; at this therefore, I am even discouraged,
and awakned: I think I had as good go no further, I am indeed under
conviction, but I may perish, & if I go on in my sins I can but perish,
and 'tis ten, twenty, a hundred to one, if I be saved should I be never so
earnest for heaven.

Answ. That few will be saved must needs be a truth, for Christ hath
said it; that many go far, and come short of heaven, is as true, being
testified by the same hand: but what then? why then I had as good
never seek: who told thee so? must no body seek, because few are
saved, this is just contrary to the text, that bids us, *therefore* strive: *strive
to enter in, because the gate is strait, and because many will seek to enter in,
and shall not be able.* But why go back again, seeing that is the next way
to hell, never go over hedge and ditch to hell, if I must needs go
thither, I will go the fardest way about; but who can tell though there
should not be saved so many as there shall, but thou mayst be one of

that few. They that miss of life perish because they will not let go their sins, or because they take up in profession short of the saving faith of the Gospel: They perish I say, because they are content with such things as will not prove graces of a saving nature, when they come to be tryed in the fire, otherwise the promise is free and full, and everlasting. *Him that cometh to me*, says Christ, *I will in no wise cast out: for God so loved the world, that he gave his only begotten son, that whosoever believeth in him might not perish but have everlasting life. Ioh. 6. 37.* Wherefore let not this thought, *few shall be saved*, weaken thy heart, but let it cause thee to mend thy pace, to mend thy crys, to look well to thy grounds for heaven; let it make thee fly faster from sin, to Christ, let it keep thee awake and out of carnal security, and thou maist be saved.

Thirdly, my third word is to professors, sirs, give me leave to set my trumpet to *your* ears again a little, *when every man hath put in all the claim they can for heaven, but few will have it for their inheritance.* I mean but few professors, for so the text intendeth, and so I have also proved, *for many, I say unto you, will seek to enter in, and shall not be able.*

Let me therefore a little expostulate the matter with you, O ye thousands of professors.

First, I begin with you whose religion lieth only in your tongues, I mean you who are little or nothing known from the rest of the rabble of the world, only you can talk better than they: hear me a word or two. *If I speak with the tongue of men and angels, and have not charity*, that is, love to God, and Christ, and saints, and holyness, *I am nothing*, no child of God; and so have nothing to do with heaven. *1. Cor. 13.* A prating tongue will not unlock the gates of heaven, nor blinde the eyes of thy judge; look to it: *the wise in heart will receive commandments but a prating fool shall fall. Pro. 10. 8.*

Secondly, covetous professor, thou that mak'st a gain of religion, that usest thy profession to bring grist to thy mill; look to it also, gain is not godlyness; *Iudas's* religion lay much in the bag, but his soul is now burning in hell; all covetousness is Idolatry, but what is *that* or what will you *call it*, when men are religious for filthy lucre sake. *Ezek. 33. 31.*

Thirdly, wanton professors I have a word for you; I mean, you that can tell how to misplead Scripture, to maintain your pride, your banqueting, and abominable idolatry: reade what *Peter* says, you are

4 when they] then they

the snare and damnation of others; *you allure through the lust of the flesh, through much wantonness, those that were clean escaped from them who live in errour. 2. Pet. 2. 18.* Besides the holy Ghost hath a great deal against you, for your feastings, and eating without fear, not for health, 5 but gluttony. *Jud. 12.* Further *Peter* saies, that you that count it pleasure to riot in the day time, *are spots and blemishes, sporting your selves with your own deceivings. 2. Pet. 2. 13.* And let me ask, did God give his word to justifie your wickedness, or doth grace teach you to plead for the flesh, or the making provision for the lusts thereof; of 10 these, also are they that feed their bodyes to strengthen their lusts under pretence of strengthning frail nature. But pray remember the text, *many, I say unto you, will seek to enter in, and shall not be able.*

Fourthly, I come next to the *opinionist*, I mean to him whose religion lieth in some circumstantials of religion; with this sort this kingdom 15 swarms at this day; these think all out of the way that are not of their mode, when themselves may be out of the way in the midest of their zeal for their opinions, pray do you also observe the text, *many, I say unto you, will seek to enter in, & shall not be able.*

Fifthly, neither is the *formalist* exempted from this number: he is a 20 man that hath *lost all* but the *shell* of religion, he is hot indeed for his form, and no marvel, for that is his *all* to contend for, but his form being without the power and spirit of godlyness, it will leave him in his sins; nay, he standeth now in them, in the sight of God, 2. *Tim.* 3. 5. *and is one of the many that will seek to enter in, and shall not be able.*

25 Sixthly, The *legalist* comes next, even him that hath no life but what he makes out of duties, this man, hath chosen to stand and fall by *Moses* who is the condemner of the world, *there is one that accuseth you, even* Moses *in whom ye trust. Joh.* 5. 45.

Seventhly, There is in the next place the *libertine*, he that pretendeth 30 to be against forms, and duties, as things that gender to bondage, neglecting the order of God: this man pretends to pray always, but under that pretence, prays not at all; he pretends to keep every day a sabbath, but this pretence serves him only to cast off all set times for the worship of God. *This is also one of the many that will seek to enter in and* 35 *shall not be able. Tit.* 1. 16.

Eightly, There is the *temporizing Latitudinarian*, he is a man that hath no God but his belly, nor any religion but that by which his belly is worshiped, his religion is always like the times, turning this way and that way, like the cock on the steeple, neither hath he any conscience but a benumned or seared one, and is next door to a down right athiest, *and also is one of the many that will seek to enter in, and shall not be able.*

Ninthly, There is also the *wilfully ignorant* professor, or him that is afraid to know more, for fear of the cross; he is for picking and chusing of truth, and loveth not to hazzard his all for that worthy name by which he would be called: when he is at any time overset by arguments, or awaknings of conscience, he uses to heal all, by, *I was not brought up in this faith*, as if it were unlawful for Christians to know more then hath been taught them at first conversion, there are many Scriptures that lie against this man, *as the mouths of great guns*, and *he is one of the many that will seek to enter in and shall not be able.*

Tenthly, we will add to all these, the professor that would prove himself a Christian by comparing himself with others, instead of comparing himself with the word of God. This man comforts himself because he is as holy as such, and such: he also knows as much as that old professor, and then concludes he shall go to heaven: as if he certainly knew, that those with whom he compareth himself would be undoubtedly saved, but how if he should be mistaken, nay may they not both fall short; but to be sure he is in the wrong that hath made the comparison, 2. *Cor.* 10. 12. and a wrong foundation will not stand in the day of Judgment. This man therefore *is one of the many that will seek to enter in & shall not be able.*

Eleventhly, There is yet another professor; and he is for God and for Baal too, he can be *any* thing, for *any* company: he can throw stones with both hands, his religion alters as fast as his company: he is a frog of *Egypt* and can live *in* the water, and *out* of the water, he can live in religious company and again as well out, *nothing* that is *disorderly* comes a miss to him, he'll *hold* with the *hair*, and *run* with the *hound*, he carries *fire* in *one* hand, and *water* i'th *t'other*, he is a very *any* thing but what he *should* be: *This is also one of the many that will seek to enter in, and shall not be able.*

Twelfthly, There is also that *free-willer* who denies to the holy Ghost

5

10

15

20

25

30

---

4 the] them
34 that *free-willer* . . .] *that* free-willer . . .

the sole work in conversion, and that *Socinian*, who denieth to Christ that he hath made to God satisfaction for sin: and that *Quaker* who takes from Christ the two natures in his person, & I might add as many more: touching whose damnation (they dying as they are) the Scripture
5 is plain: *these will seek to enter in & shall not be able.*

But Fourthly, if it be so, what a strange disapointment, will many professors meet with at the day of Judgment: I speak not now to the open profaner, every body (as I have said) that hath but common understanding between good and evil, knows that they are in the broad
10 way to hell and damnation, and they must needs come thither, nothing can hinder it, but repentance unto salvation, except God should prove a lier to save them, & tis hard ventring of that.

Neither is it amiss, if we take notice of the examples that are briefly mentioned in the Scriptures concerning professors that have miscarried.
15 1. *Judas* perished from among the Apostles. *Acts.* 1. 2. *Demas* as I think perished from among the Evangelists. 2. *Tim.* 4. 10. 3. *Diotrephes* from among the Ministers, or them in office in the Church. 3. *Ioh.* 9. 10. 4. And as for Christian professors, they have fell by heaps, and almost by whole Churches. 2. *Tim.* 1. 15. *Revel.* 3. 14, 15, 16, 17.
20 5. Let us adde to these, that the things mentioned in the Scriptures about these matters, are but brief hints, and *items* of what is afterwards to happen; as the Apostle said; *some mens sins are open before hand, going before unto judgment, and some men they follow after.* 1. *Tim.* 5. 24. So that, fellow-professor, let us fear, lest a promise being left us of entring
25 into this rest, any of us should seem to come short of it: O to come short! nothing kills like it, nothing will burn like it.

I intend not discouragements but awaknings, the Churches have need of awakning and so hath all professors, do not despise me therefore, but hear me over again! what a strange disappointment will
30 many professors meet with at the day of God almighty! a disappointment, I say and that as to several things.

1. They will look to escape hell, & yet fall just into the mouth of hell! what a disappointment will here be.

1-2 . . . that *Socinian* . . . that *Quaker*] . . . *that* Socinian . . . *that* Quaker
3 two] true
19 *Revel.* 3. 14, 15, 16, 17.] *Revel.* 3. 4, 15, 16, 17.   24 again!] again?

2. They will look for heaven but the gate of heaven will be shut against them! what a disappointment is here?

3. They will expect, that Christ should have compassion for them, but will finde that he hath shut up all bowels of compassion from them! what a disappointment is here?

Again, fifthly, As this disappointment will be fearful, so certainly it will be very full of amazement.

1. Will it not amaze them to be unexpectedly excluded from life and salvation?

2. Will it not be amazing to them to see their own madness and folly, while they consider how they have dallyed with their own souls, and took lightly for granted, that they had that grace that would save them but hath left them in damnable state.

3. Will they not also be amazed one at another, while they remember how in their life time, they counted themselves fellow-heirs of life. To allude to that of the prophet: *they shall be amazed one of another, their faces shall be as flames. Isa.* 13. 8.

4. Will it not be amazing to some of the damned *themselves*, to see some come to *hell* that then they shall see come *thither*. To see preachers of the word, professors of the word, practisers in the word, to come thither; what wondring was there among *them* at the fall of the king of *Babilon*, since he thought to have swallowed up all because he was run down by the *Medes* and *Persians, how art thou fallen from heaven Lucifer, son of the morning?* how art thou cut down to the ground that didst weaken the nations? If such a thing as this, will with amazement, surprize the damned, what an amazement will it be to them to see such an one as he, *whose head reached to the clouds*: to see him come down to the pit, and perish for ever like his own dung. *Hell from beneath is moved for thee, to meet thee at thy coming, it stirreth up the dead for thee, even all the chief ones of the earth. Isa.* 14. they that see thee, shall narrowly look upon thee and consider thee, saying, *is this the man?* Is this he that professed and disputed, and forsook us, but now he is come to us again? is this he that separated from us, but how is he fallen with us into the same eternal damnation with us?

Sixthly, yet again, one word more, if I may awaken professors. 1. consider, though the poor carnal world shall certainly perish, yet they

36 world] world,

will want these things to aggravate their sorrow which thou wilt meet with in every thought that thou wilt have of the condition thou wast in when thou wast in the world.

1. They will not have a profession to bite them when they come thither.

2. They will not have the tasts of a lost heaven, to bite them when they come thither.

3. They will not have the thoughts of, *I was almost at heaven*, to bite them when they come thither.

4. They will not have the thoughts of, how they cheated saints, Ministers, Churches, to bite them, when they come thither.

5. They will not have the dying thoughts of false faith, false hope, false repentance, and false holyness to bite them when they come thither. *I was at the gates of heaven, I looked into heaven, I thought I should have entred into heaven! O how will these things sting! they will, if I may call them so, be the sting of the sting of death in hell fire.*

Seventhly, Give me leave now in a word, to give you a little advice.

1. Doest thou love thine own soul, then pray to Jesus Christ for an awakned heart, for an heart so awakned, with all the things of another world, that thou maiest be allured to Jesus Christ.

2. When thou comest there, beg again for more awaknings about sin, hell, grace, and about the righteousness of Christ.

3. Cry also for a spirit of discerning, that thou maist know that which is saving-grace indeed.

4. Above all studies, apply thy self to the study of those things, that shew thee the evil of sin, the shortness of mens life, and which is the way to be saved.

5. Keep company with the most godly among professors.

6. When thou hearest what the nature of true grace is, defer not to ask thine own heart, if this grace be there; and here take heed,

1. That the preacher himself be sound, and of good life.

2. That thou takest not seeming graces for real ones, nor seeming fruits for real fruits.

3. Take heed that *a sin and thy life goes not unrepented of*, for that will make a *flaw* in thine *evidence*, a *wound* in thy *conscience*, and a *breach* in thy *peace*, and an hundred to one if at last, it doth not drive all the grace

in thee into so dark a corner of thy heart, that thou shalt not be able, for a time, by all the torches that are burning in the Gospel to finde it out to thine own comfort and consolation.

FINIS.

THE HEAVENLY FOOT-MAN

The Heavenly
FOOT-MAN:
OR,
A Description
OF
The Man that gets to Heaven.

TOGETHER,

With the Way he Runs in, the Marks he Goes by: Also some Directions, how to Run, so as to Obtain.

Briefly Observed, and Published
By *John Bunyan.*

To which is added,

A Catalogue of all Mr. *Bunyan's* Books, being Sixty, with the Title-Pages at length.

And it came to pass, when they had brought them forth abroad, that they said, escape for thy Life, look not behind thee, neither stay thou in all the plain: Escape to the Mountain, lest thou be Consumed. Gen. 19. 17.

LONDON,
Printed for *Charles Doe,* Comb-maker, in the *Borough Southwark,* near *London-Bridge.* 1698.

Title-page of the 1698 edition of *The Heavenly Foot-man,* from the British Library (pressmark c.59. a. 15)

THE HEAVENLY FOOT-MAN

Note on the Text

No edition of *The Heavenly Foot-man* was published in Bunyan's lifetime, the first edition being printed for Charles Doe in 1698. It was not printed in Doe's Folio of 1692, and at the end of the list of Bunyan's works which he appended to the 1698 edition of *The Heavenly Foot-man*, he wrote, '*The four Books* following [the others being *A Christian Dialogue, A Pocket Concordance* and *An Account of his Imprisonment*] *were never yet Printed, except this now of the* Heavenly Footman, *which I bought in* 1691, *now six years since, of Mr.* John Bunyan, *the Eldest Son of our Author; and I have now put it into the World in Print, Word for word, as it came from him to me.*'

The date of composition of the treatise is a matter for conjecture, but a reasonable suggestion may be based on those lines in *The Author's Apology for his Book* prefaced to the First Part of *The Pilgrim's Progress* in 1678:

> When at the first I took my Pen in hand,
> Thus for to write; I did not understand
> That I at all should make a little Book,
> In such a mode . . .
> . . . I writing of the Way
> And Race of Saints, in this our Gospel-Day,
> Fell suddenly into an Allegory
> About their Journey and the way to Glory.

Brown concluded that the book Bunyan was at work on when the first notions of *The Pilgrim's Progress* entered his imagination was *The Strait Gate* of 1676, adding, 'No other work published during his long imprisonment, or for years after, at all meets the requirements of the case.' (p. 262) In fact, *The Strait Gate* meets very few of the requirements of the case. It is not about the race of saints along the way to heaven, nor of the dangers and encouragements of the pilgrim, but rather a discussion of the qualifications needed to enter the gate at the end of the journey. There are, admittedly, some similarities to *The Pilgrim's Progress*. The entrance to heaven is called 'some little pinching wicket' (above, p. 76, l. 24) and in its concluding pages we meet the 'man that hath *lost all* but the *shell* of religion' (p. 125, l. 20) who reminds us of Formalist; and the man who 'can be anything for any company; he can throw stones with both hands; his religion alters as fast as his company; he is a frog of Egypt, and can live in the water and out of the water . . .' is the same weak professor as By-Ends. But these are only incidental reminders. *The Heavenly Footman* seems much more likely to be the book Bunyan refers to, for it is truly about 'the Way and Race of Saints', an allegory developing from St. Paul's image of the race for a prize to that of a long journey to a goal through dangerous and difficult lands. If we accept this, then the date of composition of *The Heavenly Foot-man* is pre-1678 and, depending on the date accepted for the actual writing on *The Pilgrim's Progress*, possibly pre-1672. Other pieces of internal evidence support this early date. Bunyan speaks of 'that little time which I have been a professor' (below p. 152, l. 16) and the books he refers to—*A Few Sighs from Hell* (p. 178, l. 6) and *The Doctrine of the Law and Grace Unfolded* (p. 153, l. 7)—are his earlier books. All this suggests a date of *c.* 1671 for the composition of the treatise, or even earlier, according as to how short 'that little time' since Bunyan's conversion in 1660 had been, and, despite its late publication, brings it nearer in time to *The Strait Gate* and *The Barren Fig-tree*.

THE FIRST EDITION, 1698

Title-page: **The Heavenly** | FOOT-MAN: | OR, | A Description | OF | *The Man that gets to Heaven.* | TOGETHER, | With the Way he Runs in, the | Marks he Goes by: Also some | Directions, how to Run, so as | to Obtain. | [rule] | Briefly Observed, and Published | By *John Bunyan.* | [rule] | *To which is added,* | A Catalogue of all Mr. *Bunyan's* Books, being | Sixty, with the Title-Pages at length. | [rule] | *And it came to pass, when they had brought | them forth abroad, that they said, escape for thy | Life, look not behind thee, neither stay thou in all | the plain: Escape to the Mountain, lest thou be | Consumed.* Gen. 19. 17. | [rule] | *LONDON,* | Printed for *Charles Doe,* Comb-maker, in the | *Borough Southwark,* near *London-Bridge.* 1698. |

Collation: 8°: A–F⁸, G⁴ [$4–A1, G3, G4]. Pages: [i–xvi] 72 + 16 = 104. Pages 1–72 correctly numbered, last 16 pages unnumbered.

Contents: A1ʳ title page, A1ᵛ blank. A2ʳ AN | EPISTLE, | To all the Slothful, and | Careless People. | —A6ᵛ Farewel | I wish our Souls may | meet with Comfort, | at the Journeys end. | J.B. | catch-word THE. A7ʳ THE | CONTENTS, | Of the whole of this Book. | —A8ᵛ [rule] These be the Contents of this little Book; | If thou wilt see farther, then thorow it look. B1ʳ [double rule] THE | *Heavenly Foot-Man*: | OR, | A Description of the Man that | gets to Heaven, *Ec.* | —F4ᵛ text, Farewel. | ERRATA. | *Some litteral Faults, I question not but you will | easily pass by without error, and for the rest, I | here direct you to mend them.* [5 lines of errata.] F5ʳ [Advertisement] Mr. *Bunyan's* Books. | Running Reader! | I *That now help you to this* Heavenly Foot-Man | *in Print* [12 lines] | *Charles Doe.* | *This Catalogue, is word for word, as it is in | the several Title-Pages, except the Texts.* [list of 60 titles] —G2ᵛ. G3ʳ Some Account of Mr. *Bunyan,* | —G4ᵛ *Your Christian Brother,* Charles Doe.

Running titles: Running title of 'An Epistle, To all the Slothful, and Careless People.' The Epistle. Running title of 'The Contents', The Contents. Running title to the text *The Heavenly Foot-man; or,* | *The Man that gets to Heaven.* Pages 5 and 21 *The Man that gets to Haveen.* Pages 31, 47, and 59 *The Heavenly Foot-man; or,* instead of *The Man that gets to Heaven.* Pages 2, 6, 11, 18, 22, 27, 31, 34, 38, 43, 47, 50, 54, 58, 63, 66, 71 have u.c. T in *The* from a different fount. Page 73 has headline Mr. *Bunyan's* Books. Pages 74–84 have running titles *A Catalogue of all* | Mr. Bunyan's *Books.* Page 85 has headline *Of Mr. Bunyan, and's Ministry.*

Catchwords: E4 posture, [Posture;] F1 he [he?].

The text is that of the first edition, of which the spelling has been retained, with a few exceptions (which have been noted). Obvious typographical spelling errors have been silently corrected. The original punctuation has for the most part been retained. It has been silently corrected where stops and commas, exclamation and question marks have obviously been confused and dropped about. Where clumsy but possible puctuation has been emended slightly, and where radical repunctuation has been necessary to clarify the sense, this has been noted.

The Biblical references have, where necessary, been corrected, and the incorrect references noted at the foot of the page.

The edition is on the whole carefully printed, but goes most often astray in its use of italic type. Where it is quite obvious that italicization has 'spilled over' into words outside quotations, or where an obvious confusion of roman and italic within a quotation has occurred, these cases have been silently corrected. Where there is any doubt, any emendation appears in the footnotes.

The short list of *Errata* supplied by the Printer of the first edition has been incorporated into the text and such corrections have been noted.

The single occurrence of black letter type, on the title page of the 1698 edition, has been represented by bold type.

AN EPISTLE,

To all the Slothful, and
Careless People.

FRIENDS!
Solomon *saith, that* The desire of the slothful killeth him: Pro. 21. 25.
And if so, what will slothfulness *it self do to those that entertain*
it. The Proverb is, He that sleepeth in Harvest, is a Son that Pro. 10. 5.
causeth shame: *And this I dare be bold to say, no greater shame can befal a*
Man, than to see that he hath fool'd away his Soul, and sinned away eternal
Life. And I am sure this is the next way to do it; namely to be slothful,
slothful I say, in the work of Salvation. The Vinyard of the slothful Man, in
reference to the things of this Life, is not fuller of Briars, Nettles, and stinking
Weeds, than he that is slothful *for Heaven, hath his Heart full of heart-*
choaking, and Soul-damning Sin.
Slothfulness *hath these two Evils, first, to neglect the time in which it*
should be getting of Heaven; and by that means, doth in the second place bring
in untimely Repentance. I will warrant you, that he who shall lose his Soul in
this World through slothfulness, *will have no cause to be glad thereat, when*
he comes to Hell.
Slothfulness, *is usually accompanied with carelesness, and carelesness is*
for the most part begotten by senslesness; and senslesness doth again put fresh
strength into slothfulness: *And by this means the Soul is left remediless.*
Slothfulness *shutteth out Christ.* Slothfulness *shameth the Soul.* Cant. 5. 2,
Slothfulness, *it is condemned even by the feeblest of all the Creatures.* Go 3, 4.
to the Ant, thou sluggard, consider her ways, and be wise. The sluggard Pro. 13. 4.
will not plow, by reason of the cold; (*that is, he will not break up the* Pro. 6. 6.
Fallow Ground of his Heart, because there must be some pains taken by him Pro. 20. 4.
that will do it,) therefore he shall beg in Harvest, (*that is, when the Saints*
of God shall have their glorious Heaven and Happiness given to them;) *but*
the Sluggard *shall* have nothing, *that is, be never the better for his crying for*
Mercy, according to that in Mat. 25. 10, 11, 12.

If you would know a Sluggard *in the things of Heaven, compare him with one that is* slothful *in the things of this World. As*

I. *He that is* slothful, *is loth to set about the Work he should follow: So is he that is* slothful *for Heaven.*

II. *He that is* slothful, *is one that is willing to make delays: So is he that is* slothful *for Heaven.*

III. *He that is a* Sluggard, *any small matter that cometh in between, he will make it a sufficient* excuse *to keep him off from plying his Work: So it is also with him that is* slothful *for Heaven.*

IV. *He that is* slothful *doth his Work by the* halves: *And so it is with him that is* slothful *for Heaven. He may* almost, *but he shall never* altogether *obtain perfection of deliverance from Hell; he may* almost, *but he shall never (without he mend) be* altogether *a Saint.*

V. *They that are* slothful, *do usually* lose *the season in which things are to be done: And thus it is also with them that are* slothful *for Heaven, they* miss *the season of Grace. And therefore,*

VI. *They that are* slothful, *have* seldom, *or never good Fruit: So also it will be with the Soul-sluggard.*

VII. *They that are* slothful, *they are* chid *for the same: So also will Christ deal with those that are not active for him.* Thou wicked, *or slothful,* servant out of thine own mouth will I judge thee, thou said'st I was thus, *and thus*; wherefore then gavest not thou my money to the bank, *&c.* Take the unprofitable servant, and cast him into outer darkness, where shall be weeping and gnashing of teeth.

I. *What shall I say,* time *runs, and will you be* slothful?

II. *Much of your Lives are* past, *and will you be* slothful?

III. *Your Souls are* worth *a thousand Worlds: and will you be* slothful?

IV. *The day of* Death *and Judgement is at the Door, and will you be* slothful?

V. *The* Curse *of God hangs over your Heads: And will you be* slothful?

VI. *Besides, the* Devils *are earnest, laborious, and seek by all means every day, by every Sin, to keep you out of Heaven, and hinder you of Salvation: And will you be* slothful?

VII. *Also your* Neighbours *are diligent for things that will perish: And will you be slothful for things that will endure for ever?*

VIII. *Would you be* willing *to be Damned for* slothfulness?

Luk. 19. 22, 23.

Mat. 25. 30.

5

10

15

20

25

30

35

23 marg. Mat. 25. 30] Mat. 25. 26, 30

IX. *Would you be willing the* Angels *of God should neglect to fetch your Souls away to* Heaven, *when you lye a* Dying, *and the* Devils *stand by, ready to scramble for them?*

X. Was Christ *slothful in the work of your Redemption?*

5 XI. *Are his* Ministers *slothful in tendering this unto you?*

XII. *And Lastly, if* all this *will not move, I tell you,* God *will not be slothful or neglegent to damn you;* (whose damnation now of a long time slumbereth not;) *nor the* Devils *will not neglect to fetch thee, nor* Hell *neglect to shut its mouth upon thee.*

10 Sluggard, *Art thou* Asleep still, *art thou resolved to sleep the sleep of Death? will neither tidings from* Heaven *or* Hell *awake thee? wilt thou say* Prov. 6. 10. *still,* Yet a little sleep, a little slumber, and a little folding of the arms to sleep? *Wilt thou yet turn thy self in thy sloth, as* the door is turned upon the hinges? *O that I was one that was skilfull in lamentation, and had but a* 15 *yearning heart towards thee! how would I pity thee! how would I bemoan thee! O that I could with* Jeremiah, *let* my Eyes run down with Rivers of Water for thee! *poor Soul, lost Soul, dying Soul, what a hard Heart have I, that I cannot mourn for thee: if thou shouldest lose but a Limb, a Child, or a Friend, it would not be so much, but poor Man 'tis thy Soul; If it was to ly in* 20 Hell *but for a day, but for a year, nay ten thousand years, it would (in comparison) be nothing: But Oh! it is for ever, O this cutting ever, what a Soul-mazing word will that be, which saith,* Depart from me ye Cursed into EVERLASTING Fire? &c.

Object. *But if I should set in, and run as you would have me, then I must* 25 Run from all my Friends, *for none of them are Running that way.*

Answ. *And if thou do'st, thou wilt* Run *into the bosom of* Christ, *and of* God: *and then what harm will that do thee?*

Object. *But if I* Run *this way, then I must* Run *from all my Sins.*

Answ. *That's true indeed; yet if thou doest not, thou wilt* Run *into* Hell 30 Fire.

Object. *But if I* Run *this way, then I shall be* hated, *and lose the love of my Friends and Relations, and of those that I expect benefit from, or have reliance on, and I shall be* mocked *of all my Neighbours.*

Answ. *And if thou doest not, thou art sure to* lose *the love and favour of* 35 God *and* Christ, *the benefit of heaven and glory, and be mocked of God for thy folly,* (I will laugh at your calamities, and mock when your fear cometh;

8 *thee*] the   11 marg. Prov. 6. 10] Prov. 6. 11

Prov. 1. 26) *and if thou wouldest not be hated and mocked, then take heed*
thou by thy folly doest not procure the displeasure, and mockings of the great
God; for his mocks and hatred will be terrible, because they will fall upon thee
in terrible times; even, when tribulation and anguish taketh hold on thee;
which will be when *Death* and *Judgment* comes, when all the Men in the   5
Earth and all the Angels in Heaven *cannot help thee.*

Object. *But surely I may begin this* time *enough a year or two hence,*
may I not?

Answ. *First hast thou any* lease *of thy life? did ever God tell thee thou*
shalt live half a year, or two months longer? nay, it may be thou mayest not   10
live so long. And therefore,

Secondly, *Wilt thou be so sottish, and unwise, as to* venture *thy Soul*
upon a little uncertain time?

Thirdly, *Doest thou know whether* the day of grace *will last a Week*
longer, or no? for the day of grace is past with some before their life is ended;   15
and if it should be so with thee, wouldest thou not say, O that I had begun to
Run *before* the day of Grace *had been past, and the Gates of Heaven shut*
against me, But,

Fourthly, *If thou shouldest see any of thy Neighbours neglect the making*
sure of either House or Land to themselves, if they had it proffered to them;   20
saying, time enough hereafter, when the time is uncertain: And besides, they
do not know whether ever it will be proffered to them again, or no: I say,
wouldest thou not then call them Fools? And if so, then dost thou think that
thou art a Wise Man to let thy Immortal Soul hang over Hell by a Thread of
uncertain time, which may soon be cut asunder by Death.   25

But to speak plainly, all these are the words of a slothful *Spirit. Arise*
Man, be slothful *no longer, set Foot, and Heart and all into the way of God,*
and Run, *the Crown is at the end of the Race; there also standeth the loving*
forerunner, even Jesus, *who hath prepared Heavenly Provision to make thy*
Soul welcom, and he will give it thee with a willinger Heart than ever thou   30
canst desire it of him. O therefore do not delay the time no longer, but put into
practice the words of the Men of Dan *to their Brethren, after they had seen the*
goodness of the Land of Canaan. *Arise (say they) &c. for we have seen the*
Land, and behold, it is very good, and are ye still, *(or do you forbear*

1 Prov. 1. 26] inserted. No reference.
3 marg. Prov. 1. 27] Prov. 1. 26, 27, 28   9 thee] the

Running,) *Be not* slothful *to go, and to enter to possess the Land*, Judges 18. 9.

Farewel.

I wish our Souls may meet with Comfort, at the Journeys end.

J.B.

5

THE
CONTENTS,

Of the whole of this Book.

17 *Christ,*] Christ   27 Gazing] Garing

7. Not *to be* Daunted *with the Enemies thou art like to meet with, between this and the Kingdom of Heaven.*

8. *To take heed of* Stumbling *at the* Cross.

9. *To cry hard to God for an inlightened Heart, and a willing Mind.*

Motives.

The Motives are Nine.

1. *To consider, there is* no ways *but this, thou must either* win *or* lose: *If thou* win, *thou* winnest all, *if thou* lose, *thou* losest all.

2. *The* Devil *and* Sin *do the best they can to make thee* lose.

3. *If* they *get the better of thee, thou* shall lose.

4. *Now the* Gates *of* Heaven, *and the* Heart *of* Christ, *are both* open *to thee.*

5. *Therefore keep thy* Eye *upon the* Prize.

6. *Think* Much *of them that are gone before. First, how* Really *they got in. Second, how* Safe *they are, now they are there.*

7. *Do but* Set *to the Work, and when thou hast* Run *thy self* down weary, Christ *will* carry *thee in* his Bosom.

8. *Or else, convey* new Strength *to thee.*

9. *Let the very* Industry *of the Devil and wicked Men, (I say, let the Consideration of their diligence to bring their Designs to pass) provoke thee.*

The Uses.

The uses are Nine also.

1. *To* Examin *thy self, whether thou art in the way or no.*

2. *The* Danger *they are in, that grow weary before they come to their Journeys end.*

3. *The* Sad Estate *of them that are* Running *quite back again.*

4. *Their* Wo *also that to this day* Sit still, *and* Run *not at all.*

5. *This* Doctrin *calleth aloud to them that* began *but a while since, to mend their pace.*

6. *That* Old *Professors should not let* Young *Striplings outrun them.*

7. *They behave themselves* basely, *that count they run fast enough, if they keep Company with the* hindmost *and laziest Professors.*

8. *That* Lazy Professors *are apt to keep others besides themselves out of* Heaven.

9. *The Conclusion, or last Use, wherein to* provoke *thee, thou hast the* Heavenly Carriage of Lot *as he went from* Sodom, *and the fearful Doom of his* Wife.

Also, to consider, if thy Soul *be lost, it is thy* own loss, *and thou only wilt feel the smart thereof;*

Together with a short Expostulation.

These be the Contents of this little Book;
If thou wilt see farther, then thorow it look.

THE
Heavenly Foot-Man:
OR,

A Description of the Man that
gets to Heaven, &c.

I. Cor. 9. 24.

So Run, that ye may Obtain.

HEAVEN and Happiness, is that which every one desireth, in so much that wicked *Balaam* could say, *Let me* die the death of the righteous, and let my last end be like his: Yet for all this, there are but very few that do obtain that ever-to-be-desired Glory: In so much that many Eminent Professors drop short of a welcom from God into his pleasant place. The Apostle therefore, because he did desire the Salvation of the Souls of the *Corinthians*, to whom he writes this Epistle, layeth them down in these words such Counsel, which if taken, would be for their help and advantage.

First, Not to be wicked, and sit still, and wish *for Heaven; but to Run for it.*

Secondly, Not to content themselves with every kind of *Running:* But saith he, *SO Run, that you may obtain.* As if he should say, some, because they would not lose their Souls, they begin to *Run* betimes, they *Run* apace, they *Run* with patience, they *Run* the right way: Do you *SO Run.* Some *Run* from both Father, Mother, Friends and Companions, and this that they may have the Crown: Do you *SO Run.* Some *Run* through Temptations, Afflictions, good Report, evil Report, that they may win the Pearl: Do you so *Run. SO Run that you may obtain.*

Numb. 23. 10.

Eccle. 12. Heb. 12.

1 Cor. 9. 25.

2 Cor. 6.

23 marg. Matth. 14. 26 omitted   25 marg. 1. Cor. 9. 25.] 1 Cor. 4. 13.

These words, they are taken from Mens *Running* for a Wager: A very apt Similitude to set before the Eyes of the Saints of the Lord. *Know you not that they which Run in a Race, Run all, but one obtains the Prize? so Run that ye may obtain.* That is, Do not only Run, but be sure you *Win* as well as *Run. SO Run, that you may obtain.*

I shall not need to make any great ado in opening the words at this time, but shall rather lay down one Doctrine that I do find in them, and in prosecuting that, I shall shew you in some measure, the scope of the words.

The Doctrine is this.

They that will have Heaven, they must Run for it; I say, *they that will have Heaven, they must Run for it.* I beseech you to heed it well. *Know you not that they which Run in a Race, Run all, but one obtaineth the Prize, so Run ye.* The Prize is Heaven, and if you will have it, you must *Run* for it. You have another Scripture for this in the 12 of the *Hebrews*, the 1, 2, and 3. Verses. *Wherefore seeing also,* saith the Apostle, *that we are compassed about with so great a Cloud of Witnesses, let us lay aside every weight, and the Sin which doth so easily beset us, and let us Run with Patience the Race that is set before us.* And let us Run, saith he.

Again, saith *Paul, I so run, not as uncertainly, so Fight I,* &c.

But before I go any farther:

First, Flying.

Observe, that this *Running* is not an ordinary, or any sort of Running; but it is to be understood of the swiftest sort of Running: And therefore in the 6 of the *Hebr.* it is called a Flying. *That we might have strong Consolation, who have fled for refuge to lay hold on the hope set before us*; mark, who have *Fled.* It is taken from that 20 of *Joshua,* concerning the Man that was to *Flee* to the City of Refuge when the Avenger of Blood was hard at his Heels, to take Vengeance on him, for the Offence he had committed; therefore it is a *Running* or *Flying* for ones Life. A running with all might and main, as we use to say; so *Run.*

2. *Pressing.*

Secondly, This running in another place, is called a pressing, *I press* Phil. 3. 14. *towards the mark*; which signifieth, that they that will have Heaven, they must not stick at any difficulties they meet with; but press, crowd and 5 thrust thorow all that may stand between Heaven and their Souls. *So run.*

3. *Continuing.*

Thirdly, This *Running* is called in another place a *Continuing* in the Colos. 1. 23. way of Life. *If you continue in the faith grounded, and setled, and be not* 10 *moved away from the hope of the Gospel of Christ.* Not to *Run* a little now and then, by Fits and starts, or halfway, or almost thither; but to *Run* for my Life, to *Run* thorow all difficulties, and to continue therein to the end of the *Race*, which must be to the end of my Life. *So Run, that ye may obtain.* And the Reasons for this Point, are these.

15 *First*, Because all or every one that *Runneth doth not obtain* the Prize; there be many that do *run*, yea and *run* far too, who yet miss of the Crown that standeth at the end of the Race. You know, that all that *Run* in a Race do not obtain the victory, they all *Run*, but one wins: And so it is here, it is not every one that *runneth*, nor every one that seeketh, Luk. 13. 23, 20 nor every one that striveth for the mastery, that hath it. *Though a Man* 24. *do strive for the mastery*, saith Paul, *yet he is not Crowned, unless he strive* 2 Tim. 2. 5. *lawfully*; that is, unless he *so Run* and *so* strive, as to have Gods approbation. What do you think, that every heavy-heel'd Professor will have Heaven? what *every lazy one*? *every wanton and foolish Professor*, that 25 will be stopped by any thing, kept back by any thing, that scarce *Runneth* so fast Heavenward as a Snail creepeth on the ground? nay there are some Professors, do not go on so fast in the way of God, as a Snail doth go on the Wall; and yet these think that Heaven and Happiness is for them; but stay, there are many more that *Run*, than 30 there be that obtain; therefore he that will have Heaven must *Run* for it.

Secondly, Because you know, that though a Man do *Run*, yet if he do not overcome, or win, as well as *Run*, what will they be the better for

8 marg. Colos. 1. 23.] Col. 1. 14.   19 marg. Luk. 13. 23, 24.] Luk. 13.

their running? they will get nothing. You know the Man that runneth, he doth do it that he may win the Prize; but if he doth not obtain, he doth lose his Labour, spend his Pains and Time, and that to no purpose, I say he getteth nothing. And ah how many such *Runners* will there be found at the day of Judgment? even multitudes, multitudes that have *Run*, yea *run so far as to come to Heaven Gates, and not able to get any farther*, but there stand knocking when it is too late; crying Lord, Lord, when they have nothing but rebukes for their pains. *Depart from me*, you come not here, you come too late, you *Run* too lazily, the door is shut. *When once the Master of the House is risen up*, saith Christ, *and hath shut to the Door, and ye begin to stand without and to knock, saying, Lord, Lord, open to us; I will say, I know you not, Depart*, &c. O sad will the Estate of those be, that *Run*, and *Miss*; therefore if you will have Heaven, you must *Run* for it. And *So run, that you may obtain*.

Thirdly, Because the *way is long*, (I speak Metaphorically) and there is many a dirty step, many a high Hill, much Work to do, a wicked Heart, World and Devil to overcome. I say, there are many steps to be taken by those that intend to be Saved, by running or walking in the steps of that Faith of our Father *Abraham*. Out of *Egypt*, thou must go thorow the *Red Sea*; thou must Run a long and tedious Journey, thorow the wast howling Wilderness, before thou come to the Land of Promise.

Fourthly, They that will go to Heaven, they must Run for it; because, as the way is long, so the time in which they are to get to the end of it, is very *uncertain*; the time present is the only time, thou hast no more time alotted thee, than that thou now enjoyest. *Boast not thy self of to morrow, for thou knowest not what a day may bring forth*. Do not say, I have time enough to get to Heaven seven Years hence: For I tell thee the Bell may Toll for thee before seven Days more be ended, and when Death comes, away thou must go, whether thou art provided or not; and therefore look to it, make *no delays*, it is not good dallying with things of so great Concernment, as the Salvation or Damnation of thy Soul. You know he that hath a great way to go in a little time, and less by half than he thinks of, he had need *Run* for it.

Fifthly, They that will have Heaven, they must Run for it; because *the Devil, the Law, Sin, Death and Hell, followeth them*. There is never a poor Soul that is going to Heaven, but the *Devil*, the *Law*, *Sin*, *Death*

Pro. 27. 1.

1 Pet. 5. 8.

and *Hell* makes after that Soul. *The Devil your adversary, as a roaring Lion goeth about, seeking whom he may devour.* And I will assure you the *Devil is nimble*, he can run apace, he is light of Foot, he hath overtaken many, he hath turn'd up their Heels, and hath given them an
5 everlasting fall. Also the *Law*, that *can shoot a great way*, have a care thou keep out of the reach of those great Guns, the Ten Commandments. *Hell* also *hath a wide Mouth*, it can stretch it self farther than you are aware of; and as the Angel said to *Lot, Take heed, look not behind*   Gen. 19. *thee, neither tarry thou in all the plain,* (that is, any where between this
10 and Heaven) *lest thou be consumed.* So say I to thee, take heed, tarry not, lest either the *Devil, Hell, Death,* or the fearful Curses of the *Law* of God, do overtake thee, and throw thee down in the midst of thy Sins, so, as never to rise and recover again. If this were well considered, then thou, as well as I, wouldst say, *They that will have Heaven, must Run for it.*
15   *Sixthly,* They that will go to Heaven, must run for it; because, *perchance the Gates of Heaven may be shut shortly.* Sometimes Sinners have not Heaven Gates open to them, so long as they suppose: And if they be once shut against a Man, they are so heavy, that all the Men in the World, nor all the Angels in Heaven, are not able to open them. *I*   Rev. 3. 7.
20 *shut, and no man can open,* saith Christ. And how if thou shouldst come but one quarter of an Hour too late, I tell thee it will cost thee an Eternity to bewail thy misery in; *Francis Spira* can tell thee what it is to stay till the Gate of Mercy be quite shut; or to run so lazily, that they be shut before thou get within them. What to be shut out! What out of
25 Heaven! Sinner, rather than lose it, *Run for it*; yea, and *So Run that thou mayst obtain.*
   Lastly, Because, *If thou lose, thou losest all; thou losest Soul, God, Christ, Heaven, Ease, Peace, &c.* Besides, thou layst thy self open to all the Shame, Contempt and Reproach, that either God, Christ, Saints,
30 the World, Sin, the Devil and all can lay upon thee. As Christ saith of the foolish Builder, so will I say of thee, if thou be such a one who runs and missest; I say, even all that go by, will begin to mock at thee, saying, *this Man began to Run well, but was not able to finish.* But more of   Luke 14. 28, this anon.   29, 30.
35   *Quest.* But how should a poor Soul do to *run*? For this very thing is

12 throw thee] throw the
33 marg. Luke 14. 28, 29, 30.] Luke 14. 28, 29, 20.

that which afflicteth me sore, (as you say) to think that *I may Run, and yet fall short*. Methinks to fall short at last, O it fears me greatly! Pray tell me *therefore, how I should Run?*

Answ. That thou mightst indeed be satisfied in this particular, consider these following things.

The First Direction.

If thou wouldest so Run as to obtain the Kingdom of Heaven, then *be sure that thou get into the Way* that leadeth thither: For it is a vain thing to think, that ever thou shalt have the Prize, though thou runnest never so fast, unless thou art in the *Way* that leads to it. Set the case that there should be a Man in *London*, that was to run to *York* for a Wager: Now though he run never so swiftly, yet if he run full *South*, he might run himself quickly out of Breath, and be never the nearer the Prize, but rather the farther off. Just so is it here, it is not simply the Runner, nor yet the hasty Runner, that winneth the Crown, unless he be in the *way* that leadeth thereto. I have observed, that little time which I have been a Professor, that there is a great *Running* to and fro, some this way, and some that way: Yet it is to be feared most of them are out of the way, and then though they run as swift as the Eagle can fly, they are benefited nothing at all.

Here is one runs a *Quaking*, another a *Ranting*; one again runs after the *Baptism*, and another after the *Independency*: Here's one for *Free-will*, and another for *Presbytery*, and yet possibly most of all these Sects run quite the wrong way, and yet every one is for his Life, his Soul, either for Heaven or Hell.

If thou now say, which is the way? I tell thee it is CHRIST THE SON OF MARY, THE SON OF GOD. *Jesus saith, I am the Way, the Truth and the Life, no Man cometh to the Father, but by me.* So then thy business is, (if thou wouldest have Salvation) to see *if Christ be thine*, with all his Benefits: Whether *he hath covered thee with his Righteousness*, whether he hath shewed thee that *thy Sins* are *washed away with his Heart-Blood*, whether thou art *planted* into *him*, and whether thou have *Faith* in *him*, so as to make a *Life* out of *him*, and to *Conform* thee to *him*: That is, such Faith, as to conclude, that *thou art Righteous, because*

John. 14. 6.

17 Professor] Prosessor   Corrected in the Errata.

Christ is thy Righteousness, and so constrained to walk with him as the joy of thy Heart; because he saveth thy Soul. And for the Lords sake take heed, and do not deceive thy self, and think thou art in the *way*, upon too slight grounds; for if thou miss of the *way*, thou wilt miss of
5 the Prize, and if thou miss of that, I am sure thou wilt lose thy Soul, even that Soul which is worth more than the whole World.

But I have Treated more largely on this in my Book of *the Two Covenants*; and therefore shall pass it now; only I beseech thee to have a Care of thy Soul, and that thou mayest so do, take this Counsel.
10 *Mistrust* thy own *Strength*, and throw it away, down on thy Knees in *Prayer* to the Lord, for the *Spirit* of Truth, search his Word for direction, fly *Seducers* Company, keep Company with the soundest Christians, that have most Experience of Christ, and be sure thou have a care of *Quakers, Ranters, Free-Willers:* Also do not have too much
15 Company with some *Anabaptists*, though I go under that name my self. I tell thee, this is such a serious matter, and I fear thou wilt so little regard it, that the thoughts of the worth of the thing, and of thy too light regarding of it, doth even make my Heart ake whilst I am a writing to thee. The Lord Teach thee *the way by his Spirit*, and then I am sure
20 thou wilt know it. *So Run.*

Only by the way, let me bid thee have a Care of *two things*, and so I shall pass to the next thing.

First, have a Care of relying on the *outward Obedience* to any of Gods Commands, or thinking thy self ever the better in the sight of God for
25 that.

Secondly, Take heed of fetching Peace for thy Soul from any *Inherent* Righteousness: But if thou canst believe, that *as thou art a Sinner, so thou art justified freely by the Love of God through the Redemption that is in Christ*; and that God for *Christ's* sake hath *forgiven* thee, not because he
30 saw any thing *done*, or to be done in or by thee, to move him thereunto, do it; for that's the *right way*, the Lord put thee into it, and keep thee in it.

The Second Direction.

As thou shouldest get into the way, so thou shouldest also be *much in*
35 *Studying*, and musing *on the way*. You know Men that would be expert

in any thing, they are usually much in studying of that thing, and so likewise is it with those that quickly grow expert in any way: This therefore thou shouldest do. Let thy Study be much exercised about *Christ*, which is the *way*; what he is, what he hath done, and why he is, what he is, and why he hath done what is done; as why *he took upon him* 5

Phil. 2. 7. *the form of a Servant*, why he was *made in the likeness of men*. Why he *Cried*, why he *Died*, why he *bare the Sin of the World*, why he was made

2 Cor. 5. 21. *Sin*, and why he was made Righteousness, why he is in Heaven in the *nature* of Man, and *What* he doth there; be much in musing and considering of these things; be thinking also enough of *those places* 10 *which thou must not come near*, but leave some on this Hand, and some on that Hand, as it is with those that Travel into other Countries, they must leave such a Gate on this Hand, and such a Bush on that Hand, and go by such a place, where standeth such a thing; thus therefore thou must do, *Avoid such things which are expressly forbidden in the Word* 15

Prov. 5 & 7. *of God*. Withdraw thy Foot far from her, *And come not nigh the Door of her house, for her steps take hold of Hell, going down to the Chambers of death*: And so of every thing that is not in the way, have a care of it, that thou go not by it, come not near it, have nothing to do with it, *So Run*.

The Third Direction. 20

Not only thus, but in the next place, thou must *strip thy self* of those things that may hang upon thee to the hindering of thee in the way to the Kingdom of Heaven, as Covetousness, Pride, Lust, or whatever else thy Heart may be inclining unto, which may hinder thee in this Heavenly Race. Men that run for a Wager, if they intend to win as well 25 as run, they do not use to incumber themselves, or carry those things

1 Cor. 9. 25. about them that may be an hinderance to them in their Running. *Every man that striveth for the mastery, is temperate in all things*. That is, he layeth aside every thing that would be any ways a disadvantage to him;

Heb. 12. 1. as saith the Apostle, *Let us lay aside every weight, and the sin that doth so* 30 *easily beset us, and let us run with patience the race that is set before us*. It is but a vain thing to talk of going to Heaven, if thou let thy Heart be incumbered with those things that would hinder. Would you not say that such a Man would be in danger of losing, though he Run, if he fill his Pockets with Stones, hang heavy Garments on his Shoulders, and 35 great lumpish Shoes on his Feet? So it is here, thou talkest of going to Heaven, and yet fillest thy Pocket with Stones (*i.e.*) fill'st thy Heart with this World, let'st that hang on thy Shoulders with its profits and pleasures; alas, alas, thou art widely mistaken: If thou intendest to win, 5 thou must *Strip*, thou must lay aside every weight, thou must be temperate in ALL things. Thou must, *So Run*.

The Fourth Direction.

Beware of by-paths, take heed thou dost *not turn into those Lanes* Isa. 59. 8.
which lead out of the way. There are crooked Paths, Paths in which Men Prov. 3. 17.
Prov. 7. 25.
10 go astray, Paths that lead to Death and Damnation: But take heed of all those. Some of them are *dangerous*, because of *Practice*, some because of *Opinion*, but mind them not; mind the Path before thee, *look right before thee*, turn neither to the right Hand nor to the Left, but let thine Eyes look right on, even right before thee, *Ponder the path of thy feet*, 15 and let all thy ways be established. Turn not to the right Hand, nor to the left: *Remove thy Foot far from evil.* This Counsel being not so Prov. 4. 26, seriously taken as given, is the reason of that starting from Opinion to 27. Opinion, reeling this way and that way, out of this Lane into that Lane, and so missing the way to the Kingdom. Though the way to Heaven be 20 but one, yet there are many crooked Lanes and by-paths shoot down upon it, as I may say. And again, notwithstanding *the Kingdom of Heaven be the biggest City*: yet usually those by-paths are the most beaten, most Travellers go those ways; and therefore the way to Heaven it's hard to be found, and as hard to be kept in, by reason of 25 these. Yet nevertheless it is in this case, as it was with the *Harlot* of Josh. 2. 18. *Jericho*, she had one *Scarlet thread* tied in her Window, by which her House was known. So it is here, *the Scarlet Streams of Christ's Blood, run throughout the way to the Kingdom of Heaven*: therefore mind that, see if thou do find the besprinkling of the Blood of Christ in the way, and if 30 thou do, *be of good chear, thou art in the right way*: but have a care thou beguile not thy self with a *fancy*: For then thou mayst light into any Lane, or way; but that thou mayst not be mistaken, consider, though it seem never so pleasant: Yet if thou do not find that in the very middle of the Road, there is Writing with *the Heart-Blood of Christ, that he came* 35 *into the World to save Sinners, and that we are justified, though we are*

Ungodly; shun that way: For this it is which the Apostle meaneth, when he saith, *We have boldness to enter into the holiest by the BLOOD of Jesus, by a new and living way which he hath consecrated for us, through the vail, that is to say, his flesh.* How easy a matter is it in this our day, for the Devil to be too cunning for poor Souls? By calling his *by-paths* the way to the Kingdom, if such an opinion, or Fancy be but cryed up by one or more, this Inscription being set upon it, by the Devil, [this is the Way of God] how speedily, greedily, and by heaps do poor simple Souls throw away themselves upon it: especially if it be daubed over with a few external *Acts of Morality*, if so good: but this is because Men do not know painted By-Paths from the plain way to the Kingdom of Heaven. They have not yet learned the true Christ, and what his Righteousness is, *neither have they a Sense of their own insufficiency*; but are Bold, Proud, Presumptuous, Self-conceited. And therefore,

The Fifth Direction.

Do not thou be too much in *looking too high* in thy Journey Heavenwards. You know Men that Run in a Race, do not use to stare and gaze this way and that, neither do they use to cast up their Eyes too high, lest happily, through their too much gazing with their Eyes after other things, they in the mean time stumble, and catch a fall. The very same case is this, If thou gaze and stare after every opinion and way that comes into the World: Also if thou be *prying overmuch into Gods Secret Decrees*, or let thy Heart too much entertain Questions about some nice, foolish curiosities, thou mayst stumble and fall, as many Hundreds in *England* have done, both in *Ranting* and *Quakery*, to their own eternal overthrow, without the Marvelous operation of Gods Grace be suddenly stretched forth, to bring them back again. Take heed therefore, follow not that proud and lofty Spirit, that *Devil-like*, cannot be content with his own Station. *David* was of an excellent Spirit, where he saith, *Lord my Heart is not haughty, nor mine Eyes lofty; neither do I exercise my self in great matters, or things too high for me. Surely I have behaved and quieted my self as a Child that is weaned of his Mother, my Soul is even as a weaned Child.* Do thou so Run.

Psal. 131. 1, 2.

25 Ranting] Canting   Corrected in the Errata.

The Sixth Direction.

Take heed that you have not an *Ear open* to every one that calleth
after you, as you are in your Journey. Men that Run, you know, if any
do call after them, saying, I would speak with you; or go not too fast,
5 and you shall have my Company with you, if they Run for some great
matter, they use to say, alas I cannot stay, I am in haste, pray talk not to
me now; neither can I stay for you, I am now running for a Wager: *If I*
win I am made, if I lose I am undone, and therefore hinder me not. Thus
wise, are Men when they *Run* for Corruptible things. And thus
10 shouldest thou do, and thou hast more cause to do so then they,
forasmuch as they *Run* but for things that last not; but thou for an
incorruptible Glory. I give thee notice of this betimes, knowing that
thou shalt have enow call after thee, even the Devil, Sin, this World, vain
Company, Pleasures, Profits, Esteem among Men, Ease, Pomp, Pride,
15 together with an innumerable Company of such Companions; one
crying *stay for me*, the other saying, *do not leave me behind*, a third saying,
and take me along with you. What will you go, saith the Devil, without
your Sins, Pleasures and Profits; are you *so hasty*, can you not stay and
take these along with you? will you *leave* your Friends, and
20 Companions behind you? can you not *do as your Neighbours do*, carry
the World, Sin, Lust, Pleasure, Profit, Esteem among Men, along with
you? have a care thou *do not let thy Ear now be open* to the tempting,
enticing, alluring, and Soul-intangling flatteries of such *sink-Souls* as
these are. *My Son*, saith *Solomon*, *if Sinners intice thee, consent thou not.* Prov. 1. 10.
25 You know what it cost the *Young Man*, which *Solomon* speaks of in
the seventh of the *Proverbs*, that was inticed by a Harlot, *with much fair* Prov. 7.
speech she won him, and caused him to yield, with the flattering of her Lips 21–27.
she forced him, till he went after her as an Ox to the Slaughter, or as a Fool to
the correction of the Stocks; even so far, till a Dart struck thorow his Liver,
30 *and knew not that it was for his Life. Hearken unto me now therefore*, saith
he, *O ye Children, and attend to the Words of my Mouth, let not thine heart*
decline to her ways, go not astray in her Paths; for she hath cast down many,
Wounded, yea, many strong Men have been slain (that is, kept out of Heaven)
by her; her House is the way to Hell, going down to the Chambers of Death.
35 Soul take this Counsel, and say, Satan, Sin, Lust, Pleasure, Profit,

26 marg. Prov. 7. 21–27] Prov. 7

Pride, Friends, Companions, and every thing else, *let me alone, stand off, come not nigh me, for I am Running for Heaven, for my Soul, for God, for Christ, from Hell and everlasting Damnation.* If I win I win all, and if I lose I lose all, let me alone; for I will not hear. *So Run.*

The Seventh Direction.

5

In the next place, *be not daunted*, though thou meetest with never so many discouragements in thy Journey thither. That Man that is resolved for Heaven, *If Satan cannot win him by flatteries, he will endeavour to weaken him by discouragements*; saying, thou art a Sinner, thou hast broke God's Law, thou art not elected, thou comest too late, the day of Grace is past, God doth not care for thee, thy Heart is naught, thou art lazy, with a hundred other discouraging suggestions; and thus it was with *David*, where he saith, *I had fainted unless I had believed to see the loving kindness of the Lord in the Land of the living.* As if he should say, the Devil did so rage, and my Heart was so base that had I judged according to my own sense and feeling, I had been absolutely distracted, but I trusted to Christ in the Promise, and looked that God would be as good as his Promise, in having Mercy upon me, an unworthy Sinner; and this is that which incouraged me, and kept me from fainting. And thus must thou do, when Satan, or the Law, or thy own Conscience, do go about to dishearten thee, either by the greatness of thy Sins, the wickedness of thy Heart, the tediousness of the Way, the loss of outward Enjoyments, the hatred that thou wilt procure from the World, or the like; *then thou must encourage thy self with the freeness of the promises, the tender-heartedness of Christ, the Merits of his Blood, the freeness of his invitations to come in, the greatness of the Sin of others that have been Pardoned, and that the same God, through the same Christ, holdeth forth the same Grace as free as ever.* If these be not thy Meditations, thou wilt draw very heavily in the way to Heaven, if thou do not give up all for lost, and so knock off from following any farther; therefore I say, take heart in thy Journey, and say to them that seek thy destruction, *Rejoyce not against me, O mine Enemy; for when I fall I shall rise; when I sit in darkness, the Lord shall be a light unto me.* So Run.

10

15

20

25

30

Psal. 27. 13.

Micah 7. 8.

13 marg. Psal. 27. 13.] Psal. 27. 13, 14.

The Eighth Direction.

Take heed of being offended at the Cross that thou must go by, before thou come to Heaven. You must understand (as I have already touched) that there is no Man that goeth to Heaven, but he must go by the Cross; *the* 5 *Cross is the standing way-mark, by which all they that go to Glory must pass by.*

We must through much tribulation enter into the Kingdom of Heaven. Acts 14. 22.
Yea, and all that will live Godly in Christ Jesus, shall suffer Persecution. If 2 Tim. 3.
thou art in the way to the Kingdom, *my life for thine, thou wilt come at the* 12.
10 *Cross shortly*, (the Lord grant thou dost not shrink at it, so as to turn thee back again). *If any Man will come after me* saith Christ, *let him deny* Luke 9. 23.
himself, and take up his Cross daily, and follow me. The Cross, it stands, and hath stood from the beginning, as a *way-mark* to the Kingdom of Heaven. You know if one ask you the way to such and such a place, you
15 for the better direction, do not only say this is the way, but then also say you must go by such a Gate, by such a Stile, such a Bush, Tree, Bridge, or such like: why so it is here, art thou enquiring the way to Heaven, why I tell thee, *Christ is the way*, into him thou must get, into his *Righteousness* to be justified; and if thou art in him, thou wilt
20 presently see the *Cross*, thou must go close by it, thou must touch it, nay, thou must take it up, or else thou wilt quickly go out of the way that leads to Heaven, and turn up some of those crooked Lanes that lead down to the Chambers of Death.

How thou mayest know the Cross, by these
25 ### Six things.

First, It's known in the Doctrine of *Justification*. 2. In the Doctrine of *Mortification*. 3. In the Doctrine of *Perseverance*. 4. In *Self-denial*. 5. *Patience*. 6. *Communion with poor Saints.*

First, In the Doctrine of *Justification*, there is a great deal of the *Cross*
30 *in that; a Man is forced to suffer the destruction of his own Righteousness, for the Righteousness of another;* This is no easie matter for a Man to do, I assure to you it stretcheth every Vein in his Heart before he will be brought to yield to it. *What for a Man to deny, reject, abhor, and throw*

11 again).] again)   15 this is the way] this is way   18 thee] the

away all his Prayers, Tears, Alms, keeping of Sabbaths, Hearing, Reading, with the rest, in the point of Justification, and to count them accursed, and to *be willing in the very midst of the Sense of his Sins, to throw himself wholly upon the Righteousness, and Obedience of another Man, abhorring his own, counting it as deadly Sin, as the open breach of the Law?* I say, to do 5 this indeed and in Truth, is the biggest piece of the Cross, and therefore *Paul* calleth this very thing a suffering, where he saith, *And I have* SUFFERED *the loss of all things* (which principally was his *Righteousness) that I might win Christ, and be found in him, not having* (but rejecting) *my own Righteousness.* That's the first. 10

Secondly, In the Doctrine of *Mortification,* is also much of the *Cross.* Is it nothing for a Man to *lay hands on his vile Opinions,* on his *vile Sins,* of his *bosom Sins,* of his *beloved, pleasant, darling Sins?* that stick as close to him as the flesh sticks to the Bones? what to lose all these *brave* things that my Eyes behold, for that which I never saw with my Eyes? 15 what to lose my *Pride,* my *Covetousness,* my *vain Company, Sports* and *Pleasures,* and the rest? I tell you this is no *easie* matter, if it were, what need all those Prayers, Sighs, Watchings? what need we be so backward to it? nay, do you not see, that some Men before they will set about this work, they will even venture the loss of their *Souls,* Heaven, 20 God, Christ, and all? what means else all those delays and put offs, saying, stay a little longer, *I am loth to leave my Sins while I am so young, and in health.* Again, what is the reason else that others do it so by the halves, coldly, and seldom, notwithstanding they are Convinced over and over, nay, and also promise to amend, and yet all's in vain. I will 25 assure you, *to cut off right Hands, and to pluck out right Eyes is no pleasure to the flesh.*

Thirdly, The Doctrine of *Perseverance* is also *cross* to the flesh, which is *not only to begin but for to hold out,* not only to bid fair, and to say would I had Heaven; but so to know Christ, to put on Christ, and walk 30 with Christ so as to come to Heaven. *Indeed it is no great matter to begin to look for Heaven, to begin to seek the Lord, to begin to shun Sin. O but it is a very great matter to continue* with God's approbation. *My Servant Caleb,* saith God, *he is a man of another Spirit, he hath followed me,* (followed me always, he hath continually followed me) *fully, he shall* 35 *possess the land.* Almost all the many Thousands of the Children of

Phil. 3. 8, 9.

Num. 14. 24.

8 marg. Phil. 3. 8, 9.] Phil. 3

Israel in their Generation fell short of *Perseverance*, when they walk'd
from *Egypt* towards the Land of *Canaan*. Indeed they went to the work
at first pretty willingly, but they were very short-winded, they were
quickly out of Breath, and *in their Hearts they turned back again into*
5 *Egypt*.

It is an easy matter for a Man to *Run hard for a spurt*, for a Furlong,
for a Mile or two: 'O but to hold out for a Hundred, for a Thousand,
for *Ten Thousand Miles*; that Man that doth this, he must look to meet
with Cross, Pain, and Wearisomness to the Flesh, especially, if as he
10 goeth, he meeteth with Briers and Quagmires, and other incumbrances,
that make his Journey so much the more Painfuller.

Nay, do you not see with your Eyes daily, that *Perseverance* is a very
great part of the *Cross*; why else do Men so soon grow weary? I could
point out a many, that after they have followed the ways of God about a
15 Twelve-Month, others it may be two, three, or four, (some more, and
some less) Years, *they have been beat out of Wind*, have taken up their
Lodging and Rest, before they have got half way to Heaven: Some in
this, and some in that Sin, and have secretly, nay, sometimes openly
said, that the *Way* is too *strait*, the *Race too long*, the Religion too *Holy*,
20 and cannot hold out, I can go no farther.

And so likewise of the other three, (to wit) *Patience, Self-denial,*
Communion, and *Communication* with, and to the *poor* Saints: how hard
are these things? *It is an easy matter to deny another Man, but it is not so*
easy a matter, to deny ones self; to deny my *self* out of Love to God, to his
25 Gospel, to his Saints; of this advantage, and of that gain, nay, of that
which otherwise I might lawfully do, were it not for offending them.
That Scripture is but seldom read, and seldomer put in practice; which
saith, *I will eat no flesh while the world standeth, if it make my Brother to*   1 Cor. 8. 13.
offend; again, *We that are strong, ought to bear the infirmities of the weak,*   Rom. 15. 1.
30 *and not to please our selves*. But how froward, how hasty, how peevish
and self-resolved are the generality of the Professors at this Day? Also,
how little considering the Poor? unless it be to say, *be thou warmed, and*
filled: But to give, is a *seldom* work; Also, especially to give to any Poor. I   Gal. 6. 10.
tell you all things are *cross* to Flesh and Blood, and that Man that hath
35 but a watchful Eye over the Flesh, and also some considerable measure
of strength against it, he shall find his Heart in these things like unto a

33 work; Also,] work Also   33 Poor. I tell you] Poor, I tell you.

starting Horse, that is Rid without a Curbing Bridle, ready to start at every thing that is offensive to him; yea, and ready to Run away too, do what the Rider can.

It is the *Cross* which keepeth those that are kept from Heaven. I am perswaded, were it not for the *Cross*, where we have one Professor, we should have twenty, but this *Cross*, that is it which spoileth all.

Some Men, as I said before, *when they come at the Cross, then they can go no farther: But back again to their Sins they must go*. Others, they stumble at it, and break their Necks; others again, when they see the *Cross* is approaching, they turn aside to the Left Hand, or to the Right Hand, and so think to get to Heaven another way, but they will be deceived; *For all that will live Godly in Christ Jesus, shall*, mark, *shall be sure to suffer Persecution*. There are but few when they come at the *Cross*, cry, *welcome Cross*, as some of the Martyrs did to the Stake they were Burn'd at: Therefore if thou meet with the *Cross* in thy Journey, in what manner soever it be, be not daunted, and say alas what shall I do now? But rather take courage, knowing that *by the Cross is the way to the Kingdom*. Can a Man believe in Christ, and not be hated by the Devil? Can he make a Profession of this Christ, and that Sweetly and Convincingly, and the Children of Satan hold their Tongue? Can Darkness agree with Light? Or the Devil endure that Christ Jesus should be Honoured both by Faith and a Heavenly Conversation, and let that Soul alone at quiet? Did you never Read, that *The Dragon persecuteth the Woman?* And that Christ saith, *In the World you shall have tribulations?*

The Ninth Direction.

Beg of God, that he would do these two things for thee. First, *enlighten thine Understanding*. And Secondly, *inflame thy Will*. If these two be but effectually done, there is no fear but thou wilt go safe to Heaven.

One of the great Reasons why Men and Women do so little regard the other World, it is *because they see so little of it:* And the reason why they see so little of it, is because they have their Understandings darkned; and therefore saith Paul, *Do not you* Believers, *walk as do other Gentiles, even in the vanity of their minds, having their understanding*

Margin notes:

2 Tim. 3. 12.

Rev. 12.
John. 16. 33.

Eph. 4. 17, 18.

darkned, being alienated from the Life of God through the ignorance (or
foolishness) *that is in them, because of the blindness of their heart.* Walk not
as those, Run not with them; alas poor Souls, they have their
Understandings *Darkned*, their Hearts *Blinded*, and that's the reason
5 they have such undervaluing Thoughts of the *Lord Jesus Christ*, and the
Salvation of their Souls. For when Men do come to see the things of
another World, what a God, what a Christ, what a Heaven, and what
an eternal Glory there is to be enjoyed; also when they see that it is
possible for them to have a share in it, I tell you, it will make them *Run*
10 *thorow thick and thin to enjoy it. Moses* having a sight of this, because his
Understanding was enlightned, *He feared not the wrath of the King; but*   Heb. 11. 24,
chose rather to suffer afflictions with the people of God, than to enjoy the   25, 26, 27.
pleasures of Sin for a season. He refused to be called the Son of the King's
Daughter, accounting it wonderful Riches, to be counted worthy of so
15 much, as to suffer for Christ with the poor despised Saints; and that
was because *he saw him who was invisible, and had respect unto the*
recompence of reward. And this is that which the Apostle usually Prayeth
for in his Epistles for the Saints, namely, *That they might know what is*   Eph. 1. 17,
the hope of Gods calling, and the riches of the glory of his inheritance in the   18.
20 *Saints. And that they might be able to comprehend with all Saints, what is*   Eph. 3. 18,
the breadth, and length, and depth, and height, and to know the love of   19.
Christ, which passeth knowledge. Pray therefore, that God would
enlighten thy Understanding, that will be a very great help unto thee. It
will make thee endure many a *hard brunt* for Christ; as *Paul* saith, After
25 you were illuminated, *ye endured a great fight of afflictions,—You took*   Heb. 10. 32,
joyfully the spoiling of your goods, knowing in your selves, that ye have in   34.
Heaven a better and an enduring substance. If there be never such a rare
Jewel lye just in a Man's way: Yet if he sees it not, he will rather
trample upon it than stoop for it, and it is because he sees not. Why so
30 it is here, though *Heaven* be worth never so much and thou hast never
so much need of it; yet if thou see it not, that is, have not thy
Understanding opened, or *enlightned* to see it, thou wilt not regard at all;
therefore cry to the *Lord for enlightning Grace,* and say, *Lord, open my*
Blind Eyes, Lord, take the vail off of my dark Heart, shew me the things of

11 marg. Heb. 11. 24, 25, 26, 27.] Heb. 11. 24, 25, 26, 17.
25 marg. Heb. 10. 32, 34.] Heb. 10. 32, 34, 35, 36.

the other World, and let me see the Sweetness, Glory, and excellency of them, for *Christ his sake*. This is the first.

The Second Direction.

Cry to God that he would *inflame thy Will also with the things of the other World*; for when a Man's Will is fully set to do such or such a thing, then it must be a very hard matter that shall hinder that Man from bringing about his end. When *Paul's* Will was set resolvedly to go up to *Jerusalem*; (though it was signified to him before, what he should there suffer,) he was not daunted at all, nay saith he, *I am ready*, (or willing) *not only to be bound, but also to Dy at* Jerusalem, *for the Name of the Lord Jesus. His Will was inflamed with love to Christ*, and therefore all the perswasions that could be used, wrought nothing at all.

Your *Self-will'd People, no Body knows what to do with them*; we use to say, he will have his own Will, do all what you can. Indeed to have *such a Will* for Heaven, is an admirable advantage to a Man that undertaketh the Race thither; a Man that is resolved, and hath his Will fixed, saith he, I will do my best to advantage my self, I will do my worst to hinder my Enemies, I will not give out as long as I can stand, *I will have it, or I will lose my Life; Though he kill me, yet will I trust in him. I will not let thee go, except thou Bless me. I will, I will, I will*, O this Blessed, *inflamed Will* for Heaven! What is like it? If a Man be *willing*, then any Argument shall be matter of encouragement, but if unwilling, then any Argument shall give discouragement; this is seen both in Saints and Sinners; in them that are the Children of God, and also those that are the Children of the Devil. As,

First, The Saints of old, they being *willing* and resolved for Heaven, what could stop them? could *Fire* and *Faggot, Sword* or *Halter*, stinking *Dungeons, Whips, Bears, Bulls, Lions, cruel Rackings, Stoning, Starving, Nakedness*, &c. *and in all these things they were more than Conquerours, through him that loved them*; who had also made them *willing in the day of his Power*.

Secondly, See again on the other side, the Children of the Devil; because they *are not willing, how many shifts and starting-holes will they*

Acts 21. 12, 13.

Job 13. 15.

Gen. 32. 26.

Heb. 11.

Rom. 8. 37.

---

have. I have Married a Wife, I have a Farm, I shall offend my
Landlord, I shall offend my Master, I shall lose my Trading, I shall
lose my Pride, my Pleasures, I shall be mocked and scoffed, therefore,
I dare not come. I, saith another, will stay till I am older, till my Children
5 are out of sight, till I am got a little aforehand in the World, till I have
done this, and that, and the other business: But alas, the thing is, *they
are not willing;* for were they but soundly *willing,* these and a Thousand
such as these, would hold them no faster than the *Cords* held *Sampson,*
when *he broke them like burnt Flax.* I tell you *the Will is all,* that's one of   Judg. 15. 14.
10 the chief things which turns the Wheel either backwards or forwards;
and God knoweth that full well, and so likewise doth the Devil, and
therefore they both endeavour very much to strengthen the Will of
their servants: God, he is for *making of his a willing People* to serve him:
And the Devil he doth what he can to possess the Will and Affection of
15 those that are his, with love to Sin; and therefore when *Christ comes*   John. 5. 40.
close to the matter indeed, saith he, *you will not come to me. How often*   Luke 13. 34.
would I have gathered you, as a Hen doth her Chickens, but you would not.
The Devil had possessed their *Wills,* and so long he was sure enough
of them. O therefore cry hard to God, to *inflame thy will for Heaven and*
20 *Christ;* Thy Will, I say, if that be rightly set for Heaven, thou wilt not be
beat off with discouragements: and this was the reason, that when
Jacob wrestled with the Angel, though he lost a Limb as it were, and *the
hollow of his Thigh* was put *out of joynt* as he wrestled with him: yet saith
he, *I will not,* mark, *I will not let thee go, except thou Bless me.* Get thy *Will*   Gen. 32. 24,
25 *tipt* with the Heavenly Grace, and resolution against all discouragments,   25, 26.
and then thou goest *full speed* for Heaven; but if thou faulter in thy *Will,*
and be not sound there, thou wilt *Run hobling* and halting all the way
thou runnest, and also to be sure, thou wilt *fall short at last.* The Lord
give thee a Will, and Courage.
30   Thus have I done with directing thee how to *Run to the Kingdom;* be
sure thou keep in Memory what I have said unto thee, lest thou lose
thy *way:* But because I would have thee think of them, take all in short,
in this little bit of Paper.

    First, get into the way. 2. Then *Study* on it. 3. Then *strip,* and lay
35 aside every thing that would hinder. 4. *Beware* of By-Paths. 5. Do not
gaze and stare too much about thee, but be sure to ponder the Path of

    5 sight] sit Corrected in the Errata.

thy Feet. 6. Do not *stop* for any that call after thee, whether it be the World, the Flesh, or the Devil; for all these will hinder thy Journey, if possible. 7. Be not *Daunted* with any discouragements thou meetest with as thou goest. 8. Take heed of *stumbling* at the *Cross*. And 9. *Cry hard* to God for an *enlightened* heart, and a *willing* mind, and God give thee a prosperous Journey.

Yet before I do quite take my leave of thee, let me give thee a few *Motives* along with thee. It may be they will be as good as a pair of *Spurs*, to prick on thy lumpish Heart in this rich Voyage.

The First Motive.

Consider there is *no way but this*; thou must either *win* or *lose*: If thou winnest, then Heaven, God, Christ, Glory, Ease, Peace, Life, yea Life Eternal is thine, thou must be made equal to the Angels in Heaven, thou shalt Sorrow no more, sigh no more, feel no more pain; thou shalt be out of the reach of *Sin, Hell, Death, the Devil*, the *Grave*, and whatever else may endeavour thy hurt: But Contrariwise, and if thou lose, then thy loss is *Heaven, Glory, God, Christ, Ease, Peace*, and whatever else which tendeth to make *Eternity* comfortable to the Saints; besides, thou procurest *Eternal Death, Sorrow, Pain, Blackness*, and *Darkness*, fellowship with *Devils*, together with the everlasting *Damnation* of thy own *Soul*.

The Second Motive.

Consider, that *this Devil, this Hell, Death and Damnation followeth after thee as hard as they can drive*, and have their *Commission* so to do by the *Law*, against which thou hast *Sinned*; and therefore for the Lords sake make hast.

The Third Motive.

If they *seize upon* thee before thou get to the *City of Refuge*, they will put an everlasting stop to thy Journey: This also cries, *Run for it.*

The Fourth Motive.

Know also, that now Heaven Gates, *the Heart of Christ, with his Arms, are wide open to receive thee.* O, methinks that this Consideration, that the Devil followeth after to destroy, and that Christ standeth open
5 Arm'd to receive, should make thee reach out and *fly* with all haste and speed. And therefore,

The Fifth Motive.

Keep thine Eye upon the Prize, be sure that thy Eyes be continually upon the profit thou art like to get. The reason why Men are so apt to
10 faint in their Race for Heaven, it lyeth chiefly in either of these two things.

First, they do not seriously consider the worth of the *Prize*; or else if they do, they are afraid it is *too good* for them: But most lose Heaven, for want of considering the price, and the worth of it. And therefore
15 that thou maiest not do the like, keep thy Eye much upon the *Excellency*, the *Sweetness*, the *Beauty*, the *Comfort*, the *Peace* that is to be had there, by those that win the *Prize*. This was that which made the Apostle *Run* thorow any thing; *good report, evil report, Persecution, Affliction, Hunger, Nakedness, Peril by Sea, and Peril by Land, Bonds and*
20 *Imprisonments:* Also it made others endure to be *Stoned, Sawn asunder,* to have their Eyes bored out with *Augers*, their Bodies broiled on *Gridirons*, their Tongues *cut* out of their mouths, boiled in *Cauldrons*, thrown to the *wild Beasts*, burned at the *Stakes*, whipt at *Posts*, and a thousand other fearful Torments, *while they looked not at the things that* 2 Cor. 4. 18.
25 *are seen* (as the things of this World,) *But at the things that are not seen; for the things which are seen, are temporal, but the things which are not seen, are eternal.* O this word *Eternal*, that was it that made them, that when they might have *had deliverance, they would not accept of it*, for they knew Heb. 11. 35.
in the world to come they should have a better *Resurrection*.
30   2. And do not let the thoughts of the *rareness of the place* make thee say in thy Heart, this is too good for me; for I tell thee, *Heaven is prepared for whosoever will accept of it*, and they shall be entertained with hearty good welcom: Consider therefore, that *as bad as thou have got*

16 the *Comfort*,] the *Comfort*   28 marg. Heb. 11. 35.] Rom. 11. 35.

Jam. 2. 5.

thither, thither went scrubbed beggarly *Lazarus, &c.* nay, it is prepared for the poor, *Hearken my beloved brethren,* saith James, take notice of it, *hath not God chosen the poor of this World rich in faith, and heirs of the Kingdom? therefore* take Heart and *Run,* Man. And,

The Sixth Motive.

Think much of them that are gone before. First, how really they got into the Kingdom. *Secondly,* how safe they are in the Arms of *Jesus;* would they be here again for a thousand Worlds; or if they were, would they be afraid that God would not make them welcom? *Thirdly,* what they would *judge* of thee, if they knew thy Heart began to *fail thee* in thy Journey; or thy Sins began to allure thee, and to perswade thee to stop thy Race, would they not call thee a thousand Fools? and say, *O that he did but see what we see, feel what we feel, and taste of the dainties that we taste of.* O if he were here one quarter of an hour, to behold, to see, to feel, to taste and enjoy, but the thousand part of what we enjoy! what would he do? what would he suffer, what would he leave undone. Would he favour Sin, would he love this World below, would he be afraid of Friends, or shrink at the most fearful threatnings that the greatest *Tyrants* could invent to give him? nay, those who have had but a sight of these things by faith, when they have been as far off from them as Heaven from Earth; yet they have been able to say with a comfortable and merry Heart, as the Bird that sings in the Spring; that *this and more shall not keep them from running to Heaven.* Sometimes, when my base Heart hath been inclining to this World, and to loiter in my Journey towards Heaven, the very consideration of the glorious Saints and Angels in Heaven, what they enjoy, and what *low thoughts they have of the things of this World* together, how they would befool me, if they did but know that my Heart was drawing back, hath caused me to rush forward, to disdain these poor, low, empty beggarly things, and to say to my Soul, *come Soul let us not be weary,* let us see what this Heaven is, let us even venture all for it, and try if that will quit for cost. Surely *Abraham, David, Paul* and the rest of the Saints of God were as wise as any are now, and yet they lost all for this Glorious Kingdom, O therefore, *throw away stinking lusts,* follow after Righteousness, love the

28 drawing back, hath] drawing back; hath

Lord Jesus, devote thy self unto his fear, I'll warrant thee he will give
thee a goodly recompence. Reader, what sayest thou to this? Art
resolv'd to follow me, nay, resolve if thou canst to get before me. *So
Run, that ye may obtain.*

5   *The Seventh Motive.*

To encourage thee a little farther, *set to the work*, and when thou hast
Run thy self down weary, then *the Lord Jesus will take thee up and carry
thee*; is not this enough to make any poor Soul begin his Race? thou
(perhaps) cryest, O but I am feeble, I am lame, *&c.* well, but Christ
10 hath a bosom, consider therefore when thou hast *Run* thy self down
weary, he will put thee in his bosom, *He shall gather the Lambs with his*   Isa. 40. 11.
*Arms, and carry them in his bosom, and shall gently lead those that are with
young.* This is the way that Fathers take to encourage their Children,
saying, run sweet Babe while thou art weary, and then I will take thee
15 up and carry thee. *He will gather his Lambs with his Arms, and carry them
in his bosom*; when they are weary, they shall ride.

The Eighth Motive.

Or else, he will convey new strength from Heaven into thy Soul,
which will be as well. *The Youths shall faint and be weary, and the young*   Isa. 40. 30,
20 *Men shall utterly fail. But they that wait upon the Lord, shall* RENEW   31.
*their strength, they shall mount up with wings like Eagles, they shall run and
not be weary, they shall walk and not be faint.* What shall I say besides
what hath already been said? Thou shalt have *good* and *easy Lodging,*
good and wholsom Diet, *the Bosom of Christ to ly in,* the joyes of Heaven
25 to feed on: Shall I speak of the society, and of the duration of all these?
Verily to discribe them to the height, is a Work too hard for me to do.

The Ninth Motive.

Again, Methinks the very Industry of the Devil, and the Industry of

1–2 give thee] give the   14–15 thee up] the up
19 he will convey new strength . . . which will be as well.] *he will convey new strength
. . . which will be as well.*   25 society] saciety Corrected in the Errata.

his Servants, &c. should make you that have a desire to Heaven and Happiness, to *Run apace*. Why the Devil, he will lose no time, spare no pains, also neither will his Servants; both to seek the destruction of themselves and others, and shall not we be as Industrious for our own Salvation; shall the World venture the Damnation of their Souls for a poor *Corruptible Crown*; and shall not we venture the loss of a few trifles, for an *eternal Crown?* Shall they venture the loss of eternal Friends, as *God to love, Christ to Redeem*, the *Holy Spirit to Comfort, Heaven for Habitation, Saints and Angels for Company*: And all this, to get, and hold Communion with Sin, and this World, and a few base Drunken, Swearing, Lying, Covetous Wretches, like themselves? And shall not we *Labour* as hard, *Run* as fast, seek as diligently, nay, a hundred times more diligently for the Company of *these Glorious eternal Friends*, though with the loss of such as these; nay, with the loss of Ten Thousand times better than these Poor, Low, Base, Contemptible things? Shall it be said at the last Day, that *wicked Men made more haste to Hell, than you did make to Heaven?* That they spent more Hours, Days, and that early and late, for Hell, than you spent for that which is Ten Thousand, Thousand of Thousands times better? O let it not be so: But *Run* with all might and main.

Thus you see I have here spoken something, though but little. Now I shall come to make some Use and Application of what hath been said, and so conclude.

The First Use.

You see here, that he that will go to Heaven, he *must Run for it*: Yea, and not only Run, but SO *Run*, that is, (as I have said) to Run *earnestly*, to Run *continually*, to *Strip* off every thing that would hinder in his Race, with the rest; well then, do you *So Run*.

1. And now let us examin a little, Art thou got into the *right Way?* Art thou in *Christ's Righteousness?* Do not say yes, in thy Heart, when in truth there is no such matter. It is a dangerous thing you know, for a Man to think he is in the right way, when he is in the wrong. It is the next way for him to *lose his way*, and not only so; but if he Run for Heaven, as thou sayst thou do'st, even to lose that too. O this is the misery of most Men! To perswade themselves that they Run right,

when they never had one Foot in the way! *The Lord give thee Understanding here; or else thou art undone for ever.* Prethee Soul search, *when wast thou turned out of thy Sins, and Righteousness, into the Righteousness of Jesus Christ?* I say, dost thou see thy self *in him?* And is
5 *he* more precious to thee than the whole World? Is thy mind always musing on *him?* Dost thou love to be talking of *him?* And also to be walking with *him?* Dost thou count *his* Company preciouser than the whole World? Dost thou count all things but Poor, Lifeless, Empty, Vain things, without Communion with *him?* Doth *his* Company
10 sweeten all things? And *his* Absence embitter all things? Soul, I beseech thee be serious, and lay it to Heart, and do not take things of such weighty Concernment as the Salvation or Damnation of thy Soul, without good ground.

2. Art thou *unladen* of the things of this World, as Pride, Pleasures,
15 Profits, Lusts, Vanities? What, dost thou think to *Run* fast enough, with the World, thy Sins, and Lusts in thy Heart? I tell thee Soul; they that have laid all aside, every weight, every Sin, and are got into the nimblest posture, they find *work enough to Run; so to run, as to hold out.*

To *Run thorow* all that opposition, *all* them Jostles, *all* them Rubs,
20 over *all* them Stumbling-blocks, over *all* them Snares, from *all* those Intanglements, that the Devil, Sin, the World, and their own Hearts lay before them. I tell thee, if thou art a going Heaven-ward, thou wilt find it no small, or easy matter. Art thou therefore discharged, and unladen of these things; never talk of going to Heaven, if thou art not.
25 It is to be feared, thou wilt be found among them, *Many that will seek to* Luke 13. 24. *enter in, and shall not be able.*

The Second Use.

If so, Then in the next place, *what will become of them that are grown weary, before they are got half way thither?* Why Man, it is he that holdeth
30 out to the end that must be saved, it is he that *overcometh* that shall *inherit all things,* 'tis not every one that begins. *Agrippa* gave a fair step for a sudden, he stept almost into the Bosom of Christ in less than half Act. 26. 28 an Hour. Thou (saith he to *Paul*) hast *Almost perswaded me to be a Christian.* Ah! But it was but *almost,* and so he had as good have been

33 marg. Act. 26. 28.] Act. 17. 28

never a whit; he stept fair indeed, but yet he *stept short*; he was hot while he was at it, but he was quickly out of Wind. O this but *almost*! I tell you, *this but almost, it lost his Soul*. Methinks I have seen sometimes, how these poor Wretches that get but almost to Heaven, how fearfully their *almost*, and their but *almost* will torment them in Hell. When they shall cry out in the bitterness of their Souls, saying, *I was almost a Christian*, I was *almost* got into the Kingdom, *almost* out of the Hands of the Devil, *almost* out of my Sins, *almost* from under the Curse of God, *Almost*, and that was all, *almost, but not all together*. O that I should be *almost* at Heaven, and should not go quite thorow! Friend, it is a sad thing to sit down before we are in Heaven, and to grow weary before we come to the place of rest. And if it should be thy case, I am sure thou dost not *so Run, as to obtain*. But,

The Third Use.

Again, In the next place, *What then will become of them that some time since were Running Post-haste to Heaven* (insomuch, that they seemed to out-strip many) but now are Running as fast *back again?* Do you think those will ever come thither? What to Run *back again, back again* to Sin,

2 Pet. 2. 21.

to the World, to the Devil, *back gain* to the lusts of the Flesh. Oh! *It had been better for them not to have known the way of righteousness, than after they have known it, to turn* (to turn back again) *from the holy Commandment.* Those Men shall not only be Damned for Sin, but *for professing to all the World, that Sin is better than Christ*: For the Man that Runs back again, he doth as good as say, I have tried Christ, and I have tried Sin; and I do not find so much profit in Christ, as in Sin. I say, this Man declareth this, even by his Running *back again*. O sad! What a

Heb. 10. 38.

Doom will they have, who were *almost* at Heaven Gates, and then Run *back again. If any Man draweth back*, saith Christ, *My Soul shall have no*

Luke 9. 62.

pleasure in him. Again, *No Man having put his Hand to the Plough*, that is, set forward, (in the ways of God,) *and looking back*, turning back again, *is fit for the Kingdom of Heaven*. And if not fit for the Kingdom of Heaven, then for certain he must needs be fit for the Fire of Hell: And therefore saith the Apostle, those that *bring forth* these Apostatizing

1 whit;] whit,   1 indeed,] indeed: 1 *short*;] short,
19 marg. 2 Pet. 2. 21.] 2 Pet. 21, 22.

Fruits as *Briers and Thorns, are rejected, being nigh unto cursing, whose end is to be Burned.* O there is never another Christ to save them by Bleeding and Dying for them. And if they *shall not escape, that neglect* (then how shall they escape, that *reject and* turn their *backs* upon) *so* Heb. 2. 3.
5 *great salvation. And if the Righteous,* that is, they that Run for it, will find work enough to get to Heaven, *then where will the ungodly* backsliding *Sinner appear?* O if *Judas* the Traitor, or *Francis Spira* the *backslider,* were but now alive in the World to whisper these Men in the Ear a little, and tell them what it hath cost their Souls for *backsliding,* surely it
10 would stick by them, and make them afraid of *Running* back again, so long as they had one day to live in this World.

The Fourth Use.

So again *Fourthly,* how unlike to these Mens Passions will those be, that *have all this while sat still,* and have not so much as set one foot
15 *forward* to the Kingdom of Heaven. Surely he that *backslideth,* and he that *sitteth still* in Sin, they are both of one mind, the one he *will not stir,* because he loveth his Sins, and the things of this World; the other he Runs *back again,* because he loveth his Sins, and the things of this World. Is it not one and the same thing? *they are all one here, and shall*
20 *not one and the same Hell hold them hereafter.* He is an *ungodly* one that never looked after Christ, and he is an *ungodly* one, that did once look after him, and then Ran quite back again, and therefore that word must certainly drop out of the mouth of Christ against them both, *Depart from me ye Cursed into everlasting fire, prepared for the Devil and his* Mat. 25. 41.
25 *Angels.*

The Fifth Use.

Again, here you may see in the next place, that is, *they that will have Heaven, must Run for it*; then this calls aloud to those that began but a while since to *Run,* I say, for them, *to mend their pace, if they intend to*
30 *win*; you know that they which come hindmost, had need Run fastest. Friend, I tell thee, there be them that have Run ten years to thy one, nay, twenty to thy five; and yet if thou talk with them, sometimes they

13 how] now   Corrected in the Errata.   24 marg. Mat. 25. 41.] Mat. 25.

will say they doubt they shall come late enough. How then will it be with thee? look to it therefore, that thou delay no time, not an hours time, but speedily part with all, with every thing that is an hindrance to thee in thy Journey; and run; yea, *and so Run that thou mayest obtain.*

The Sixth Use.

Again, Sixthly, You that are old Professors, *Take you heed, that the young striplings of Jesus,* that began to strip but the other day, *do not out-run you,* so as to have that Scripture fulfilled on you, *The first shall be last, and the last first.* Which will be a shame to you, and a credit for them. What for *a young Soldier* to be more courageous, then he that hath been used to Wars. To you that are hindmost, I say, strive to *out-run* them that are before you; and you that are foremost, I say *hold your ground,* and keep before them in faith and love, if possible; for indeed *that is the right Running, for one to strive to out-run another,* even for the hindmost to endeavour to overtake the formost, and he that is before, should be sure to lay out himself to keep his ground, even to the very utmost. But then,

The Seventh Use.

Again, How basely do they behave themselves, *how unlike are they to win, that think it enough to keep Company with the hindmost.* There are some Men, that profess themselves such as Run for Heaven as well as any, yet if there be but any *lazy, slothfull, cold, half-hearted Professors in the Country, they will be sure to take Example by them,* they think if they can but keep pace with them, they shall do fair; but these do not consider, that *the hindmost lose the Prize.* You may know it if you will, that it cost the foolish Virgins dear for their coming too late. *They that were ready went in with him, and the door was shut. Afterward,* mark, *Afterward came the other* (the foolish) *Virgins, saying Lord, Lord, open to us: But he answered and said, Depart, I know you not.* Depart lazy Professor, cold Professors, *slothful Professors.* O! methinks the word of God is so plain for the overthrow of your *lazy Professors,* that it is to be wondered, Men do take no more notice of it. How was *Lot's* Wife

Mat. 25. 10, 11, 12.

26 Mat. 25. 10, 11, 12.] Mat. 25.

served for Running *lazily*, and for giving but one *look behind* her, after the things she left in *Sodom?* How was *Esau* served, for staying too long before he came for the *blessing?* And how was they served that are mentioned in the thirteenth of *Luke*, for *staying till the door was shut?*
5 Also the *foolish Virgins*; A heavy aftergroan will they give, that have thus stayed too long. It turned *Lot's Wife* into *a Pillar of Salt*. It made *Esau* Gen. 19. 26. *weep* with an exceeding loud and *bitter Cry*. It made *Judas hang himself*, Heb. 12. 17. yea, and it will make thee *Curse the day* in which thou wast Born if thou miss of the Kingdom, as thou wilt certainly do, if this be thy course.
10 But,

The Eighth Use.

Again, How and if thou by thy *lazy Running* shouldest not only destroy thy self, but also *thereby be the cause of the damnation of some others*; for thou being a Professor, thou must think that others will take
15 notice of thee, and because thou art but a poor, cold, *lazy Runner*, and one that seeks to drive the World, and pleasure along with thee: Why thereby others will think of doing so too. Nay, say they, why may not we as well as he? He is a *Professor* and yet he seeks for *pleasures*, riches, profits, he loveth vain Company, and he is Proud, and he is so and so,
20 and professeth that he is going for Heaven; yea, and saith also he doth not fear but he shall have entertainment; let us therefore keep pace with him, we shall fare no worse than he. *O how fearful a thing will it be, if that thou shalt thus be instrumental of the ruin of others, by thy halting in the way of righteousness*: Look to it, thou wilt have strength little enough
25 to appear before God, to give an account of the *loss* of thy own Soul, thou needest not have to give an account for others, why thou didst stop them from entering in. How wilt thou answer that saying, *You would not enter in your selves, and them that* would, you hinder; for that saying will be eminently fulfilled on them, that through their own
30 *Idleness* do keep themselves out of Heaven, and by giving of others the same example, hinder them also.

6 Lot's] Lots   26 why] why,   27 from entering] for entering

The Ninth Use.

Therefore, Now to speak a word to both of you, and so I shall conclude.

First, I beseech you in the Name of our Lord Jesus Christ, that none of you do Run so lazily in the way to Heaven, as to hinder either your selves, or 5 *others.* I know that even he which *Runs Laziest,* if he should see a Man running for a temporal Life, if he should so much neglect his own well-being in this World, as to venture, when he is a running for his Life, to *pick up* here and there *a lock of wool* that hangeth by the way side; or to step now and then aside *out* of the *way,* for to gather up a 10 *straw* or two, or any rotten stick. I say, if he should do this when he is a running for his Life, thou wouldest Condemn him; and dost thou not *Condemn thy self,* that doest the very same, in effect; nay worse, that *Loiterest* in thy Race, notwithstanding *thy Soul, Heaven, Glory, and all is at stake.* Have a care, have a care, poor *wretched Sinner, have a care.* 15

Secondly, If yet there shall be any, that notwithstanding this advice, will still be staggering, and *Loitering* in the way to the Kingdom of Glory, be thou so wise as not to take example by them, *Learn of no Man farther, then he followeth Christ. But look unto Jesus, who is* not only *the author and finisher of Faith.* But *who did for the joy that was set before him,* 20 *endure the Cross, despise the shame and is now set down at the right hand of God.* I say, look to no Man to learn of him, no further than he followeth Christ. *Be ye followers of me* (saith *Paul*) *even as I am of Christ.* (1. Cor. 11. 1.) Though he was an eminent Man; yet his exhortation was, that none should follow him any further, then he followed Christ. 25

Heb. 12. 1, 2.

Provocation.

Now that you may be *provoked* to Run with the foremost, take notice of this. When *Lot* and his Wife was running from Cursed *Sodom* to the Mountains, to save their lives, it is said, that his Wife looked back from behind him, and she became *a Pillar of Salt*; and yet you see that 30 neither her practice, nor the judgment of God that fell upon her for the same, *would cause Lot to look behind him.* I have sometimes wondered at *Lot* in this particular; his Wife looked behind her, and Died immediately, but *let what would become of her,* Lot *would not so much as*

look behind him to see her: We do not Read, that he did so much as once look where she was, or what was become of her, his Heart was indeed upon his Journey, and well it might, *there was the Mountain before him, and the Fire and Brimstone behind him, his Life lay at Stake, and he had lost*
5 *it,* if he had but look'd behind him. Do thou *so Run:* And in thy Race *Remember* Lot's *Wife,* and remember her *Doom,* and remember for *what that* Doom did *overtake her,* and remember that God made *her an Example,* for all *lazy* Runners, to the end of the World, and take heed thou fall not after the same Example. But,

10 If this will not provoke thee, Consider thus, 1. Thy Soul is thy own Soul, that is either to be sav'd or lost, *thou shalt not lose my Soul by thy laziness:* It is thy own Soul, thy own Ease, thy own Peace, thy own Advantage or Disadvantage. If it were my Soul that thou art desired to be good unto, methinks reason should move thee somewhat to pity it:
15 But alas, it is thy own, thy own Soul. *What shall it profit a man, if he shall* Mark 8. 36. *gain the whole world, and lose his own Soul.* Gods People wish well to the Souls of others, and wilt not thou wish well to thy own? And if this will not provoke thee, then think,

Again, 2. If thou lose thy Soul, it is *thou* also that must *bear* the blame. *In a Spiritual*
20 It made *Cain* stark mad, to consider that he had not looked to his *Sence.* Brother *Abel's* Soul. How much more will it perplex thee, to think that thou hadst not a care of thy own? And if this will not provoke thee to bestir thy self, Think, again,

3. That if thou wilt not Run, *the People of God are resolved to deal with*
25 *thee even as* Lot *dealt with his Wife,* that is, leave thee behind them. It may be thou hast a Father, Mother, Brother, *&c.* going Post-hast to Heaven, wouldst thou be willing to be left behind them? Surely no!

Again, 4. Will it not be a Dishonour to thee to see the very *Boys and Girls* in the Country, to have more Wit than thy self. It may be the
30 Servants of some Men, as the Horse-keeper, Plough-man, Scullion, *&c.* is more looking after Heaven, than their Masters. I am apt to think sometimes, that *more Servants than Masters, that more Tenants than Land-lords will inherit the Kingdom of Heaven.* But is not this a shame for them that are such? I am perswaded you scorn that your Servants
35 should say, that they are wiser than you in the things of this World; and yet I am bold to say, that many of them are wiser than you in the things of the World to come, which are of greater Concernment.

Expostulation.

Well then, *Sinner*, what sayst thou? Where is thy Heart? Wilt thou Run? Art thou resolved to Strip? Or art thou not? Think quickly Man, it is no dallying in this matter. Confer not with Flesh and Blood, look up to Heaven, and see how thou likest it; also to Hell, (of which thou mayst understand something in my Book, called *A few Sighs from Hell, or the Groans of a Damned Soul*, which I wish thee to Read seriusly over) and accordingly Devote thy self. If thou dost not know the way, *imquire at the Word of God*. If thou wantest Company, cry for God's Spirit, if thou wantest Incouragement, entertain the *Promises*: But be sure thou begin betimes, *get* into *the way*, Run apace, and hold out to the *end*. And the Lord give thee a prosperous Journey.

Farewel.

NOTES TO *THE BARREN FIG-TREE*

The image of the barren fig-tree is a favourite one with Bunyan. He uses it later in *The Pilgrim's Progress*, part II, in the Interpreter's garden: '... a Tree whose *inside* was all rotten, and gone, and yet it grew and had leaves'. Poem XXXIII of *A Book for Boys and Girls* concentrates the theme of this sermon into its twenty-odd lines. Other contexts where he uses the parable or the image are in *The Jerusalem Sinner Saved* (Offor, i. 99), *The Acceptable Sacrifice* (Offor, i. 711), *The Desire of the Righteous Granted* (Offor, i. 749), *Of the Resurrection of the Dead* (Offor, ii. 112), *The Holy War* (ed. Sharrock and Forrest, pp. 158–9), *The Life and Death of Mr. Badman* (Offor, iii. 662).

p. 9, l. 6. *Complexion*: disposition, temperament.

p. 9, l. 8. Cf. *The Jerusalem Sinner Saved* where he uses similar language of fruitless fig-trees and tares planted by the Devil: 'But why doth the devil do thus? Not of love to them, but to make of them offences and stumbling blocks to others. For he knows that a loose professor in the church does more mischief to religion than ten can do to it that are in the world.' (Offor, i. 99.)

p. 11, l. 15. *prodigious*: unnatural, monstrous.

p. 12, l. 3. *Salvo*: a dishonest mental reservation, a quibbling evasion.

p. 14, l. 1. *Them words also*. This was still a normal usage of 'them' as a demonstrative adjective.

p. 17, l. 34. *not in any honor*. If we retain the text's 'humor', Bunyan appears to mean, 'a neglecting of the body which does not spring from a mind and character naturally inclined to such action'. But the reference he gives is to Col. 2: 23, which ends with '... neglecting of the body; not in any honour to the satisfying of the flesh', supporting the emendation of 'humor' to honor'.

p. 19, l. 26. *Austerity*: stern, rigorous, or severe treatment.

p. 20, l. 6. *daubing*: covering with finery or ornaments in a vulgar and tasteless way. Now obs. or dialect.

p. 20, l. 7. Bunyan frequently attacks contemporary fashions as immodest and lascivious. Cf. *Christian Behaviour* (Offor, ii, 569), 'The attire of an harlot is too frequently in our day the attire of professors; a vile thing, and argueth much wantonness and vileness of affections ... Doth a wanton eye argue shamefacedness? Doth wanton talk argue chastity? And doth immodest apparel, with stretched-out necks, naked breasts, a made speech, and mincing gaits, &c, argue mortification of lusts?' Cf. also *A Book for Boys and Girls*, Poem XVI, 'Upon Apparel'.

p. 20, l. 10. *carriages*: habitual conduct or behaviour.

p. 20, l. 35. *where ever he defers to be*. This reading is from the Errata in the first edition—'for *desire*, read *defer*.' In the Alberta copy there is an MS. correction of 'desires' to 'defers', showing this to be acceptable and comprehensible to at least one reader. The *O.E.D.* records no intransitive use without a preposition in any sense which fits this context. Bunyan seems to be using it in the sense of 'agrees', 'condescends', but this usage without a subsequent preposition and noun is not recorded. The second edition of 1688 returns to the more easily understood 'desires' obviously finding difficulty in 'defers'. One is tempted to emend to the 1688 reading, but the Errata is difficult to ignore.

p. 21, l. 32. *End-ship*: a small suburb, a hamlet.

p. 24, l. 11. *righteousness imputed*. Cf. *The Desire of the Righteous Granted* (Offor, i. 766), 'That that which makes me righteous is the obedience of Christ to his Father's will, that this righteousness is before the throne of God, and that it is made mine by an act of God's free grace ... for the Spirit comes with the gospel down from heaven to such an one, and fills his soul with good; by which he is capacitated to bring forth fruit, true fruit, which are the fruits of righteousness imputed, and of righteousness infused, to the glory and praise of God.'

p. 25, l. 5. *only Saints before men*. In *A Holy Life the Beauty of Christianity* Bunyan depicts in greater detail those 'that shew like Saints abroad yet act the part of Devils when they are at home' (Oxford Bunyan, ix. 319).

p. 25, l. 31. *Contentment*: would here seem to mean 'being content with one's lot', 'not desiring more'.

p. 28, l. 14. *run*: a normal past indicative until the end of the seventeenth century.

p. 28, l. 36. *convenient*: fitting, appropriate to the circumstances.

p. 31, l. 2. *Citations*: either summonings to reform, or the quotation and citing of the Scriptures.

p. 31, l. 21. *thy Closet fruits, thy Family Fruits*. Bunyan deals at greater length with 'closet iniquity' and 'family iniquity' in *A Holy Life the Beauty of Christianity* (Oxford Bunyan, ix. 319–26).

p. 32, l. 18. *a hitting Season*: A 'hit' is an abundant crop of fruit, so a hitting season is a season of a full fruit harvest.

p. 38, l. 25. *a thief in the Candle*: an excrescence in the wick of a candle which causes it to gutter and waste.

p. 39, l. 6. *prefixed*: fixed and appointed beforehand.

p. 47, l. 11. *the day of grace ends with some men before God takes them out of this world.* This terrible state is often referred to by Bunyan. In *A Few Sighs from Hell* he warns 'that for ought thou knowest the day of grace may be past to thee before thou diest, not lasting so long as thy uncertain life in this world. And if so, then know for certain that thou art as sure to be damned as if thou wert in hell already; if thou convert not in the mean while.' (Oxford Bunyan, i. 366.) Mr. Badman dies in this state–'God gave him up now to a reprobate mind, to hardness and stupidity of spirit; and so was that Scripture fulfilled upon him, "He hath blinded their eyes." Is. vi. 10. And that, "Let their eyes be darkened that they may not see." Ro. xi. 10.' (Offor, iii. 656.) In *Law and Grace* he gives his readers ways of knowing that the day of grace is not yet ended with them (Oxford Bunyan, ii. 212).

p. 48, l. 20. *a lot with the Saints*: a share with the Saints.

p. 49, l. 5. *gamesom*: sportive, given to sport.

p. 50, l. 31. *liveless*: lifeless.

p. 51, l. 33. This scene of the terrors of the death-bed is a favourite with all awakening preachers, and Bunyan is no exception. A similar example is this from *A Treatise of the Fear of God* (Oxford Bunyan, ix. 45), '. . . when thou liest a dying, he can license him then to assault thee with great temptations . . . God can tell how to tumble thee from off thy death-bed in a cloud, he can let thee die in the dark; when thou art dying, thou shalt not know whither thou art going, to wit, whether to Heaven or to Hell.' Mr. Badman's first approach to death closely resembles this scene. 'To my best remembrance, he lay crying out all one night for fear; and at times he would so tremble that he would make the very bed shake under him. But O! how the thoughts of death, of hell-fire, and of eternal judgment did then wrack his conscience. Fear might be seen in his face, and in his tossings to and fro; it might also be heard in his words, and be understood by his heavy groans. He would often cry, I am undone, I am undone; my vile life has undone me!' (Offor, iii. 649.)

p. 52, l. 27. Bunyan suspects repentance made in the face of tribulation, sickness, and the fear of death. He shows it often fading with the removal of the fear. Cf. *A Treatise of the fear of God* (Oxford Bunyan, ix. 94), 'Hast thou not cried for health when sick, for wealth when poor, when lame for strength, when in prison for liberty, and then spent all that thou gottest by thy prayer, in the service of Satan, and to gratify thy lusts?' And again in *The Life and Death of Mr. Badman* (Offor, iii. 651), 'I have known many that, when they have been sick, have had large measures of this kind of repentance, and while it lasted, the noise and sound thereof has made the town to ring again. But, alas! how long has it lasted? Ofttimes scarce so long as until the party now sick has been well . . .'

p. 52, l. 35. *to-side*: out of the way.

p. 53, l. 23. *They go far as never turn*: proverbial. (Tilley, R. 210.)

p. 58, l. 17. *Spira's complaint.* Bunyan had read the story of Francis Spira in Nathaniel Bacon's *A Relation of the Fearful State of Francis Spira in the year 1548,* published in 1649. Spira had deserted his Protestant faith to become a Roman Catholic, from unworthy motives, and later died in despair. In *G.A.* Bunyan recounts the terrifying effect on him when Spira's experience seemed to parallel his own (p. 49, ll. 21–34). Spira's words here are echoed by that other hopeless apostate, the Man in the Iron Cage, in the House of the Interpreter (*P.P.*, p. 34, ll. 24–5), 'I cannot get out; O now I cannot get out'. He refers to him again in *The Greatness of Soul* (Oxford Bunyan, ix. 167), 'Behold *Spira* in his book, *Cain* in his guilt, and *Saul* with the Witch of *Endor*, and you shall see men ripened, men inlarged and greatned in their fancies, imaginations and apprehensions, tho' not about God, and Heaven and glory; yet about their Loss, their misery, and their woe, and their Hells.' '*Francis Spira* the *backslider*' appears again, in company with Judas, in *The Heavenly Foot-man* (above, p. 151).

p. 58, l. 23. *Lot's wife.* This is a reference to the popular superstition that the pillar of salt was still to be seen. Christian and Hopeful pass by it (*P.P.*, pp. 108–10) and conclude that 'specially since the Judgment which overtook her, did make her an example within sight of where they are'.

p. 59, l. 31. *tenour:* meaning, import.

p. 61, l. 4. *Devices:* pleasures, inclinations, as in 'We have followed to much the devices and desyres if our owne heartes.' (Book of Common Prayer.)

p. 64, l. 22. There is a similarly powerfully imagined death-bed scene in *The Desire of the Righteous Granted* (Offor, i. 764), 'And now the bed shakes, and the poor soul is loath to go out of the body, for fear the devil should catch it, as the poor bird is to go out of the bush, while it sees the hawk waits there to receive her.'

NOTES TO *THE STRAIT GATE*

The metaphor of the strait gate, from Matt. 7: 13, 14 appears often in Bunyan's work, signifying the way into the saving faith of the church, or into the Kingdom of Heaven. In *G.A.* (pp. 19–20) it is the way through the wall around the mountain, from the cold and clouds to the warmth and sunshine within: '. . . at the last I saw as it were, a narrow gap, like a little door-way in the wall, thorow which I attempted to pass: but the passage being very straight, and narrow, I made many offers to get in, but all in vain . . .'. It reappears as the Wicket Gate of *P.P.* and, at the very end of his life, in *Israel's Hope Encouraged*, he frequently uses it: 'Hope will point and show it the gate afar off.' (Offor, i. 590.) 'Look behind thee, take a view of the path thou hast trodden these many years. Dost thou think that the way thou art in will lead thee to the strait gate, sinner?' (Offor, i. 620.)

p. 69, l. 5. *not about things controverted among the godly.* Bunyan is most probably referring to such previous works as *A Confession of my Faith and a Reason of my Practice* (1672), *A Defence of the Doctrine of Justification by Faith* (1672), and *Differences about Water-baptism no Bar to Communion* (1673) rather than to the controversies with the Quakers of twenty years before.

p. 69, l. 10. *The text calls for sharpness, so do the times.* Bunyan frequently expresses his outrage at the immorality and sinfulness of Restoration England, and especially of its clergy. Cf. *The Life and Death of Mr. Badman* (Offor, iii. 594), 'Wolves in sheep's clothing swarm in England this day: wolves both as to doctrine, and as to practice too. Some men make a profession, I doubt, on purpose that they may twist themselves into a trade; and thence into an estate; yea, and if need be, into an estate knavishly, by the ruins of their neighbour. Let such take heed, for those that do such things have the greater damnation.'

p. 69, l. 13. *Some (say they) make the gate of heaven too wide, and some make it too narrow.* The latter accusation had been levelled at Bunyan, when he was preaching a sermon upon which this treatise is possibly built. Charles Doe gives the story in *The Struggler*: 'As Mr. Bunyan was preaching in a barn, and showing the fewness of those that should be saved, there stood one of the learned to take advantage of his words: and having done preaching, the schoolman said to him, You are a deceiver, a person of no charity, and therefore not fit to preach; for he that (in effect) condemneth the greatest part of his hearers hath no charity, and therefore is not fit to preach.'

p. 71, l. 18. *retort*: a sharp and possibly angry reply.

p. 71, l. 19. *resolve*: an answer (obs.).

p. 72, l. 15. *gally-pots*: earthenware pots, especially those used by apothecaries.

p. 77, l. 14. The symbolism of the gates of the Temple and the duties of the Porters is expounded at greater length in *Solomon's Temple Spiritualized*, chs. XXV and XXVI (Offor. iii. 477–8).

p. 82, l. 37. *over there is*: over and above what there is.

p. 83, l. 19. *thou that art like the heartless dove*. 'Ephraim also is like a silly dove without heart: they call to Egypt, they go to Assyria.' Hos. 7: 11 That is, Israel is rebuked for turning anywhere but towards God, for failing, as the listener addressed here, to strive Godwards.

p. 83, l. 25. Such professors are a frequent object of Bunyan's denunciation. Cf. *A Treatise of the Fear of God* (Oxford Bunyan, ix. 27), 'And thus do all those that retain the name, and shew of religion, but are neglecters, as to the power, and godly practice of it. These will live like *Dogs* and *Swine* in the house, they pray not, they watch not their hearts, they pull not their hands out of their bosoms to work, they do not strive against their lusts, nor will they ever resist unto blood striving against sin.'

p. 85, l. 34. *nippeth*: any of three possible meanings could be intended here: concerns closely, affects painfully, or rebukes sharply.

p. 86, l. 20. *and also white raiment . . . that thou maiest see*. Rev. 3: 18.

p. 91, l. 4. *to make conscience of*: to make a conscientious observance of.

p. 91, l. 8. *and his ways a stalking-horse*. Cf. *The Life and Death of Mr. Badman* (Offor, iii. 632), 'Go, Professors, go; leave off profession, unless you will lead your lives according to your profession. Better never profess, than to make profession a stalking horse to sin, deceit, to the devil, and hell.'

p. 91, l. 29. *a smart and thundring Sermon*: a sharp, severe sermon such as that preached by Captain Boanerges, the son of thunder in *The Holy War* (ed. Sharrock and Forrest, pp. 158–9), 'His Text was this, *Cut it down, why cumbreth it the ground?* and a very smart Sermon he made upon the place . . .'.

p. 94, l. 35. *that I have done elsewhere*. The sin against the Holy Ghost is one which much exercised the Puritan moral theologian. Bunyan's major discussion of this prior to *The Strait Gate* is when he describes his own terror of having committed it in *G.A.*, pp. 47 ff. He also discusses it in *The Jerusalem Sinner Saved* (Offor, i. 102–3) and in *Law and Grace* (Oxford Bunyan, ii. 201–10).

p. 98, l. 5. *set by with no body*: not regarded or esteemed by anybody.

p. 99, l. 14. *respecteth*: deals with, is concerned with.

p. 99, l. 21. *their naked knowledge*: mere knowledge, not strengthened or increased into belief.

p. 99, l. 24. Cf. *The Life and Death of Mr. Badman* (Offor, iii. 606), 'If the master have one guise for abroad, and another for home; that is, if his religion hangs by in his house as his cloak does, and he seldom in it, except he be abroad'.

p. 100, l. 6. *this kingdom belongs to the elect*. Bunyan passes very swiftly over this doctrine of the elect, and elsewhere in his work he shows a similar tendency, especially over the notion of election to damnation. In *Instruction for the Ignorant* he makes no mention of election, and election to damnation is not spoken of in *A Confession of my Faith* although he is orthodox in his statement of belief that 'this faith is effectually wrought in none, but those which before the world were appointed unto glory' (Offor, ii. 598). He is keenly aware of the mental and spiritual agony which the hopes and fears of election can bring to a believer, and his teaching is nearly always directed towards the awakening and answering the calling of Christ in the seeker for salvation, and to repressing an anxious questioning of his election. In *The Jerusalem Sinner Saved* (Offor, i. 102) he advises his reader to 'lay the thoughts of thy election by, and ask thyself these questions: Do I see my lost condition? Do I see salvation is nowhere but in Christ? Would I share in his salvation by faith in him? . . . Wherefore, sinner, when Satan, or thine own heart, seeks to puzzle thee with election, say thou, I cannot attend to talk of this point now, but stay till I know that I am called of God to the fellowship of his Son, and then I will show you that I am elect, and that my name is written in the book of life. If poor distressed souls would observe this order, they might save themselves the trouble of unprofitable labour under these unseasonable and soul-sinking doubts.' He teaches a similar order in *Law and Grace* (pp. 214–6). In *The Resurrection of the Dead* (Offor, ii. 123), in playing down the doctrine of predestined damnation, he stresses rather the freedom of will and choice which a man has in turning to sin: 'Now men will tattle and prattle at a mad rate about election and reprobation, and conclude, that because all are not elected, therefore God is to blame that any are damned: but then they will see, that they are not damned because they were not elected, but because they sinned; and also they sinned, not because God put any weakness into their souls, but because they gave way, and that wilfully, knowingly, and desperately, to Satan and his suggestions.' In *Come, & Welcome to Jesus Christ* (Oxford Bunyan, viii. 353) Bunyan is so strongly influenced by his text 'All that the Father giveth me, shall come to me; and him that cometh to me, I will in no wise cast out', that he plays down even more the doctrine of election and damnation, and preaches with great warmth and conviction the breadth and compulsiveness of Christ's saving grace, and that the mark of salvation in a man is his turning and coming to Christ: 'If Satan therefore objecteth, *but thou art not elected*; Answer. But I am coming, Satan, I am coming; and that I would not be, but that the Father draws me; and I am coming to such a Lord Jesus, as *will in no wise cast me out*. Further, Satan, were I not elect, the Father would not draw me, nor would the Son so graciously open his bosom to me. I am perswaded, that not one of the non-elect, shall ever be able to say (no, not in the day of judgement) I did sincerely come to Jesus Christ. Come they may feignedly, as Judas and Magus did; But that is not our question: Therefore, O thou honest-hearted coming sinner, be not afraid, but come!'

p. 100, l. 27. *when we can tend it*: when we can listen, pay attention to it.

p. 101, l. 6. *Gospel-holyness*. The life of good works which springs from conversion and the acceptance of Christ as the only means of salvation, as opposed to the attempted life of good works under the Law. Cf. *The Desire of the Righteous Granted* (Offor, i. 766), '. . . for the Spirit comes with the gospel down from heaven to such an one, and fills his soul with good; by which he is capacitated to bring forth fruit, true fruit, which are the fruits of righteousness imputed, and of righteousness infused, to the glory and praise of God.'

p. 103, l. 7. *distinctly*: in a separate section.

p. 105, l. 25. *the shew of the countenance*: the outward bearing and conduct.

p. 108, l. 16. *Eightly*. Bunyan or the printer has lost count here. This should be 'Seventhly'.

p. 112, l. 21. *countenanceth*: bears out, backs up.

p. 115, l. 13. *awakenings*. Cf. *Light for them that sit in Darkness* (Oxford Bunyan, viii. 127), 'By awakened men I mean, such as through the Revelation of their Sin and Misery, groan under the want of Jesus to save them, and that continue sensible that they needs must perish if his benefits be not bestowed upon them.'

p. 115, l. 20. *in order to*: with a view to bringing about.

p. 115, l. 27. *notions*: the merely intellectual grasp of the idea of grace, without it being accepted by the heart and soul, through the power of the Holy Spirit. See also p. 122, l. 23 above.

p. 120, l. 31–2. This description tallies exactly with the plate at the beginning of the 3rd edition of *The Barren Fig-Tree* (1692). See p. 5, above.

p. 123, l. 13. *doubt thy thoughts*: call in question your thoughts.

p. 123, l. 34. *go back again*. Cf. *P.P.*, p. 43, ll. 12–13, where Timrous and Mistrust 'are going back again from the hill Difficulty'.

p. 123, l. 35. *go over hedge and ditch*. This has a proverbial ring, but I do not find it recorded. The image is from hunting—one who rides a straight line across country, looking for neither gates nor roads.

p. 124, l. 20–27. *whose religion lieth only in your tongues*. Cf. *P.P.*, p. 80, l. 1, where Talkative who 'dwelt in Prating-row' is rebuked with the words,

'Talking is not sufficient to prove that fruit is indeed in the heart and life.'

p. 124, l. 29. *covetous professor*. Cf. *The Life and Death of Mr. Badman* (Offor, iii. 594), 'Some men make a profession, I doubt, on purpose that they may twist themselves into a trade; and thence into an estate; yea, and if need be, into an estate knavishly, by the ruins of their neighbour'.

p. 125, l. 13. *opinionist*. A good example of Bunyan's position as opposed to the 'opinionist' is his teaching on water-baptism. In *A Confession of My Faith, and a Reason of my Practice* (Offor, ii. 611), he writes: 'I am therefore for holding communion thus, because the edification of souls in the faith and holiness of the gospel, is of greater concernment than an agreement in outward things . . . And know that the edification of the church of God dependeth not upon, neither is tied to this or that circumstance.'

p. 125, l. 19. *the formalist*. He is a frequent object of Bunyan's attack. In *P.P.*, p. 39, l. 25, Christian meets Formalist in the company of Hypocrisie. In *The Jerusalem Sinner Saved* (Offor, i. 99) we read of those who 'have a form of godliness and deny the power thereof', and in *The Desire of the Righteous Granted* (Offor, i. 765) of 'the desires of the cold formal professor; the desires, I say, of him whose religion lies in a few of the shells of religion'. A fuller picture of the formalist's practice appears in *A Holy Life the Beauty of Christianity* (Oxford Bunyan, ix. 254): 'There are a great many Professors now in *England*, that have nothing to distinguish them from the worst of Men, but their Praying, Reading, hearing of Sermons, Baptism, Church Fellowship, and Breaking of Bread. Separate them but from these, and everywhere else they are as black as others, even in their whole Life and Conversation.'

p. 125, l. 36. *temporizing Latitudinarian*. Bunyan's special use of this word is further illustrated in *A Defence of the Doctrine of Justification* (Offor, ii. 322): 'Behold you here then, good reader, a glorious Latitudinarian, that can, as to religion, turn and twist like an eel on the angle; or rather like the weather cock that stands on the steeple.' It is personified in the figures of Mr. By-ends and Mr. Hold-the-world in *P.P.* (pp. 101–2) with their statements of belief, 'For my part I like that Religion best, that will stand with the security of God's good blessings unto us,' and 'I am for Religion in what, and so far as the times, and my safety will bear it.'

p. 126, l. 5. *the wilfully ignorant professor*. He also appeared in *P.P.* when Christian and Hopeful 'met with a very brisk Lad . . . and his name was Ignorance,' whose response to knowledge offered by Christian is to tell him to 'be content to follow the Religion of your Countrey, and I will follow the Religion of mine.' (p. 123).

p. 126, l. 34. *that free-willer*. Bunyan uses this word in a special sense, and not in its more accepted context of free-will as opposed to predestination. Words from *Mr. Bunyan's Last Sermon* (Offor, ii. 756) expand what he says here: '. . . there is not only in carnal men a will to be vile, but there is in them a will to be saved also; a will to go to heaven also. But this it will not do; it will not privilege a man in the things of the kingdom of God; natural desires after the things of another world, they are not an argument to prove a man shall go to heaven whenever he dies. I am not a free-willer, I do abhor it . . .'

p. 127, l. 1. *that Socinian.* The Socinian heresy is primarily an anti-Trinitarian or Unitarian doctrine. God is the supreme lord of all, single and alone in his supremacy. It is the Socinian teaching on Christ which especially arouses Bunyan's wrath, for this denied the central tenet of his faith, the atoning sacrifice of the Cross, and man's salvation through the imputed righteousness of Christ. The Socinian Christology saw Christ as one to whom God once and above all delegated his power, sending him with supreme authority to man, to show man the hidden will of God and to teach the precepts he must follow to obey him. Through these observances the Christian believer lays hold on eternal life. Bunyan's hatred of the doctrine often inspires such outbursts as that in *Israel's Hope Encouraged* (Offor, i. 611): 'Wherefore usually, when they come at this doctrine, they belch out their frumps, their taunts, their scoffs, and their scorns against it; and in opposition thereto, comment, exalt, cry up, and set on high, Socinianism, Mahometanism, man's ragged righteousness, or anything.'

p. 127, l. 2. *that Quaker.* For a full discussion of the Quakers and Bunyan's controversies with them see Oxford Bunyan, i. xvi–xxxv. Here the Quaker's reluctance to admit the full and true humanity of the incarnate Christ is chosen for special mention, although many more Quaker doctrines were opposed to Bunyan's theology of the atonement, to salvation through Christ's imputed righteousness.

p. 127, l. 12. *hard ventring of that*: dangerously daring to do that, i.e., to express such an opinion.

NOTES TO *THE HEAVENLY FOOT-MAN*

p. 137, l. 17. *untimely*: at the wrong time, i.e., too late.

p. 137, l. 23. *Cant. 5. 2, 3, 4.* This reference to The Song of Solomon is either inaccurate or is being very ingeniously applied. The words of 5: 2, 'I sleep, but my heart waketh: it is the voice of my beloved that knocketh, saying Open to me, my sister, my love . . .' being taken as a type of Christ knocking on the door, the slow rising of the sleeper to open the door, only to find the beloved gone, making an illustration of slothfulness.

p. 138, l. 31. *earnest*: zealous and intense. The word could still be used for violent and ungoverned feeling, which present usage excludes.

p. 139, l. 7. *now of a long time*: now for a long time.

p. 139, l. 13. *as the door is turned upon the hinges.* Proverbs 26: 14. 'As the door turneth upon his hinges, so doth the slothful upon his bed.'

p. 139, l. 21. *But Oh! it is for ever, O this cutting ever.* Bunyan often expresses the terror of this 'for ever'. Cf. *One Thing is Needful* (Oxford Bunyan, vi. 191–4) and *A Few Sighs from Hell* (Oxford Bunyan, i. 276), 'O this one word Ever, how will it torment thy Soul!' In *P.P.* (p. 35) the man in the iron cage of Despair cries out 'O, Eternity, eternity! how shall I grapple with the misery that I must meet with in eternity.'

p. 139, l. 22. *Soul-mazing*: confusing and perplexing the soul.

p. 139, l. 24. *if I should set in*: if I should begin.

p. 140, l. 15. *the day of grace is past with some before their life is ended.* See note to p. 47, l. 11, above.

p. 143, l. 10. *clearing*: elucidation.

p. 145, l. 4. *the Heavenly Carriage*: such behaviour as led him towards heaven.

p. 147, l. 7. *So run, that ye may Obtain.* This text has appeared in *P.P.* (p. 85. ll. 31–2) in Evangelist's words to Christian and Faithful, 'The Crown is before you, and it is an incorruptible one; so run that you may obtain it.' It is also handled in *A Treatise of the Fear of God* (Oxford Bunyan, ix. 77–8), 'Well, but the Lord whom thou fearest will not leave thee to thy ignorance, nor yet to thine enemies power or subtilty, but will take it upon himself to be thy teacher and thy guide, and that in the way that thou hast chosen . . . and who ever wanders, turns aside, and swerveth from the way of Salvation: whoever is benighted, and lost in the midst of darkness, thou shalt find the way to Heaven and the glory that thou hast chosen . . . he hath the heart and mind of God still discovered to him in the way that he hath chosen even all the way from this world, to that which is to come, even until he shall come to the very gate and door of Heaven.' *Israel's Hope Encouraged* frequently uses the image of the way and the journey, with its dangers and temptations (Offor, i. 582, 590, 598–9, 620).

p. 149, l. 19. The reference of the 1698 text 'Luk. 13' is very general. Verses 23–4 are the relevant ones: 'Then said one unto him, Lord are there few that be saved? And he said unto them, Strive to enter in at the strait gate: for many, I say unto you, will seek to enter in, and shall not be able.'

p. 149, l. 23. *heavy-heel'd*: as opposed to a heeler, a quick runner who has light heels.

p. 149, l. 27. *as a Snail doth go on the Wall.* This has a proverbial ring but there is only 'Slow as a snail' recorded in Tilley (S. 579).

p. 150, l. 16. *many a dirty step, many a high Hill.* These are hints to be developed into such fuller allegories as the Slough of Despond and the hill Difficulty in *P.P.*

p. 150, l. 21. *the wast howling Wilderness.* Deut. 32: 10.

p. 151, l. 4. *turn'd up their heels*: knocked them down, killed them.

p. 151, l. 22. *Francis Spira.* See note to p. 58, l. 17, above.

p. 152, l. 21–25. This is typical of Bunyan's attacks on sectarian teaching, its emphasis on parts and not the whole, on its preaching 'another gospel! Cf. *Some Gospel Truths Opened* (Oxford Bunyan, i. 63), 'And then, O poor Soul, if thou comest but hither, thou wilt never have an itching ear after another gospel. Nay, thou wilt say, if a presbyter, or anabaptist, or independent, or ranter, or quaker, or papist, or pope, or an angel from heaven, preach any other doctrine, let him be accursed again and again.'
Quakers. See note to p. 127, l. 2, above.
Ranters. An Antinomian sect, exalting reliance on the inner light above the authority of the scriptures, and with a reputation for licentiousness and a rejection of the necessity of obeying any moral code. It is as debauched perverters of the faith that Bunyan frequently attacks them, as in *The Resurrection of the Dead* (Offor, ii. 106), 'they do both allow and maintain the chief doctrine of the Ranters, with most of the debauched persons in the world', and *A Few Sighs from Hell* (Oxford Bunyan, i. 381–2), '. . . else through a notion of the gospel, the devil bewitching and beguiling thy understanding, will, and affections, thou wilt, Ranter-like, turn the grace of God into wantonness . . .'.

p. 152, l. 21. *runs after the Baptism.* Bunyan sets out his beliefs on baptism in *A Confession of My Faith* (1672) and *Differences in Judgment about Water Baptism no Bar to Communion* (1673). He held that water baptism was an outward show of the inner baptism of the Spirit, and did not 'run after baptism' in demanding believer's baptism as a requisite for full church membership and communion.
Independency. The principles of church organization and government held by

the Independents (or Congregationalists) where each group of self-governing Christians is held to be a part and a representative of the universal church.

p. 152, l. 22. *Free-will.* See note to p. 126, l. 34, above.

Presbytery. The principles of church government by Presbyters and elders of the church. Bunyan's inclusion of this and Independency is not so much an attack on the religious beliefs of these sects, but on their making a—to Bunyan—peripheral matter of organization a central and fundamental issue.

p. 153, l. 7. *my Book of the Two Covenants.* i.e., *The Doctrine of the Law and Grace unfolded* (1659).

p. 153, l. 15. *Anabaptists, though I go under that name my self.* In the seventeenth and eighteenth centuries Baptists were often described as Anabaptists, without being in any way connected with the continental churches. Bunyan, while accepting the name of Baptist rejected believer's baptism as a necessity for church communion. See note to p. 152, l. 21 above. It is against such 'anabaptists' that he warns his readers here. Cf. *A Confession of my Faith, and a Reason of my Practice*: 'And as for those titles of Anabaptists, Independents, Presbyterians, or the like, I conclude that they came neither from Jerusalem, nor Antioch, but rather from hell and Babylon, for they naturally tend to divisions.' (Offor, ii. 593.)

p. 153, l. 26. *Inherent Righteousness.* Righteousness inherent in our own natures, as opposed to the righteousness of Christ imputed to us. Cf. Book of Common Prayer Collect for Lent II, 'Almighty God, who seest that we have no power of ourselves to help ourselves . . .'.

p. 154, l. 16. *Prov. 5 & 7.* Bunyan only gives chapter references here as he is conflating quotations from different verses, 5: 8, 'Remove thy way from her, and come not nigh the door of her house'; 5: 5, 'Her feet go down to death; her steps take hold on hell'; 7: 27, 'Her house is the way to hell, going down to the chambers of death.'

p. 154, l. 25. The casting aside of the burden is reminiscent of the bundle falling from the back of Christian at the foot of the Cross, but there the burden was the burden of sin and guilt; here it represents an over-attachment to the profits and pleasures of this world, as it does in *Solomon's Temple Spiritualized*: 'The straitness, the narrowness, must not be understood of the gate simply, but because of that cumber that some men carry with them, that pretend to be going to heaven. Six cubits! What is sixteen cubits to him who would enter in here with all the world on his back . . . Wherefore he that will enter in at the gate of heaven . . . must go in by himself, and not with his bundles of trash on his back.' (Offor, iii. 476.)

p. 155, l. 8. *by-paths.* Another hint of *P.P.* (p. 111, l. 29)—'. . . a *Meadow*, and a Stile to go over into it, and that *Meadow* is called *By-Path-Meadow*'.

p. 156, l. 19. *too much gazing* etc. The story has an almost proverbial quality as a very old and popular improving anecdote. Plato tells it of Thales in *Theatetus*, Chaucer of the astronomer who looked

> Up-on the sterres, what there sholde bifalle,
> Til he was in a marle-pit y-falle, (*Miller's Tale*, 273.)

and Sidney repeats it in *A Defence of Poetry* (*Miscellaneous Prose of Sir Philip Sidney*, ed. Duncan-Jones and van Dorsten, p. 82).

p. 156, l. 25. *Ranting and Quakery*. See note to p. 152. ll. 210–25.

p. 156, l. 26. *without*: unless.

p. 157, l. 12–17. The tempting cries to the pilgrim are reminiscent of Christian's experience as he set out on the Way, 'So I saw in my Dream that the Man began to run; Now he had not run far from his own door, but his Wife and Children perceiving it, began to cry after him to return: but the Man put his fingers in his ears, and ran on crying, Life, Life, Eternal Life: so he looked not behind him, but fled towards the middle of the Plain.' (*P.P.*, p. 10.)

p. 158, l. 29. *thou wilt draw very heavily*: you will pull yourself along with great difficulty.

p. 159, l. 4. Cf. *P.P.*, p. 38, l. 2, 'He ran thus till he came at a place somewhat ascending; and upon that place stood a *Cross*, and a little below in a bottom, a *Sepulcher*.'

p. 159, l. 5. *the standing way-mark*: the sign-post.

p. 160, l. 2. *in the point of Justification*: with reference or respect to Justification.

p. 160, l. 33. *Num. 14. 24.* Bunyan appears to be quoting from memory and not quite accurately, 'But my servant Caleb, because he had another spirit with him and hath followed me fully, him will I bring into the land whereunto he went: and his seed shall possess it.'

p. 161, l. 10. *Briers and Quagmires.* A faint hint of the more developed landscapes of *P.P.*, '... they drew near to a very *Miry Slow* that was in the midst of the Plain, and they being heedless, did both fall suddenly into the bogg' (p. 14); and 'Again, behold on the left-hand, there was a very dangerous Quagg, into which, if even a good Man falls, he can find no bottom for his foot to stand on.' (*P.P.*, p. 62.)

p. 161, l. 33. *a seldom work*: a rare, infrequent work.

p. 161, l. 36. *a starting horse, that is Rid without a Curbing Bridle.* Based on the proverbial saying 'a boysterouse horse must have a rough bridle' (Tilley, H. 684).

p. 162, l. 4. *It is the Cross which keepeth those that are kept from Heaven*: those that are kept from Heaven are kept from Heaven by the Cross.

p. 162, l. 9. In *P.P.* this becomes the doctrine of Mr. Worldly Wiseman who 'loveth that Doctrine best, for it saveth him from the Cross' and which involves '1. His turning thee out of the way. 2. His labouring to render the Cross odious to thee.' (p. 22.)

p. 163, l. 11. *Heb. 11. 24, 25, 26, 27.* Bunyan conflates pieces of several verses and reorders them: v. 24 '. . . refused to be called the son of Pharoah's daughter'; v. 25. 'Choosing rather to suffer affliction with the people of God, than to enjoy the pleasures of sin for a season'; v. 26, '. . . for he had respect unto the recompense of the reward'; v. 27, '. . . not fearing the wrath of the king'.

p. 164, l. 33. *shifts and starting-holes*: evasive stratagems and loop-holes, the latter a figurative use from the hole where a hunted animal takes refuge.

p. 165, l. 25. *tipt*: fitted with a protecting cap, or a plate for the toe of a shoe.

p. 166, l. 28. *the City of Refuge.* The image is from Josh. 20, where six cities are appointed as sanctuaries for manslaughterers fleeing from their avengers.

p. 167, l. 21. *Augers*: tools for boring holes in wood.

p. 167, l. 21–23. The variety of torments inflicted on the martyrs, and which are not in the list of the author of the Epistle to the Hebrews, are all recorded in the first book of Foxe's *Acts and Monuments*, 'containing the three hundred years next after Christ, with the ten persecutions of the Primitive Church'. The reference here to 'Augers' suggests that these torments had been impressed on Bunyan's memory by a plate at page 1018 of vol. i of the 1632 edition which is that possessed by Bunyan. This illustrates the 'martyrdom of good bishops under wicked emperours in the primitive Church', and shows whipping at the post, burning at the stake, tearing by wild beasts, and boring out the eyes where a very large auger is being employed. The text merely refers to 'the thrusting out of eyes' (p. 108) without any mention of the instrument used.

p. 168, l. 1. *scrubbed*: squalid, insigniificant.

p. 168, l. 27. *befool me*: treat me as a fool, call me a fool.

p. 168, l. 31. *quit for cost*: to balance the cost, to be an equivalent of the cost,

p. 169, l. 14. *while*: until.

p. 171, l. 19. *Jostles*: struggles, tussles.

p. 171, l. 19. *rubs*: obstacles, impediments.

p. 171, l. 32. *for a sudden*: for an instant.

p. 171, l. 34. *he had as good have been never a whit*: he had as well not done it even to the smallest extent. Cf. *The Holie Citie* (Offor, iii. 436), 'Thou must enter in by every whit of Christ, or thou shalt enter in by never a whit of him.'

p. 173, l. 7. *Francis Spira, the backslider.* See note to p. 58. l. 17, above.

p. 174, l. 1. *they doubt they shall come late enough*: they fear they will come very late, 'enough' being used as an intensive as in 'well enough' and 'sure enough'.

p. 176, l. 18. *Heb. 12: 1–2*. Another example of Bunyan quoting, slightly inaccurately, from memory.

p. 177, l. 19. The margin has *In a Spiritual Sence*. It is not clear whether this refers to the subject of the whole paragraph or simply to Cain looking to his brother Abel's soul.

p. 178, l. 6. *A few Sighs from Hell*. Published in 1658 (Oxford Bunyan, vol. i).

p. 178, l. 8. *Devote thy self*: apply yourself zealously.